SURVIVING THE FAMILY KINGDOM

A Memoir of Growing Up in Mom's Cult, Escaping, and Reclaiming a Life

Peggy Sharr

Preface

This is a true story. The events in this memoir are based on my lived experience, filtered through the lens of memory, emotion, and time. I have done my best to tell the truth as I experienced it. That said, memory is deeply personal. Others may remember things differently, and that's okay. Some names and identifying details have been changed to protect the privacy of some involved.

There are moments in these pages that may be hard to read. They were harder to live and even harder to write. But I believe in the power of stories to illuminate, to connect, and to mend what's been broken. If you find yourself in these pages, please know: your truth matters, too.

Memory is a slippery thing. It shapeshifts, fades, and resurfaces when we least expect it, sometimes in fragments, sometimes like a tidal wave. This story is told through my memories, as I lived and experienced them. This is not a book written in anger, revenge, or judgment. It is a book written in clarity, healing, and the hope that by telling my story, others will feel less alone in theirs.

I didn't write Surviving the Family Kingdom to expose anyone. I wrote it to reclaim the pieces of myself I had to bury in order to survive. For years, I believed obedience was love, silence was strength, and suffering was holy. I believed it because I was taught to. I was raised in a world ruled by my mother's version of God—a world she called "The Kingdom," where fear was cloaked in scripture and control was sold as salvation.

It took decades to unlearn what I thought was truth. It took becoming a mother myself to understand the cost of continuing a cycle I never asked to be part of. And it took nearly losing everything to finally find the courage to leave.

This is not a story of blame. It's a story of becoming. Of questioning. Of clawing my way out of a life that was never truly mine. And if you've ever been made to feel small, silenced, or unworthy, whether by religion, family, or fear. I hope my story reminds you that survival is not the end of the story. It's the beginning.

Paledon, Iowa, 1984

I can't let her read my mind. I have to stay awake.

My nine-and-a-half-month pregnant body aches—bone-deep, organ-deep. I've been up since six, chasing my one-year-old, feeling like a whale with a foot jammed in my ribs. I say nothing. Saying I want to go to bed would be "giving in to the flesh."

Gravity drags on my eyelids. I want to smack my cheeks, anything to stay alert, but attention is worse than exhaustion. We're a small group: seven adults and two babies. Mom will surely notice if I'm smacking myself. Though, she hasn't looked my way all night.

The ornate clock above Mom's head reads 2:10 a.m. Twenty hours awake; six of them being preached at by my drunk, chain-smoking mother, who believes she's Jesus. I'm scared shitless she'll read my thoughts and accuse me of harboring a demon. In our house, that's enough to put you in the hot seat until dawn.

Mom drones on, in her rocking chair, Bible in her lap, cigarette burning in the ashtray, her third rum and Diet Coke sweating on the table. Her emerald eyes glint behind her wire-rimmed glasses. The green leather cover of her Bible is faded to mud-brown, gold edges gone soft. "Be ye therefore perfect," she rasps, "even as your Father in heaven is perfect."

She hasn't looked at me all night, but she can smell a yawn like a shark smelling blood in the water. If she sees me nodding off, she'll put me in the hot seat, for sure.

Sitting in a chrome kitchen chair dragged in from the kitchen, I lock my spine straight like a steel rod to keep my baby from kicking my ribs, my belly so swollen I can't see my feet. I'd told Mom I was okay with sitting in a kitchen chair because the couch folded me and the baby would kick me like a soccer player. The pillow behind my back was the only thing making it bearable. I want to slide onto the floor and sleep where I drop, but I don't dare. I don't want to be confronted with giving in to the Spirit of Sleep, as Mom called it. Doesn't matter how many times I command the spirit to leave like Mom taught me, I feel even more tired. It's relentless. Stay awake, Peggy, I tell myself. Damnit, stay awake.

I loop my hair behind both ears, sit up straighter and take a deep breath. Aromas of garlicky, homemade spaghetti sauce fill the room along with cigarettes and Mom's musky, Tabu cologne. That aromatic concoction brings both comfort and dread.

On her nights off, when I was little, Mom would stand in front of her vanity puffing on cigarettes and preening before going out to the bar. With her emerald cat-eyes with black liner, and lips coated with coral lipstick, she looked like a movie star. She'd apply one last coat of mascara, rake her long aristocratic fingers through her Liza Minelli pixie, then spritz her blouse with Tabu. I'd stand in the doorway, hair feral, barefoot, watching her and daydreaming about being like her when I grew up. When she was out, I'd pose at her vanity, spray perfume on my shirt, and pretend to smoke a pencil. All the movie stars smoked. I swore I'd smoke when I turned eighteen.

On her days off I'd hang out with her in the kitchen. I'd hover, hopeful over whatever she was cooking. Sometimes she'd let me lick the cake batter from the bottom of the bowl or crunch on the leftover pie crust sprinkled with cinnamon and sugar. So yummy.

But that same scent could sour my tongue. For as many pleasant experiences as that scent trio brings, there are many more disturbing and tragic ones.

I look at Deb on the couch, blonde waves in her face, her ginger one-year-old drooling down her forearm. It's obvious Deb is tired *and* mad. Tight lips, Mom says are a sign of being possessed by the Demon of Stubbornness. Stubbornness landed her in the hot seat a lot.

Tonight, Mom lets it pass. Not sure why. Her unpredictability was one of her scariest qualities.

Randy, Deb's husband, sits beside her. He's slight but sturdy, with aviator glasses too big for his face. His eyes keep slipping closed, then he jerks his head and straightens his back trying to stay alert. Randy's a faithful devotee but his nervous laugh and awkward joke-telling come from the "Demon of Mockery," Mom says. He argues. She probes. He denies. She pushes. Eventually he crumbles, begging for forgiveness for having thoughts she claims she could read. Sometimes she would cast the demon from him, sometimes not. The rules always change, depending on her mood.

Mom's four rum and Cokes in by now and preaching damnation. I'm not in the hot seat, but I feel like I am. I always feel like I am. When someone's in the hot seat, the night could go until two, three, even four a.m. It's often Deb. Partly because she wears her feelings on her face. Mom frequently accuses her of letting in the Demon of Stubbornness. And Deb defends herself, which pisses Mom off. Mom's right. Deb *is* stubborn. She holds out. She doesn't seem to fear her like the rest of us. Still Mom always gets her to repent. But she only confesses to get free. She doesn't seem devoted. We hadn't talked about it. I'm only guessing. I'm too scared to think about it, let alone talk to her about it.

My baby's playing my ribs like a xylophone. I need to lie down. Why can't we just go to bed already? This is ridiculous. She's drunk. I rub my forehead. Stop! I yell in my head. What if she reads my mind? I can't be in the hot seat. Not tonight…I just want to sleep. I drag my focus back to Mom's sermon. So, I'm sacrificing sleep, I tell myself. Big deal. Jesus was nailed to a cross. Praise Jesus. Praise Jesus. Praise Jesus. I sigh, then widen my eyes and flit my head.

Uncle Jim, the only father figure I'd ever known, adjusts his grimy, John Deere hat, then with precision, and the bottle to his lips, spits his Red Man tobacco saliva into his make-shift spittoon: a Coke bottle held between his legs. He's very close to Mom. Does everything she tells him. He pushes back sometimes but she always gets her way. She gives him more rope than the rest of us but tightens it when it pleases her. She calls him her "right hand man." Truth is, I don't think he likes that position. Years ago, when Jim was just nineteen, she told him God called her. Told him she was "Jesus come in the flesh." She convinced him to leave their parents and travel with her, and he did. He's loyal, but like the rest of us, he's also trapped.

"I am the way the truth and the light…" She takes a deep drag from her Benson and Hedges 100s, ember flaring, then blows the smoke to the ceiling. She points her cigarette at us, and gazes around the room, slow and deliberate. "No one comes to the Father except through me."

The low light from the lamp next to Mom holds a billow of smoke that slowly orbits under the shade. It holds my attention for a moment. She doesn't notice that I'm struggling to stay awake. The more she drinks the less perceptive she becomes.

She clanks the ice of her rum and Diet Coke, swaying in the creaky rocking chair, open Bible in her lap. The multiple bookmarks, yellow highlights, and tattered corners are evidence of her years of devotion. She flips to scriptures without missing a beat. She reads passages like she wrote them. And of course, it's King James. She turns her nose up at any other version. As beat up as her Bible is, it still smells like a Bible. Ink, paper, and leather. Quite pleasant.

Narrow-eyed, she peers around the room, stopping to meet each of our gazes. She snaps open her cigarette case, slides one out and lights it with her BIC, then perches it on the amber colored, glass ashtray. While cleaning her glasses with her navy, peasant blouse, she says, "only the pure in heart will enter the kingdom of heaven. There's an unclean heart in this room."

My stomach flips. Oh God, not me. Please, not me.

Deb rolls her eyes; Randy flings his bangs by flitting his head. Jim leans forward, elbows on his knees. A small exhale ripples through the room. We know what this means: no one sleeps until someone breaks.

I'm suddenly alert. Oh man…we're gonna be up all night. My chest sinks. Well, as far as it could sink considering I'm carrying a bowling ball in my body. Mom doesn't seem to notice our reactions. But that doesn't dissuade my fear of her reading my mind or discovering that all I want to do is go to bed.

She sips her drink, her cigarette dangling between her fingers, then says, "somebody let a demon in. We're gonna stay up all night if we have to."

Did I let a demon in? Did I have an evil thought? I remember I'd had doubts about Mom's claim that she'd raised a man from the dead, something she commonly alleged in her sermons. While I'd pushed the thought from my mind, I worry it already entered my heart. Deep down I know she's lying, but I'm terrified to admit it to myself. I panic: Please, Lord, forgive me for doubting. A tremor goes through me. Then I refocus on Mom.

She turns a page in her Bible, her voice low and ominous, smoke escaping her mouth as she speaks. "The Day of the Lord will come like a thief in the night. When the end comes, you can't have no evil in your heart." She furrows her brow. "Otherwise, you'll be tossed in The Lake of Fire forever where there's burning and gnashing of teeth."

That reminder sends another surge of alertness through me. Heat rushes over my face. Old nightmares crawl out of the burrows. Me, half-naked scavenging for food because I'd refused the Mark of the Beast—666—while soldiers hunt me across a dead landscape. And the Lake of Fire itself, molten with bodies, flailing, and shrieking, with their mouths wide. I'm piled on top, screaming but no sound comes out. At twenty-one, I still wake up sweaty and breathless.

Like children, the seven of us wait for Mom's permission to go to bed. Nobody dares to excuse themselves. There's a tacit understanding that we don't go to bed until she does.

I'm no stranger to this scene; that's how most nights go. I normally have the stamina for it, but not tonight. Tonight, the only one with stamina is the baby in my belly kicking me like it's practicing for the World Cup.

The chrome chair I'm sitting on feels like concrete. I can't fight it anymore. I excuse myself to check on Matty, who's stirring in the nursery. An exit I can justify.

Rich, my husband—also fighting the Spirit of Sleep—is seated on a kitchen chair next to me, his arms crossed over his well-sculpted chest, and his gangly legs wrapped in skin-tight Levis with his ankles crossed. "The Lord used you as a vessel to bring in Rich," Mom had told me. Rich and I were drawn to each other the moment our eyes met but two weeks into our relationship Mom took over. We're about to have our second child and we don't even really know each other. We didn't experience the typical courting phase like most couples. Once Rich got saved, he became a devotee, and Mom was in charge of our relationship. Rich was lost. Divorced with two kids and distant from his family. Just the kind of convert Mom sought.

I waddle back to my seat after checking on Matty and adjust my pillow. Nothing has changed. Shit, nobody confessed yet. A small sigh slips before I catch it. Mom doesn't notice.

Mom coughs in a tissue, then wipes her mouth. She always has a little smoker's cough. She raises her Bible. "I am Jesus come in the flesh…"

How can SHE be Jesus? She's a mess. I panic. No, I can't think like that. She's the chosen one. She's gonna save me from The Lake of Fire. Praise Jesus. Praise Jesus.

Then:

"Peg, go to bed," Mom says with a softer voice.

A shiver moves through me. Is this a test? Like when she made us drink toilet water to prove our loyalty. Did she read my mind? Shit! I don't know what to do.

All eyes turn to me.

I stay seated, biting my thumbnail. "Really?"

"Yeah." Her mouth tips in an approximation of tenderness. "Go on. You must be tired." She removes a tube of lipstick from her cigarette case and applies a fresh coat, going just outside her lip line. "Makes my lips look fuller," she often says.

I'm too wrecked to question it. "Uh…okay. Thanks, Mom."

I hoist myself up and waddle to our bedroom. When I get to the doorway guilt soaks me. Everyone's just as tired as me. I glance back, taking stock. But I'm pregnant. I shoulda been able to go to bed hours ago. What right does she have…Stop! I swiftly get rid of those thoughts. I tell myself that Mom is teaching us to be warriors for the Lord. And she's saving us from The Lake of Fire. I ask Jesus for forgiveness then slip on my nightgown and crawl into our squeaky, wrought iron bed.

Merciless heartburn makes sleep impossible. Lying on my side, with the taste of stomach acid on my tongue, I can't filter out Mom's gruff voice or what I can see of her through the narrow opening of the burlap curtains between our bedroom and the living room. She'd told us the Lord didn't want us to have a bedroom door. We didn't understand why, but Rich and I didn't question it—too afraid to get put in the hot seat.

Mom raises her arched, thinly plucked brows. "Only the pure in heart will see God and only the perfect will sit at His feet. We're not going to bed until someone repents." She tips her glass, letting the last few drops slide down her throat, sets it down sharp, then scoots to the edge of the chair. "I'm going to the bathroom and when I get back youse've better figured out who's backslidden." As she walks across the room, she looks down, appraising her body. She always hated her thighs. The floor creaks under her.

***

Later, Rich falls into bed. Someone must've repented because the house is quiet. I'd been falling in and out of slumber, praying I'd go into labor. My due date of December seventh had passed three weeks prior.

"Rich, I'm worried," I whisper, pushing hair from my face. "Mom leaves in two days."

"Yeah, so?"

I sigh.

He lays down and pulls the covers over his shoulder. "What's the big deal?"

"The big deal *is* I want her to be with me when I have the baby. Remember? I told you."

"Peggy. You did it without her before."

"I know, but I don't want to this time. Can we please change her ticket? I checked. It's only fifty dollars."

"Fine. If that's what you want." He rolls over and passes out.

I lie there, fantasizing about Mom feeding me ice chips, holding my hand while I'm doing my Lamaze breathing, and telling me I'm doing a good job, like moms do on TV.

I didn't consciously know it back then, but my wanting her to be with me for the birth was a last effort to wake the mother inside the preacher. I needed her to prove she loved me and saw me as a daughter, not just another devotee.

For years, I'd yearned for her to recognize that I need her, not as a preacher, but as a mother. When she got her "calling" ten years prior, she stopped being a mother and focused on preaching, saving souls, and preparing for the End Times. I felt insignificant then. I feel insignificant now. I cling to memories from the first eleven years of my life, when I was allowed to be a kid—dancing with Mom and Deb to Beach Boys records, cooking our favorite foods, having sleepovers, attending summer camp, going skating on Friday nights. Yes, we were poor, fatherless, and moved a lot, but at least we had a mom.

We'd settled in Iowa when I was almost sixteen, after traveling the country for more than four years searching for converts into Mom's homegrown microcult she called The Kingdom. Since moving to the tiny town of Paledon, Mom reserved her sermons for family. The Lord had told her we were the chosen family, that there were no more souls to save. The new order: find mates, make babies, wait for the End Times.

***

I wake up at six buzzing with hope, energy restored, eager to talk with Mom. Today I'll ask her to stay. She'll say yes. I clean the kitchen, tend to Matty, fold laundry in neat hopeful stacks, and listen for her footsteps.

She appears around eleven with mascara-raccoon eyes and hair standing on end. She re-ties the belt of her terrycloth robe. We exchange good mornings. She sits and tries to straighten her mussed hair. "Pour your mom a coffee, will ya?"

"Eggs?" I offer.

"Let me get some coffee in me first." She lights a cigarette then flips open *Time* magazine. "Sit. You should be resting."

The high morning sun floods through the kitchen window above the sink, accentuating the dancing smoke from her cigarette. I scoot my chair out of the blinding sun and watch her, waiting for her to look up.

Finally, chewing my thumbnail, I say, "Hey, Mom."

"Don't bite your nails, Peg."

I stick my hands in my armpits. "There's something I want to ask you."

She flips a page. "What is it?"

"Me and Rich wanna pay the extra so you can stay longer—" I swallow hard, "—until I have the baby. I want you to be with me for the birth. Remember, I told you?" I chew my thumbnail again.

She looks at me with a you-understand-right? look. She pats the magazine closed. "Oh, Peg. I wanna get back…I miss my friends."

The words don't land at first. They hang there thin and ordinary. Then they hit me like a slap. My stomach turns acidic. I watch her face for a clue that she's joking, though Mom was not the joking type. My heart hammers toward something I don't have language for. Thoughts rapid fire. What!? You miss your friends? What the hell? I thought you were Jesus. I thought we were supposed to stay close for His second coming. I thought we were the chosen family. I don't ask her questions or try to talk her into it. I'm stunned. I search her face for answers, but she doesn't look up. I search myself for answers.

Then I confront a reality that I'd been carrying at the pit of my stomach for ten years. She ain't Jesus. The End Times ain't coming. This is bullshit. All these years I fought to believe, tried to be perfect, denied what I knew to be lies. All because I was afraid of the stupid Lake of Fire. Maybe there ain't even a Lake of Fire.

For the first time in nearly ten years, I'm not afraid to think for myself. She's living a double life. Here, she claims to be Jesus and controls us with fear. In Pennsylvania, she lives like a normal woman: job, friends, dating, whatever she wants. All the while—even when she's not here—we follow her rule to the letter. I don't have friends. That was never allowed. I didn't get an education. Not allowed. I don't have a life outside of the Kingdom. Not allowed. But she does.

Wow! In a moment, I make the decision to live a normal life. I don't know yet what that looks like, but I sure as hell know it doesn't include her telling me how to live.

We sit sipping coffee, her attention on the magazine, my attention on her. As I stare through her—though she doesn't notice—I decide I won't mention my revelation. I want to get away from her like she's got leprosy. And I don't feel the slightest prick of guilt.

The room looks the same. The same table, the same chipped coffee mugs, the same grease-stained walls, but now I see from a new angle. For years I'd been stacking on a shelf in my mind things I knew to be wrong. The lies, the abuse, the control, the sheer insanity. The shelf held steady most of the time. It almost toppled a few times, but I always managed to steady it by telling myself that the Lord works in mysterious ways and who am I to question Him. Mom is the chosen one and I need to be perfect to stay out of The Lake of Fire. Mom's reason for not staying with me for the birth is the lone piece that topples the shelf and sends it crashing down. Those words: "I miss my friends," are like the antidote pill to wake me from the ten-year coma I'd been in. My entire lens shifts like a film flipping to the next frame. A few seconds earlier I was yearning to be recognized, but at this moment, the hour of her departure cannot come soon enough.

That night in bed, I allow thoughts I'd repressed for a decade to unearth—unvetted. I think about Mom's claims: that she raises the dead, heals the sick, casts out demons, reads minds. I line each claim up and shine an honest light on them. I think about how she tore apart families and beat babies. I think about how when I was twelve, I pried a woman's hands from Mom's throat while being held at gunpoint, believing I'd be punished for interfering with her murder. I think about how I witnessed Mom mentally—and sometimes physically—torturing people trying to break them. I think about how I'd been plagued with mental torment and fear of the Lake of Fire and convinced myself to believe her claim that she was Jesus. And I think about my stolen adolescence and how Mom drove away my first love in shame. I think about how she controlled my life in every way.

For the first time, I allow myself to feel angry about the social isolation and denying me a high school education, all in the name of "the Lord's will." I'm angry. The anger arrives like blood to a fresh wound: painful, then hot and obvious. I'm angry about my adolescence disappearing inside a woman's appetite for power. I'm mad. I'm just so mad.

I let myself think about the future without her script. Not the apocalypse. Not the mark of the beast. Not Jesus coming like a thief in the night. But a real future. A door with a lock because I choose one; a bed I decide to lie on; laughter that isn't sin; friends I pick because I like the way they make me feel; a church or no church. School for my kids. A kitchen that smells like food and nothing else.

I think of the old nightmares. I follow them to the edge. The Lake of Fire is just a picture I was handed. I tear it up. I don't sleep. I think all night. I realize I don't need to wait for her permission for anything anymore. Not to sleep, not to wake, not to eat, not to think. What I *had* wanted dissolved into personal agency. Before, I wanted her to be a mother. To choose me. To see me. I now realize. She won't. She can't. Maybe she never could.

I realize I'd been clinging to the version of Mom that I knew early in my childhood before The Kingdom. Life was far from perfect back then, but at least I was allowed to be a kid.

Mom worked hard to support us without help from our dad who'd left when Deb and I were babies. She was a survivor. One time she burned our kitchen chairs for heat when we were out of coal. Another time, she stormed into an in-session courtroom and asked a judge for help with getting our dad to pay child support. The judge had no power to help but did give her twenty bucks from his trousers. She was a badass when she needed to be. When I was bitten by a neighborhood dog, taken to the hospital by the owner, and strapped down in the E.R. for stitches, Mom burst in to save me. I stopped flailing and screaming the moment I saw her. "She don't need no straps," she told the nurses. "My Peggy will hold still with me here." When she learned my grade-school principal paddled me for a school infraction, she got up in that principle's face and told her she better not ever lay a hand on me again, "or there will be hell to pay."

Back then, I trusted her. I loved her. I still do, somewhere under the smoke.

But she wasn't always badass. There was another side to her. She was depressed—especially after giving up our baby brother for adoption when I was four. She didn't cry daily or even weekly, but when she cried, it could go on for hours. She'd cry about her baby and Shane, a man who dumped her after she'd waited two years for him while he was away at war. And she'd cry about her mom not loving her. "Why don't my mom love me?" she'd ask Deb and me. We didn't know what to say. We'd rub her back; tell her it was going to be okay. Tell her our brother was with a good family, like she'd told us. Didn't matter. She'd keep sobbing.

I remember the day she came home from the hospital empty-handed. She hadn't told Deb and me that she was giving away our brother. We knew it was a boy because Mom had told us she had a premonition. We'd been excited about our new baby brother for months. "I can't afford to feed another mouth," she told us. At four, I didn't completely understand, but I did understand I would never meet my brother. After my dad that was my second big loss.

Mom would fall into depressive episodes saying she wanted to die. I carried fear of her suicide like a backpack full of wet sand.

To escape her heartbreaks, she flew us from Pennsylvania to California when Deb and I were six and seven. I think about how that move put into motion the events that led to Mom losing her sanity.

CHAPTER TWO
Los Angeles, 1968

Peppered with homeless people curled on park benches like weeds, and rusted cars end to end, the apartment complex stretched around the block. I didn't mind the shabby neighborhood. There were tons of kids to play with and that was enough for me. Scabs on both knees, my feet tough as rawhide. After school, I'd burst through the door, fling off my shoes, and bolt outside like the world belonged to me. Being outside was my happy place.

Because the tips were better, Mom worked nights. And because she couldn't afford childcare, Deb and I stayed home alone. We knew our bedtime and we honored it. Besides, we didn't have a TV, so there was nothing to keep us up anyway. On rainy nights we occupied ourselves by playing cards or fighting, as siblings do. We lived on food stamps and school lunches, our fridge swinging between feast and famine. On feast days, there were pot pies, TV dinners, Pop Tarts, and Mom's home-cooked leftovers. Mom cooked on her days off. I loved those days. During famine times we made do—saltines with butter, hot dogs pierced with forks roasted over the open flame of the gas stove, macaroni and ketchup, Jello. Mom told us to go to the neighbor lady if we needed anything, but we never did. We were self-sufficient.

For a brief, glorious period we even had a station wagon that Mom had bought at a fly-by-night dealership. She'd let us bring friends to run errands. Because the jump-seat door would only open from the inside, I'd fling open the squeaky door and crawl over the back seat, sometimes accidentally puncturing a hole in the delicate ceiling fabric causing dust to rain on my face. I'd open the door, and everyone would pile in. We'd sit waiting for Mom to start the engine jiggling our legs and clapping our hands near our faces. "Weeeeeee," we'd sing when she stepped on the gas. "I wish your mom was my mom," kids would say. Sure, we were poor, and our life was bumpy, but I was mostly happy.

Then the car got repossessed. Mom couldn't make the payments.

Still Mom seemed happier since arriving in California. She'd made friends, started dating, and got a cocktail waitress job. Though, she didn't like having to wear hot pants. From as far back as I can remember she hated her thighs. In an attempt to shrink her thighs, she'd do housework with multiple layers of Saran Wrap around her legs. Her boss, moving her into the coffee shop where the uniform was knee-length, felt like grace.

Mom worked hard but with her low wages we lived in constant uncertainty. We didn't know from one year to the next what Christmas would be like. We wondered about Christmas that year. The closer it got, the more Deb and I worried. The fridge was bare. No tree. No plan. No money. But Mom didn't disappoint that year. On Christmas Eve, she wrangled in a tree and a bag of food donated from a church. She'd bought a spool of red velvet ribbon and tinsel to decorate the tree.

The three of us sat at our kitchenette table, making bows, the air sweet with pumpkin-custard pie. When the last bow was hung, and the last strand of tinsel was hung, we stood back, hands on our hips, admiring our little miracle.

That night I went to bed hopeful; my letter to Santa tucked beneath my pillow.

*A Barbie Dream House

*Ken and Barbie dolls with clothes

*Sidewalk chalk

*A bike with a banana seat

I figured the bike was a stretch, but what was the harm in asking?

Morning came and there they were: two shiny new bikes. Mine purple with pink tassels and a banana seat; Deb's a blue two-speed. Mom said they were charitable gifts from the church. That's when I learned there was no Santa.

I rode that bike every free moment. I'd zip around the parking lot weaving in and out of cars, racing kids on the longest parts, screeching to a halt just before the hedges. That bike was everything to me. But one day after going in to use the bathroom, I went back out to find the bike gone—stolen. I stood frozen, staring at the empty space, my chest feeling hollow.

After a few months we moved into a one-bedroom duplex. I started third grade at a new school—a rough one. Kids brought clubs and knives for protection, and there were race wars and rumors of gang rapes. Surprisingly, I didn't feel unsafe. I made friends right away and even got my first boyfriend.

Mom told Deb and me to walk home together. You's'll get a whooping if you don't," she'd warn. She relied on Deb to keep tabs on me, so in my eyes, Deb was a fink. She was only a year older. I didn't see how *she* could be my boss. "My girls are different as night and day," Mom would say. Deb was a loner. I hated being alone. Deb got all As and glowing remarks on her report cards. My report card was a mix but never Ds or Fs and always annotated the same plea: *Peggy's a good student but talks too much*. They weren't wrong. Listening and not talking for long periods in class was torture. Homework was a last-minute scramble. If I got a bad grade, I'd wake Mom in the morning to sign it while she was half asleep from working nights. Eventually, I started forging her signature. She wasn't the wiser. She was strict about our chores, but not homework. She didn't say much about grades except that I could do better if I spent "less time socializing and more time doing homework." Work ethic—rather than achievement—was what mattered to her. She didn't hide that she only went to the tenth grade. She wore it like a badge of honor, evidence that one does not need an education to have a strong work ethic.

Mom was tough love through and through. "I gotta be mom and dad," she'd say, "That's why I'm hard on youse girls." And she was.

***

When I was in fourth grade, I told a tall tale at school that I was being advanced to fifth grade because of how smart I was, and Trina, a classmate, didn't like that one bit. She challenged me to fight after school. I agreed because backing down wasn't an option.

But Trina chickened out and sent her sixth-grade cousin, Cassandra, instead—bigger, meaner. Built like a linebacker.

I was stuck in detention that day for talking during silent time when I spotted Cassandra outside, standing behind Deb.

"I'mo kick yo ass," Cassandra mouthed, her face squeezed through the door.

Two even larger girls flanked her, scowling at me.

Mr. Legler sat at his desk in his Hawaiian shirt and flip flops, his legs propped on his desk, thumbing through a magazine, like detention was his personal vacation. He glanced up, squinting in irritation. "You 'bout done. I don't have all day."

My hand trembled as I finished writing; I swallowed hard, drew in a big breath, and slid out of my desk. I skulked to Mr. Legler's desk and slid the paper in his in-tray, then waited. I could feel words in the back of my throat: *those three girls are going to jump me.*

Mr. Legler removed his reading glasses from the perch of his nose. "Is there something else, Peggy?"

"N…no." I whispered, forcing a smile. My legs were about to buckle. I turned around, pulled my shoulders back and ambled toward Deb.

We walked at a steady clip, the three girls behind us breathing down our necks, their sneakers slapping the pavement. "You think you bad?" Cassandra said, then shoved me. "I'm go'n mess you up." I stumbled but caught myself. Then all three punched my back like a flock of birds smashing into a window. I bolted. I ran as if carried by a tailwind. I could hear their feet smacking the pavement behind me, then fading, then gone. I wasn't big, but I was fast.

Once home, I flung open the door and collapsed on the floor, lungs burning, my sweat-soaked waves mashed to my forehead, my knee-high socks slouched. Mom rushed over to me, wearing a grease-stained apron and flour streaks across her cheek. I'd forgotten it was her day off.

"Peggy, *what's wrong?*"

I tried to speak, but words came out as sobs.

She crouched, voice sharp. "Stand up. Stop crying! Tell me what happened *this minute!*"

I blubbered out the story, leaving out the lie that started it. She was mad that I came home without Deb. But when Deb showed up a couple of minutes later, she refocused on what happened.

Her eyes narrowed. "No daughter of mine runs from a fight. We're going to Cassandra's."

The blood drained from my face. "No, Mom. She's huge. She'll kill me."

"You'll be fine. I'll make sure it's fair."

I knew where Cassandra lived but boy, I wished I hadn't. I wanted to sink into the floor, but Mom was already marching down the street, apron tossed aside. Deb and I followed like baby chicks.

Mom rapped on the screen door of the modest, ranch-style home. "Get out here Cassandra. My daughter's here to fight you." Mom's voice carried like thunder.

I froze, imagining Cassandra pummeling me with her fists and I come out of it with black eyes, a bloody mouth, and knocked-out teeth.

An older girl came to the door, resembling Cassandra. Mom leaned closer to the door, "Cassandra and her two bully friends jumped my daughter after school. Get Cassandra out here…now. Peggy's gonna fight her fair and square."

A few seconds later, Cassandra peeked through the screen. "Whatchu want?"

"Peggy's here to fight you."

Cassandra giggled warily. "Don't want to fight her."

What? She don't wanna fight me? Relief.

Mom smirked, then reached for the door handle. "You scared?"

"I ain't scared," Cassandra said, holding the door shut.

I chewed the inside of my lip. "Mom, let's just go."

Mom ignored me while playing tug of war with the screen door. "Then come out here and prove it." Mom yanked at the door. Cassandra kept her grip.

After a brief standoff, Cassandra stepped out and walked out to the front yard. Her three older sisters filed behind and stood on the sidelines, arms crossed. Mom pulled me aside, knelt to my eye level, "Kick'r in the crotch as hard as you can." I swallowed hard. That's your advice? I thought.

I puffed my chest and walked toward her, our world shrinking to the dusty patch of grass beneath us. We circled each other like sumo wrestlers. I lunged. We fell. Mom shouted, "Kick'r in the crotch! Kick'r in the crotch!

My nostrils flared, I took a breath, then charged into her stomach. We fell to the ground.

"Kick'r in the crotch! Kick'r in the crotch!" Mom yelled again.

Cassandra pinning my wrists to the ground. I squirmed and wriggled. Adrenaline took over. I contorted my body, then thrust my foot at her crotch with all my might, hitting her on the inner thigh instead of her crotch. She fell back but caught her fall. I jumped to my feet.

She lunged at me. "Aaaaaahhhhhhhhhrrrrrrrrrrrrr!" Wrapping her long, thick trunk-of-an-arm around my neck in a headlock. I stomped on her foot and squirmed my way out. Then I charged her, and we landed on the ground again.

Mom kept hollering, "kick'r in the crotch!" I positioned my foot, then, BAM! She fell back, caught herself, then jumped to her feet. I was confused. I thought a crotch kick would earn me a victory. I jumped to my feet. With bulging eyes, her fist found my cheek with the force of a brick—twice. I dropped.

"Okay, that's enough," Mom called out, referee style.

Cassandra backed away wearing a half-smile. Like she wasn't quite sure how to act.

I bolted home, tears blurring my vision.

When Mom and Deb arrived, Mom pressed a bag of frozen peas to my cheek, beaming like she'd performed a miracle. "She's not gonna mess with you again."

"What? She kicked my butt."

"Word'll get around that you're tough."

"But I ain't tough. I was scared."

"Don't matter. Word'll spread."

I was happy-go-lucky Peggy, not tough Peggy. I was chatterbox Peggy, who just wanted friends. I wasn't a fighter. I was a jokester.

Mom lit a cigarette, exhaling through the corner of her mouth, "what's the lesson?"

I sniffled. "Not to…run?"

She grabbed my shoulders. "No, the lesson *is*…to always stand up for yourself. Size don't matter. It's attitude."

The next day she dabbed makeup on my bruises. "You go to school," she said. "If you stay home, you'll look weak."

Mom was right. Nobody messed with me again. Trina, the cousin who originally challenged me to the fight— pretended I didn't exist.

✳✳✳

Tiny entered our lives the night the ambulance took Mom away. He told her not to worry, that he'd take care of us until she got better. A former pimp with a baby face and a muscular build, Tiny carried himself like a man used to being obeyed. Mom said he'd hang around the bar where she worked in Compton, buying her drinks and trying to kiss her at the jukebox. She didn't like cocky men, but Tiny was the kind who didn't wait for permission.

That rainy night, Deb and I were getting ready for bed when we heard a knock at the door. Getting visitors that late was unusual. Deb and I scurried to the door in our pajamas, our eyes wide.

"Who is it?" Deb said, loudly.

"I'm a friend of your mama's," a man said. "She had to go to the hospital and asked me to take care of y'all."

Our mouths dropped.

"What should we do?" I whispered.

Deb was only eight years old, but she was in charge when Mom was working.

"Mom said not to open unless we know the person," I said.

"Do we know you?" Deb called out.

"Y'all met me one time when your mama brought y'all to the bar. Open the door. You'll remember when y'all see me."

Deb pushed up her glasses. "Why is Mom in the hospital?"

"The ambulance took her. She's sick."

The blood drained from Deb's face.

"She's going to be in for a while. I'm here to take care of y'all. C'mon' now. It's pouring out here."

Torn between fear and worry for Mom, we cracked the door.

A short man with broad shoulders stood there on the doorstep, suitcase in hand, trench coat dripping. Tiny droplets glistened on his perfectly round, tight afro. He flashed his blindingly bright ivories. "Hi girls. Remember me?"

We said we didn't. Still, he stepped inside like he belonged, shaking rain from his coat, then removing it.

He broke the uncomfortable silence. "I'm Tiny. Your mama said y'all are *good* girls. Responsible and obedient. That true?"

Deb wrinkled her nose. "Yeah, I guess."

"C'mon over here girls. Sit down," he said, pointing to the couch.

Deb sat on the couch and crossed her leg. I sat next to her, holding my arms against my chest. Part of me was suspicious, part intrigued.

Tiny knelt in front of us. He was clean-shaven and well dressed: pleated slacks, polished shoes, and a pullover that accentuated his muscular biceps. The scent of his aftershave was intoxicatingly fatherly.

"Your mama collapsed, and the ambulance took her."

The air left my lungs. My mind was cluttered with thoughts.

"She screamed about how much it hurt. You don't need to be scared. I been knowing your mama for a while now."

Deb and I exchanged glances. Confused.

"How long will she be in the hospital?" I asked.

"Maybe a week."

We believed him. We had to.

Deb stood. "Can we go see her?"

"We'll go in a few days." He stood, snapping upright. "Alright then, get your butts to bed. It's late."

That night, I lay awake, staring at the ceiling, my mind tangled with questions. Was Mom going to die? Would Tiny be our guardian? How long would he stay? How should I act around him?

The following day, we got up and went about our usual routine. For a moment, I'd forgotten he was there—until I saw him curled in a wool blanket on the tweed L-shaped couch. Deb and I tiptoed through the house.

When we got home from school, he was doing dishes, sporting a crisp, white, wife-beater and jeans with a brown leather belt. Part of me felt settled having someone there after school, while another part worried about Mom and the future. I'm not sure why, but I wasn't scared of him. He commanded reverence, yet he personified protection, something I desperately craved.

He brought a little TV—our first since moving to California. It should've felt like a gift, but it just made me wonder if he planned to stay permanently.

That afternoon he called us to the kitchen. Deb and I stood side by side, hands behind our backs. "I'm doing the dishes right now," he said, flipping a towel over his shoulder. "But from now on, that's y'all's job. Sink better be empty before school and empty before y'all go to bed. Got that?"

Then came the lessons: how to clean chrome until it shined, how to make a bed so tight a quarter could bounce. "No playin' till the work's done," he said. Mom had always said it, but he enforced it. His word carried authority, so did his belt.

It was as though we'd been dropped into an alternate reality. Mom was gone and there was a strange insta-dad sleeping on the couch. And Deb and I were just going about our lives. I didn't mind it at first. He told stories, made us laugh. I wasn't scared. Yet.

A few days later Tiny took us to see Mom. My chest buzzed with worry on the drive. How would she look? Would she be too sick to ever take care of us again?

"When is Mom coming home?" I asked.

"When y'all are supposed to know you'll know," he said, sending me a quick glare.

Kids weren't allowed in the rooms, so Mom had to come out into the hallway.

She pushed herself in a walker, hospital robe clinging to her legs, hair matted, face pale as an egg.

"Mommy," we called, running toward her.

"No running," Tiny barked.

We froze, then snailed the rest of the way forward.

Mom smiled, the corners of her mouth barely turning up. "Hiya girls." Then, opened her arms. "Give your mom a hug."

We wrapped our arms around her.

"Careful. I had an operation."

We backed away like we'd touched a fragile piece of China.

"When you are comin' home, Mommy?" I asked.

She cupped our chins and shifted her gaze back and forth between us, steadying herself by leaning her elbows on the walker. "You girls taking good care of one another?"

We said we were.

Deb teared up. "Are you going to be okay?"

"Yeah, but I can't have no more babies. They had to take my womb."

I didn't know what a womb was, but I understood there would be no more siblings. I carried a void for my baby brother and hoped someday I'd get another brother—one who could live with us.

A lump formed in my throat. I hugged her gingerly. "We miss you Mommy."

"I miss youse too." She wrapped her arm around each of us. "Give me a kiss, girls."

We didn't like kissing Mom because her breath always reeked of cigarettes, but right then I wanted to kiss her. We got up on our tippy toes and kissed her on either cheek.

Tiny hung back, wearing a half-smile, hands in his pockets.

"My girls behaving for you?" Mom asked.

"Yes indeed. Alright now girls." Tiny motioned. "Let your mama rest."

Deb and I sighed.

As we headed for the exit I turned and got another glimpse of Mom, still shocked by her fragility.

After Tiny taught us to clean to his standards, he spent his days lying around in his robe, watching TV, and barking out orders. We never backtalked. There hadn't been much backtalk going on in our home anyway. Deb and I learned backtalk could get us a slap in the mouth. It didn't happen often, but when it did, it was memorable. One time, when I was eleven, Mom backhanded me so hard my bottom teeth sank into my lip and blood gushed.

Mom came home a few days later, Tiny remained. She didn't explain anything. We didn't ask. They pulled our twin beds together so they could sleep in the bedroom. Deb and I slept on the couch.

Mom recovered slowly. Tiny took charge. I didn't like how strict he was, but I liked him. He had a miniature herculean physique but with a little paunch, which I found quite paternal. He was smart too. He told stories of growing up in the ghetto. "Made me street smart," he'd say. I'd listen while lying on my belly, fists under my chin, soaking in every word. I'd never experienced those moments with my biological father. He was a stranger.

I'd created a story in my mind that Tiny and Mom had fallen in love and kept it a secret and their secret was exposed when Mom got sick. Mom had dated interracially before so that wasn't surprising.

Mom grew up in coal country, Pennsylvania, where everyone was white and racism was as common as coffee. The N word rolled casually off tongues at the supper table. Black people were painted as poor, dumb, and scary. Mom despised it. "Everyone's the same inside," she'd say.

One time when Deb and I were four and five, our grandmother, Mammy, drove us to Harrisburg so Mom could take care of some business. Mom promised to treat us to McDonald's. I was in the backseat daydreaming about gulping bubbly root beer after crunching down a handful of fries. Out of nowhere, Mammy shrieked with her smoker's voice. "Girls! Get on the floor and hide your eyes!"

Deb looked up from her book. "Why, what's wrong?"

"Just get down."

Deb and I clambered to the floor, rolling ourselves into spheres.

"Cover your eyes!" Mammy yelled.

"Mom, stop. There's nothing up here they shouldn't see. Get up girls."

Deb and I scooted back onto the seat. Mom lit a cigarette from the car lighter, then cracked the window. "A car with some Black people went by. Your Mammy don't want youse to see no Black people. Don't listen to her." Mom exhaled smoke out the window. "Everybody's the same inside. We all bleed the same. And all colors have good people and bad people."

Mammy rolled her eyes. "If that's what you want to teach them girls, then… I'm not sayin' no more."

Dead silence the rest of the car ride.

Mom wasn't particularly religious back then, though she did proclaim to love Jesus. Not the oppressive Jesus—her dad portrayed—who damned you for wearing makeup, listening to rock and roll, or having premarital sex. She believed in a Jesus who loved her as she was: makeup wearing, drinking and smoking, dating outside her race.

Mom took us to church on special occasions like Easter, but she didn't believe attending church was required for God's love. In fact, she thought most church-goers were haughty and gossipy. "They kill people with their words. Hate in the heart is the same as murder," she'd say.

After Tiny moved in, though, we started going to his church. It was a Southern Baptist Church, full of rhythm and heart. The air filled thick with perfume and sweat.

Afterward, we'd go to Tiny's mom's house to chomp down seafood gumbo and sweet potato pie. His mom—a robust woman with a scarf tied around her hair and a greasy apron around her round waist—made the best sweet potato pie in the world. I loved those Sundays—music, dancing, good food, laughter. Tiny's nieces and nephews grooved to Motown. I danced until my feet ached. Soul music lifted me out of everything I didn't want to feel. I'd danced to Mom's Beach Boys records back in Pennsylvania, but I'd never felt music the way I did dancing to Motown Soul. It swept me away to another realm, free of worries.

The first time we attended Tiny's church nearly everyone came up and introduced themselves. They offered Mom two-handed shakes. They patted Deb and me on our heads. At the end of the service the pastor asked if any new members wanted to come up front to be saved. Mom raised her hand. Deb and I followed suit. "C'mon up here, ladies, so we can pray together," the pastor said, a very dark portly man with a long purple robe, a gravelly voice, and big glasses slid down his nose from beads of sweat.

Cupping his hands around the tops of our heads, he said, "Looooord Jesus. We call on you to bless these children. These three young ladies are ready to serve you." Members of the congregation hummed their amens. The pastor continued. "We're calling on you to bless these humble servants that come before you right now." He pushed our heads when he was accentuating words. When he finally finished the prayer, he asked what Deb and I wanted to do for the church. Tiny had explained on the cab ride that we could choose from passing the tithe plate, singing in the choir, that sort of thing.

The pastor held the microphone to my mouth. "Sing in the choir," I muttered in an exaggerated little girl's voice.

The congregation rejoiced, singing praises to Jesus and applauding.

I imagined myself up there singing and wearing one of those shiny purple robes, the congregation clapping and swaying.

***

Tiny's personality was anything but tiny. He filled a room with his humorous antics; and he was an expert at everything. His boyish face and dimples were irresistible. His sharp eyes were brilliant kaleidoscopes of brown and gold. He liked razzin' me. It was the first time a father figure showed any interest in me. I lapped up the attention. But what I got from Tiny, and his family didn't make up for the Jekyll and Hyde sleeping with our mother.

I was outside playing hopscotch when we heard shots: *Pop! Pop! Pop!* My friends and I dispersed quicker than squirrels scampering up a tree. I darted my eyes around trying to figure out where the shots were coming from. Then: *Pop!* A sharp pain pierced my thigh. I lost my balance and tumbled to the ground, clutching my thigh. I sat up then squinted and wrinkled my nose, peering into the front window. Tiny's silhouette holding a pistol filled the window. I lay on the ground frozen like prey.

Tiny came out and stood on the stoop, arms folded, wide stance. "C'mon in here girl. Let's look at that leg."

My leg felt like a lighter had been held to it. I limped inside, sniveling back each breath.

Tiny smirked. "You gotta be faster than that," he chortled, holding the door open.

I pulled up the corner of my shorts to show him.

He flopped back onto the couch and crossed his feet. "*Oh…*you alright. It's just a little BB gun. Get on back out there."

I mopped my tears with my hands. "Tiny, did you shoot me on purpose?"

He wouldn't meet my eyes. "Go on now."

I choked back tears then raced to catch up with my friends.

Despite the mean things Tiny did, my affection for him didn't waver. I focused on the good and shoved down the bad. One of my favorite things to do with him was watch Columbo. "Them murderers are dumber than stumps," he'd say.

23

"Columbo. Now there's a smart man. He's on to them from the beginning and they don't even know it. '"Cause he play dumb. That's how he do it."

I'd cuddle up next to him and he'd share his popcorn. In those moments, he felt like a real dad. I wanted him to love me. But he was unpredictable. One minute he'd be silly, dangling us from his bicep, and the next he'd be swinging the belt. One minute he'd be cooking burgers for Mom and the next he'd be beating her. We never witnessed it—but we saw the bruises.

He was harder on Deb than me. Maybe she had an expression he didn't like, or she spoke in a tone he deemed disrespectful. Still, she found ways to seek his approval.

Tiny had been taking bookkeeping classes. Mom said after he'd beaten her so badly that last time, he took classes to prove he loved her. Not having graduated from high school, he was struggling. Deb offered to help.

I was playing outside while Deb helped Tiny with his homework that day. He'd decided to take a nap on the couch and left his textbooks open, and his papers strewn about the coffee table. Deb thought she'd do him a favor and clean up. When Tiny awoke, he was furious.

He hollowed, "Debbie, get in here."

Deb came in, chin tucked and her arms around her belly.

"Why'd you mess with my papers?!"

"I was trying to help."

Tiny stood up and yelled in her face. "Well, didn't help me none. Did I ask you to clean up?"

"No." Deb's chin quivered. "Sorry."

"Damn right you're sorry." He pointed to the bedroom doorway then unbuckled his belt. "Now get in there and bend over."

"*Please* Tiny. *Please*. I won't do it again."

Tiny put his hands on his hips. "What'd I tell you girl? Now, get in there."

With wild hair and grimy knees, I flew in the door to get a drink, skipping to the kitchen.

"Peggy. Come here," Tiny called out.

My body trembled as I walked to the doorway. Deb slithered from the bed onto the floor, kneeling, light cutting stripes across her body through the blinds.

"C'mon in here now. You need to see how pathetic your sister is."

It felt like my shoes were glued to the floor.

"C'mon now. Faster than that."

"*Please* Tiny. I don't want to watch." My face soaked with tears.

Tiny towered over Deb then flung the belt. He turned and glared. "She ain't so smart, is she?"

I shuddered from head to heel as he hit her repeatedly, each lash punctuated with an insult. Deb sobbed and pleaded. I wanted to do something, *but what?* He wiped his brow. Then in a tone as if he'd had a heart-to-heart with her, he said, "C'mon now…get on back out there and make me something to eat."

I sopped up my tears with my shirt. My legs were like jelly. I assumed he'd come after me. But he didn't. My voice quivered. "Can I go outside?"

He motioned with his hand. I dashed outside, pushing the scene from my mind.

I was used to dreadful things happening. Adapting was how I survived.

***

Tiny's erratic behavior continued. I was his favorite, but I was not spared from his rage. One day my foot caught the corner of a rug. I didn't notice and kept walking. Tiny, lounged on the couch, took a gulp of his Dr. Pepper, then said, "You forgettin' somethin'?"

I froze. I didn't understand the question, so I answered literally: "No."

He pointed to the rug. "Fix it."

He took off his belt.

I stooped down to fix the rug, my body vibrating. Before my hand could reach it, he flung his belt at my bare legs. SNAP. I backed away. He swung the belt wider and caught the edge of my thigh. SNAP.

"You betta get on over here, little girl. I'm trying to teach you a lesson."

I inched toward him.

"Now, stand right here and listen to me."

I stood, legs together, hands gripping my thighs.

"You gotta be prepared in this world. You think this is the worst you go'n git? You gone git a whole lot worse before you done in this world."

I stifled my whimper.

He swatted my butt like a football coach. "Alright now, go'n.' Do what you gotta do in the kitchen."

To this day, when I walk over a throw rug, I'm try not to turn up the corner.

Tiny's Hyde personality was worse when he was drinking. One late night Deb and I awoke when he and Mom came in. We were both near-sighted, so we squinted. We couldn't see clearly but we saw enough to know something was very wrong.

Rubbing the sleep from my eyes, I tried to adjust to the light. "Mommy, why are you so dirty?"

Her white jumper was the color of earth, and her hair was tangled. Mascara streaked down her cheeks; her face was swollen and bloody. Hunched, she dragged herself to the bedroom, Tiny loomed behind her, walking wobbly with a wild look in his eyes. He followed Mom into the bedroom then turned and said, "Go back to sleep girls."

I lay there wide awake, freaking out inside.

The next morning after Tiny left, Mom came out of the bedroom barely able to stand. She told us he'd accused her of flirting at the bar. After making a scene he insisted, they leave. "He beat me the whole way home," she said. "When I tried to get up, he kicked me down. So, I crawled."

Her friend, Clara—someone who made even Tiny back off—took her to the hospital. Tiny wouldn't mess with Clara. She was big, mouthy, and didn't take shit from anybody, even Tiny. She didn't have a kind word to say about him.

Deb and I stayed home waiting, worrying. A few hours later, Mom returned. He'd fractured her spine. "There's a piece of bone dangling. They said I'll end up in a wheelchair," she said. I couldn't wrap my brain around the idea of Mom being paralyzed. Who would take care of us? Tiny?

Tiny returned that day as if nothing had happened. Mom never said another word about it.

She didn't end up in a wheelchair but years later she told the story to new converts of God's miracle more times than kernels on an ear of corn. "Because God had a plan for me, he healed me," she'd say.

For decades after the beating, she complained of back pain. I massaged her and cracked her back often. She'd plop on the floor, lying face down, and speak through her armpit, "Peg, crack my back." I'd straddle her body and press my hands on either side of her spinal column, then I'd apply enough pressure to produce a crack. I'd move my hands down one vertebra at a time. I had no idea what I was doing, but she said it helped. I liked making her feel better.

Mom hadn't talked with Deb and me about leaving Tiny—ever. Until word came that Uncle Bob and his new wife, Tonya, were coming to visit from Pennsylvania.

"This is our chance to escape," Mom told us.

"Escape? You mean leave Tiny?"

"Yes, Peggy. No more questions."

In the days leading up to their arrival, I recalled how Uncle Bob played with me when I was little back in Pennsylvania. I fantasized about wrestling matches, whisker rubs, his toothless kisses, his cackle.

Mom planned to get him alone to tell him how we were being held against our will. But Tiny never allowed her to be alone with him.

From what Mom later told me and my own recollections; I pieced together what happened.

It was Mom's night off. They stayed in, drank, and played cards in the kitchen. Deb and I were on the couch trying to sleep, though, their thunderous voices made it impossible. We lay there—still as turtles—feigning sleep. At first, they were laughing and having a good time, and then it went sideways. Tonya said something that angered Tiny.

"No whore like you is gonna disrespect *me*," Tiny yelled.

Tonya fired back. "Who you callin' a whore?"

"C'mon man, let's keep it friendly," Bob said, in a calm voice.

Tiny ignored Bob's efforts and continued to go at it with Tonya. "I don't think you know who you dealin' with. I can *mess you up*."

Tonya was unfazed. "I don't care who you are. You can't talk to me like that. Tell him, Bob."

Bob said nothing. Mom was silent too.

Tiny's chair screeched as he pushed himself back from the table. He stormed into the bedroom—blowing by Deb and me, then came out with a gun. "You better get up outa' here if you know what's good for you," he said, rage in his voice.

Bob piped up again, "C'mon man, there's no need for a gun."

"You need to get your woman under control."

Bob gasped. "Look, we'll just go."

"Yeah, you better git."

Bob let out a nervous chuckle.

Tonya got in the last word as Bob guided her toward the door. "Good riddance."

They left and our lives resumed as they were.

***

A few months later, Deb befriended Mary, a woman who worked at the laundromat. She was a pudgy woman with wiry salt and pepper hair, unmarried and childless. She and Deb shared a love of books and could talk for hours. Every day, Deb would finish her chores and homework and go to see her. Deb wasn't a lighthearted, hopeful type; she was serious and pessimistic. But after meeting Mary, she had something spry about her, smiled, and left the house more.

One night, I came home late from playing. Deb was still at the laundromat. Mom was rarely home in the early evenings, but she was that night. Tiny was strict about how we did our chores but not about when we did them. He left that to Mom. "Y'all better get your chores done before your mama git home," he'd say. Ninety-nine percent of the time, we did.

Just as the streetlights came on, I dashed through the front door out of breath. Tiny and Mom were seated on the couch, arms folded, faces tight.

"Mom, you're home," I said.

She rose, hands on her hips, forehead wrinkled. "Yeah, I got off early. Why aren't your chores done? And, where's your sister?"

My body tensed. I clenched my pant legs. "Deb's doing laundry."

Tiny stood behind her, smirking.

"When I say you do your chores before you go outside, I mean it."

"Sorry, Mommy. I'll do 'em now."

Tiny folded onto the couch and leaned back. Hands laced behind his head. "You gonna put up with them excuses? She needs a whooping."

Mom's lips tightened.

My knees went weak. Tears streamed down my nine-year-old cheeks, plastering my red curls to my chin. Tiny pulled off his belt and handed it to Mom. She planted herself on the edge of the couch. "Get over here and lay across my lap."

I backed away from her. "No, Mom. *Please.* I won't do it again."

Tiny belly laughed. "It's gone be a whole lot worse if she gotta come after you."

I'd never seen her so furious. In the past, when I got lickings, she was calm, gave us the licking, then followed with a lecture.

The veins in her neck bulged. "Don't make me come after you."

I inched toward her, wringing my hands. I draped over her lap, my body tense as a board. She flung the belt. Whoobam! Whoobam! She struck me five or six times.

She leaned back and nudged me. "Alright. Wipe that face and go do your chores."

I went to the kitchen to get the cleaning supplies, my belly shaking with sobs.

"Whatchu gone do about Debbie?" Tiny asked.

"She's finishing the laundry. I don't think she deserves a licking," Mom said.

"You can't back down now. She been spending way too much time with that lady at the laundromat. You gotta teach her a lesson. Here, go behind that door. Then, you can surprise her when she come in."

Mom squeezed behind the door, belt in hand. Periodically Tiny would get up, peel back the curtain and look out, continuing to egg Mom on.

Chortling, he whispered loudly, "Here she come." We waited quietly, as if we were throwing Deb a surprise party. She walked in carrying a laundry basket. Mom leaped out and swung. Deb dropped the basket and the clothes toppled.

"You betta pick up them clothes," Tiny glowered from the sideline.

Deb crouched, gathering up the clothes.

"That's all you go'n give her? She deserve more than that."

"Why weren't you home before dark?" Mom demanded.

Deb sidestepped away from Mom. "I'm sorry. I'm sorry it took so long."

"Don't you move away from me!"

"You better go after her," Tiny badgered.

Mom pointed to the floor next to her. "Debbie, get over here this minute."

"No, I'm not coming over there. You're gonna hit me."

Deb was more defiant than I was—I envied that in her but also thought she was stupid for making it worse for herself.

Mom swung the belt again. Whoobam! Whoobam! Deb backed away. Mom went after her.

"That's right Sandy. That's how you show her," Tiny cheered.

Mom ran after her swinging the belt over and over, landing one out of two times. Then she stopped and plopped on the couch, seemingly exhausted. "Now, get this laundry picked up."

Whimpering, Deb knelt on the floor and picked up the laundry. I wanted to help but didn't dare.

The next day Mom was home after school (which was unusual) sitting on the couch. Walking in the door, Deb and I gave each other that familiar look: What now? My abdomen tightened around a rock in my stomach. Deb pushed up her glasses by crinkling her nose.

"Girls, come sit. I need to talk to youse." She folded her body a bit, getting at Deb's eye level. "Debbie, why did you tell Mary Tiny whooped you?"

Deb looked at Mom over her glasses. "I didn't want you to get in trouble." Tears erupted.

"That Mary needs to mind her own business. You're my daughter—not hers. She don't know nothing 'bout raising kids. I was teaching you something. So, you got a few bruises. I've had worse in my life. Your Pappy used to make me get my own switch from the yard. And Mammy dragged me out from parties by the hair. Tiny's in jail because of Mary."

"But mom, Tiny can't hurt you again if he's in jail."

"Debbie, when he gets out, and he will get out, he's gonna be *real* mad." Mom turned and walked into the kitchen.

I asked Deb what had happened. She said she'd gone to the laundromat wearing shorts to expose her bruises and told Mary that Tiny had beaten her.

"Do you think Tiny *will* get out of jail?" I asked.

Mom crossed her arms. "I hope not."

I was conflicted. On the one hand I felt close to Tiny and hoped he'd get out of jail. I clung to the good moments. But on the other hand, if he stayed in jail, he wouldn't be able to hurt us again. I couldn't understand my feelings. I'd never felt so torn.

Two days later Tiny came home. Life resumed as if nothing had happened. Tiny forbade Deb to see Mary again.

Much later, Mom told us she'd bailed Tiny out because if she didn't, someone else would've, and he would've come home and beat us.

I walked into the living room one afternoon to Tiny sitting on the couch holding his head in his hands, crying. I approached him with soft steps and put my hand on his back. "What's wrong, Tiny?"

He told me to sit, then he called Deb, who was in the kitchen washing dishes. We sat on either side of him. Tiny wiped his eyes with his thumb and forefinger, then kneeled on the floor in front of us. The afternoon sun glossed his sable afro. Tears welled in his tawny-brown eyes.

"Girls, I'm go'n change. I love your mama and I love y'all," he said, with what looked like sincerity in his eyes. "I'm gone git me a real job, stop drinking and finish school."

I wanted to believe him. But I also didn't. He'd terrorized us for two years, though I didn't fully understand that back then.

***

It was Mom's day off. I was home sick from school when she called me into the bedroom. She had a frenzied look in her eyes, and her hair was mussed. She yanked clothes off hangers and sloppily folded them into a huge black metal trunk with brass hinges. "We're leaving today and never coming back."

"What? Leaving?"

"I've been hiding tips in my winter coat so we can leave Tiny, and now I have enough. He's gone all day to class, so this is the time for us to go." She packed more frantically.

I pushed up my glasses. "Where we goin'?"

"Once we get there, I'll tell you. Now, c'mon, put your stuff in this trunk. Only take what you need. Some clothes, shoes, stuff like that. Pack your sister's clothes too."

She walked to the kitchen to load a second trunk.

I wondered: Would I see my friends again? Will Tiny be sad? Will he find us like the other time we tried to leave?

About a year prior, Mom took Deb and me to her friend's apartment in an attempt to leave, but Tiny showed up the same day, pounding on the door, at first pleading with her to come home, then demanding, "or else." Mom tried ignoring him at first. "Don't make a sound," she instructed. Deb and I sat on the couch, our hands in our laps, quiet and confused. Finally, she ushered us up and out the door to return home with him. She knew there was no escaping at that point.

"What about toys?" I hollered.

"No room."

"What about the kitty?"

"Can't take the cat."

"Deb's gonna be sad. She loves that cat."

"I know. Can't do nothing 'bout that."

When we finished packing, a car honked. Mom dashed to the living room and

31

pulled back the curtain. "It's our cab. C'mon, we have to get your sister." She dragged one trunk out to the car. I grabbed the handle of the other and tried jostling it through the doorway. The cab driver jumped out to help. Jan, the neighbor, met us at the cab and talked with Mom for a minute. I crawled into the back seat and watched out the rear window. Mom was jittery, her eyes darting around. I couldn't make out what they were saying, but it seemed like Mom was giving Jan some sort of instructions. Then they hugged and Mom climbed in the front seat of the cab. I rested my chin in my hands and watched out the back window as our neighborhood disappeared.

We picked Deb up from school. I was right, she was sad about the kitty and her dolls.

The life I knew had been set in a small frame. I was going to miss my friends, my school, Tiny's cheeseburgers, watching Columbo and eating popcorn with him, dancing with his nieces and nephews, lapping up his mom's seafood gumbo and sweet potato pie, and attending the Baptist church where everyone treated me like their little sister.

Getting out of the taxi at LAX, sadness shrouded me. I thought, Tiny's gonna be so sad. Why didn't Mom see that he was changing?

The taxi driver loaded the black trunks onto a cart for us to wheel in.

Mom found seats for us by the ticket counter. "Wait here." Her trench coat trailed as she hurried to the ticket counter. She laid her cash on the counter and asked how far the three of us could get.

She walked back over, tight-lipped, her breathing shallow.

I studied her face. "Now what?"

"I told you. No questions."

I picked at the skin on my fingers. Deb buried herself in a book.

From my seat on the plane, I leaned against the window watching the airport workers loading the suitcases. Pity for Tiny enveloped me, but I distracted myself by thinking about how fun flying was going to be.

As the plane sped up on the runway my worry was replaced with delight. The massive metal bird soaring into the sky left my anxieties behind on the tarmac. A flutter went through me as the plane ascended. Then, that I'm-on-top-of-the-world-feeling overtook me. I counted the little blue dots that were swimming pools. I was awed by how organized everything looked. Then, in moments, it all vanished as we soared through thick undulant clouds with pink and orange edges.

Mom kept a sober silence throughout the short flight.

After deplaning, she sat us down in baggage claim. She smoothed the collar of her trench coat. "We're in Sacramento. That's as far as we could get." She slid a cigarette from its pack and lit it. "Okay, girls. Now I can tell you everything." She exhaled smoke, then lifted her gaze back and forth between Deb and me, as she often did when lecturing. But this wasn't a lecture. Her eyes welled. "Tiny did terrible things. Remember the times he beat me? Well, he did more than that." She hung her head. She said he'd raped women in front of her, slept with a gun under his pillow. Said he'd kill us if she tried to leave.

Deb put her nose in the air and flared her nostrils. "I knew he was bad."

Mom nodded. "He was never gonna change."

Her words sank like stones. I crossed my arms. "I don't feel sorry for him no more. I *was* sad, but now I'm mad. Why did he do them bad things? He said he was gonna change."

Mom explained that her decision to let Tiny watch us after her emergency hysterectomy was out of desperation, but she never intended for him to stay. She had never dated him; he'd decided she was his woman. "We were prisoners for two years," she said. She wiped a tear from below her eye. "I know he said that, but he was never gonna change."

Finally, I understood why Mom didn't initiate kisses, laugh with him, or cuddle on the couch as I'd seen her do with other boyfriends. I understood why she didn't talk about marrying him, and why she'd stopped singing, laughing, and kidding around.

On the cab ride to the hotel, with my forehead pressed against the glass, a graphic image appeared in my mind: Tiny kicking Mom to the ground, making her watch him rape a woman he held at gunpoint, sleeping with a gun under his pillow.

For the first time in my life, I felt hatred.

CHAPTER THREE
Sacramento, 1971

Mom found a cheap hotel room in an old brick high-rise in downtown Sacramento, the kind of place that smelled of dust and stale smoke. The room had one rickety bed, a kitchenette with peeling linoleum, and a bathroom barely big enough to turn around. Mom and Deb took the bed. I took a roll-away that sagged in the middle. We only had enough money for a week. Each morning Mom walked out the door, purse slung over her shoulder, determination in her eye searching for a job and an apartment on foot. Bus fare would drain what little we had. Deb and I stayed back and entertained ourselves playing cards or bickering as kids do.

Before the week was up, Mom was triumphant. She'd secured an apartment and a job. "We're moving in tonight," she said, even though it wasn't ideal. The previous tenants left disgruntled and trashed the place. But we didn't have the luxury of ideal.

We stayed up cleaning the place until two a.m. On our hands and knees, we removed globs of a syrupy substance and scraped dried food from the walls. On top of that, the furious tenants bashed in the furnace beyond repair. The cold set into our bones. Deb and Mom slept in the bed fully dressed and covered with a sheet. I slept on the floor beneath a pile of coats, trying to trap my breath for warmth.

After a week, the landlord replaced the furnace and the slashed furniture with brand new, plastic still clinging to the cushions. Mom slept on the couch. Deb and I took the bed.

We'd only been there a couple of weeks when a letter arrived from Tiny "Oh my God!" Mom yelled. "There's a letter from Tiny." Deb and I rushed to the couch and sat on either side of her, anchoring her like book ends. The color drained from Mom's face as she ripped open the letter.

"How did he get our address?" Deb asked.

Her hands trembled as she studied the address on the envelope. "Oh, he sent it to our old address in Los Angeles and the post office forwarded it. He don't know where we are." Her posture softened.

Mom read the letter aloud. *I love you. You know I do. Nobody loves you like I do. I'm going to be a bookkeeper. I can take care of y'all.*

His words landed on me like something rotten. Nothing in me could forgive him for what he'd done.

"Maybe we should go back." Mom said softly. "I think he's changed."

I couldn't believe my ears.

"No, Mom!" Deb and I protested in unison.

"But what if he has? Changed?"

"He don't mean it," I said. "How could he? After he did them bad things?"

Deb rested her hand on Mom's shoulder. "He doesn't mean anything he says. Can't you see that, Mom?"

Mom looked at her pleadingly. "But…he loves us."

Deb straightened like a metal pole. "It's a trick. We're here now and it's going to work out."

I rubbed Mom's arm. "He don't love you. If he did, he wouldn't've hurt you like he did."

Mom pulled a tissue from her purse and dabbed her tears. "You're right girls. After what he did to Jan, I don't know what he'd do to me."

Clara, Mom's friend, had told her that Tiny had beaten and raped Jan—our next-door neighbor—trying to get her to tell him where we were. But Mom hadn't told Jan. She hadn't even told Clara until we were in Sacramento long enough to breathe again. We were relieved Mom came to her senses.

Our neighborhood was sketchy enough that Mom made strict rules: we had to be home before the streetlights clicked on. Deb and I took that rule seriously. We assumed Mom would too.

But one night, she was determined to go out for a drink on her night off.

Leaning over the bathroom sink she applied a final coat of mascara. "It's not easy for a single girl to go out you know. We can't just walk in a bar alone. How would that look?" She spritzed her short hairdo with Aqua Net, sealed the curls in place like armor. As usual she looked striking: her hair teased and wispy bangs against her forehead, winged eyeliner, coral lipstick, hoop earrings. Her black elephant pants swished when she moved, and a green, pullover turtleneck hugged her with elegance.

She butted her cigarette in the ashtray, then put on her coat. "Take your baths, then go to bed. And don't forget to brush your teeth. I'm gonna walk since I only have two dollars."

Deb and I were playing double solitaire. Deb whispered, "Peg, we can't let Mom go."

"I know. She could get kidnapped. Let's go tell her."

Mom freshened her lipstick and headed for the door. "Girls. Remember. Don't open the door for no one. Youse hear?"

We begged her not to leave, but she assured us she was only going to the bar where she worked a few blocks away.

"Call us the minute you get there," Deb hollered as the door shut.

Her perfume, hairspray, and cigarettes lingered in the room long after she left, like she was both gone and still there.

We listened to our transistor radio as a distraction, trying to stop worrying. Still, I imagined terrible things: her body bleeding by the road, her being kidnapped, and—the worst—never seeing her again.

Half an hour later, the door jiggled.

"Who is it?" Deb hollered.

"It's Mom. Open the door. Hurry up."

Mom fell through the door and collapsed. We ran to her aid. Her beige calf-length jacket had leaves stuck onto it like needles in a cactus. Grass and dirt were tangled in her hair, her lipstick smeared, mascara streaked down her cheeks. I froze, much like in L.A. when she came home all dirty and bloody from Tiny's beating.

She said a man jumped out of a bush and dragged her into the dark, ripped off her pants and crawled on top of her, then raped her. She called out, "Help me, Jesus." She must have appealed to his religious side because he could no longer perform and stopped. After making her swear never to tell anyone, the man robbed her of the two dollars and let her go.

"See, we told you not to go," Deb said.

"I know. I should've listened."

Sitting on the floor next to her, I scooted a little closer, pulled leaves from her coat, and put them in a little pile. "Promise you'll never go out in the dark alone again. Please, Mommy. Promise."

"I promise girls."

We helped her undress and get into the bath. She didn't call the police. She said the man was down on his luck and she forgave him because he stopped when she cried out for Jesus.

"He's a God-fearing man," she said.

I couldn't understand how she could forgive a rapist. Mom often shared what little we had. Quarters to a homeless. A bed for an unwed mother-to-be. She wasn't religious then, not really, but she talked about Jesus as if he were a childhood friend who still visited her dreams. She didn't go to church because of working late Saturday nights, but she made sure that Deb and I went to Sunday school. I didn't think much about God. Church meant time away from my friends.

***

The manager of the apartment building, a plump man with glossy black hair and a round face, asked Mom if either of us girls would want guitar lessons. He said he needed practice before becoming a teacher. I jumped at the chance. Mom agreed, so long as it was at our apartment.

I regretted it instantly.

His lessons were only a way to get his hands on me. He sat me on his lap, the guitar a shield between us, his hands strayed—one showing me the cords, the other beneath my clothes. Mom cooked in the kitchen, while I was frozen on his lap, my mind slipping out of my body. I wanted to shove him and run, but my still little body couldn't move.

"See you for your next lesson," he'd say, like he was doing me a favor.

To complicate matters, he'd taken a liking to Mom. She went to his apartment a few times, but he got too rough one night. She came home with her hair and clothes mussed. "He went too far," she said, and that was the end of that.

He never gave me another guitar lesson, but that wasn't the last of him.

One day when I was home sick, restless, and bored, I called Mom at work and asked if I could plant flowers outside our door. She told me to ask the manager for seeds. I didn't want to see him, but I had my heart set on planting flowers.

Looking back on that day, I can see his apartment in my mind as clearly as if I were looking into someone's home right now. I climbed the squeaky, wooden stairs to his front door, my body stiff with dread. I lightly rapped on the screen door, stared at the dark tweed couch, and stained shag carpet the color of dirt. The console TV, which held a vase of fake flowers, was airing a daytime show.

"Who's there?" he shouted.

I hesitated. "It's Peggy from downstairs. Mom said I should ask you for some flower seeds."

"C'mon in."

My heart hammered. "That's okay. I'll wait out here."

"C'mon. I don't bite. I just have to get dressed. It's going to be a minute. So, you might as well take a seat."

I stepped inside, then waited, shuffling my feet. I focused on the funny costumes on "Let's Make a Deal" on TV. Sunlight cut through the blinds in slashes, dust particles circulating in the air.

He came out, bathrobe hanging open, naked, hairy stomach and erect penis in full view.

I looked away. "I changed my mind. I don't need no seeds."

He rushed over, grabbed me, yanked me over to the couch, and perched me on his lap. I ripped his fingers from my hips, then bolted out the door and down the steps, my legs flying before my mind caught up. I pushed open our front door, locked it, then threw myself on the couch and bawled until my chest hurt.

I told no one. Not Deb. Not Mom. Telling it would've made it real. Soon after the incident, he moved out. We never learned why.

***

After a few months, we moved into a two-bedroom duplex on L Street in a half-way-decent neighborhood. Deb and I shared a roomy bedroom with twin beds. Mom finally had a kitchen big enough to cook without elbowing the walls. The backyard was a paradise: a cherry tree (one I would later get stuck in), orange trees with fruit ripe for the picking, and a fence lined with sweet, purple grapes.

I made friends quickly. They asked many questions about L.A. Did I go to Disneyland? Did I meet movie stars? Did I play sports? I'd created an alter ego without intending to. It morphed over time. I didn't want anyone to know about Tiny, that we were poor, or that I didn't have a dad. I said we used to be rich, had a basement full of toys, was on the diving team and had won several diving competitions. Kids were intrigued by my stories, so much so that they would encircle me at recess, begging for stories. I fed them increasingly. I felt guilty, but the attention was intoxicating. That version of me felt safer than the real one.

For a couple of years, life steadied. I abandoned hope of ever having a dad and I accepted that I wouldn't have grandparents, aunts, uncles, or cousins in my life. I focused on what I *did* have: a house, a yard, friends, school. I felt stable for the first time in my nearly ten years of life, and I think Deb did too. Except for the occasional depressive episode, Mom seemed relatively content. We still had to be on food stamps and "partial welfare," as Mom called it, but life was okay on L Street. Until it wasn't.

***

Mom told the story of how she got saved so many times; I know it like I know my hair is red.

A young woman named Melinda came to the door handing out pamphlets. Mom, drawn to anyone who talked about Jesus, let in the young zealot. She had an honest face, un-plucked brows, and long frizzy hair parted down the middle. Melinda "witnessed" to Mom. Witnessing, I would later learn, is a common practice among Evangelicals, where someone shares how Jesus personally changed their life. Mom listened raptly. After Melinda left, Mom laid the leaflet on her dresser and forgot about it.

A couple weeks later, Mom was getting ready to go out on her night off. Sitting at her vanity, applying her makeup, and listening to oldies on our transistor, she heard a man call her name. "Sandy." She ignored it. He called again. She turned up the music. The voice called a third time. "Sandy!" Finally, Mom answered. "Yes, Lord." She believed it was God calling her name.

Falling to her knees, her past suffering, sorrow, and mistakes played out before her, "like I was watching a movie," she said. She had a conversation with God. "I heard the Lord in my ears, not in my head," she clarified. He said if she didn't devote her life to Him, her life would continue as it was—full of pain. She vowed to give up her fleshly life in return for the everlasting life. God said she needed a vessel, someone who could facilitate her rebirth. She grabbed the pamphlet from her dresser and called Melinda.

Melinda arrived and had Mom kneel by the bed as she crouched beside her. She laid one hand on Mom's back and the other on her head. She prayed, asking Jesus to forgive her sins. Mom wailed. Melinda spoke in tongues (the language that Pentecostals believed was a manifestation of the presence of the Holy Ghost) and sang praises to Jesus. After Mom had cried every tear she had, Melinda said her sins had been washed away. She then asked God to allow the Holy Ghost to enter her. Mom spoke in tongues immediately.

After Melinda left, Mom sat, listening to God lay it out for her. She needed to give up smoking, drinking, dieting, dying her hair, going to the bars—anything worldly. He expected her to study the Bible and serve Him. That was the day her life changed. That was the day *my* life changed.

***

It was a usual night for Deb and me; in our room, doing what adolescent girls do.

"Girls," Mom hollered. "We're going to church. Get your shoes on."

We dropped what we were doing and dashed to Mom's room. She was sitting at her vanity, spritzing perfume on her black sweater.

"Why? It's Wednesday night," I said.

"I know." She leaned forward and applied her lipstick. "We're gonna start going to church on Wednesdays now. Get your shoes on."

"Are we going to our regular church?" Deb asked.

Mom blotted around her nose with a compact puff, then snapped it shut and tossed it into her pocketbook. "No more questions. Melinda's gonna drive us. She'll be here at any minute. Hurry up."

Melinda honked twice. We threw on our jackets and hightailed it out the door. She drove us to a stucco building in a lower-middle class neighborhood. Deb had her nose in a book, while I bit my nails and stared out the window.

"This is it," Mom said, as we pulled into a packed parking lot.

"*This* is the church?" I said in disbelief.

No windows, no cross.

Deb's forehead creased. "It doesn't look like a church."

"Just c'mon girls."

Inside, though, it was one big sanctuary. A stage. Rows of metal folding chairs. People everywhere. Hippies with babies. Old ladies adorning their Sunday's best. Musicians filed onto the stage and tuned their instruments. It was chaotic. The band smoothing out notes, kids running around, adults chatting, babies fussing.

A lanky blonde guitar player counted: "One…two…one-two-three." He adjusted the microphone, leaned into it, and sang. The rock song was only recognizable as religious if you listened to the lyrics.

Parents herded their kids to their seats. The talking stopped. The congregation clapped with the music. We joined. Attendees held their arms in the air and bobbed their heads like we were at a rock concert. Mom smiled and snapped her fingers to the music. The band finished with a drum riff, and the congregation applauded. An apple-shaped man strutted out from behind the stage with a wet, silver comb-over, wearing a red velvet suit jacket and white patent leather shoes. He scooped the microphone from the top of the keyboard. With his lips brushing against the mic, he shouted, "Praise the Lord." The congregation repeated.

My eyes flitted between the preacher, the band, the congregation. I was bewildered. Deb and I sat on either side of Mom. I couldn't get a read on her. She joined in, calling out praises.

Sweat beads gathered on the preacher's forehead. Soon he removed his velvet jacket and draped it over the keyboard, exposing his extra-wide waist. "The Loooooord Jesus is calling your name. He wants to take you to his pearly gates." His belly jiggled as he took long strides across the stage. He squeezed his eyes shut and put his hands in the air. The congregation rose, put their hands up (including Mom), and babbled (which I later learned was speaking in tongues). I stood, frozen. A woman collapsed in the aisle. Several members rushed to her and knelt, trying to find a small patch of her body to hold their hand against. She was surrounded like a piece of bread on the ground covered in ants. The babbling intensified. Finally, the woman came to, sat up, put her hands in the air, and gibbered. A woman a few seats over shouted out what sounded like Bible verses. I would later learn she was prophesying. Someone makes a prophecy in tongues, and another person translates in English. The congregation roared with praise, the band resumed, and everyone leaped to their feet and danced. Soon, someone started a dance train. I decided I'd join only if Mom did. When the end of the train came by, Mom grabbed the waist of the last person. I hooked my hands around her waist, then Deb grabbed mine. Our train bobbed around the room twice. When the song ended, the preacher grabbed the mic and continued the sermon. It was like listening to the adults from Charlie Brown and The Peanuts. Whau, whau, whau, whau, whau.

Until he said, in that fire-and-brimstone cadence, "the Lord wants my wife and me to have a new car. A Cadillac. It's going to take some time, but I know the Lord will lay generosity on your hearts." I felt my stomach twist. Tithe is for the needy. I was certain we were poorer than him and his wife. I couldn't understand why Mom couldn't see through his ruse.

After that night, we attended church every Sunday, Saturday, and Wednesday. The pattern of the service was obvious: song, prayer, sermon, fainting woman, prophecy in tongues, interpretation, altar call, sometimes a dance train. A handful would go up. The preacher would lay his hand on their head, and the elders would place a hand on their back and other parts of their body. The congregation stood, arms in the air and eyes closed, speaking in tongues. The preacher would holler, "We caaaaaall upon you, Lord, to forgive this child. He comes before you… humble and repentant…" After the convert was forgiven, the preacher commanded Satan and his demons to leave. "Leave Satan! We rebuke you!" Converts yelled similar commands. He'd then ask the Holy Ghost to enter the convert. He'd speak in tongues, shaking and jerking the convert's head and yelling, "Receive! Receive the Holy Ghost!" The new convert would speak in tongues, and everyone would rejoice. I hadn't considered going up. That is, until Deb did.

One evening, after the altar call, Deb inched her way to the front, one tail of her faded, untucked flannel shirt hanging out. Her wavy locks shimmering under the fluorescent lights. The preacher, grinned and opened his arms. Deb was shy, so going to the front was monumental. I couldn't see her face, but I imagined an awkward smile. She pushed up her aviator wire-rimmed glasses and accepted his embrace. She knelt and several attendees came to the front and sat beside her, then enveloped her with their hands. Barely an open spot remained on her body. She asked for forgiveness, received the Holy Ghost, then spoke in tongues. The crowd erupted in praise.

After watching Deb get saved, I felt pressure. Some nights elders would pull newcomers from their seats and take them to the front. I was terrified of being randomly chosen. I figured it was better to get it over with.

"It's that time folks," the preacher said—per the usual pattern—in his southern twang, his comb-over mashed with sweat. "It's time for God's newest children to come up and get saved."

The congregation sang praises. The preacher paced, wide-eyed. Sweat snaked down his forehead. Periodically, he'd pull a hanky from his pocket to wipe it. "Praise Jesus. Hallelujah. Come on brothers and sisters, let Jesus guide you in your life. Let our savior give you everlasting life."

My knees were weak. What if I can't speak in tongues?

I swallowed hard and shuffled to the front. When I turned around, Mom was beaming. I stood at the base of the stage and leaned my forehead onto my folded hands like I'd seen others do. I felt pressure to cry. I dug down into myself for a pocket of sorrow. A past, lingering feeling that would set off tears. Nothing. The preacher laid one hand on my back and another on my head. Others came up and placed their hands on different parts of me. I wasn't sure if Mom's hands were there or not. The symphony of babblings moved up and down in volume. I felt like I'd been teleported to another realm. If I don't cry, will it take? Will Jesus forgive me? Heat came off the preacher like a pot belly stove.

"Are you sorry for all your sins little girl?"

I kept my forehead pressed to my folded hands. "Yes."

"Then ask the Lord to forgive you."

I wanted to disappear, but I squeezed out the words in the softest voice I could. If they couldn't hear me, they wouldn't be able to figure out that I was faking. "Please Lord, forgive me."

The preacher belted in a sing-songy tempo. "We ask that you let this child receive your Holy Ghost, Lord."

"Hallelujah! Praise Jesus!" Members called out. I shuddered. My ears hurt. Elders, and those who'd come up, closed in on me. I was trapped by a blanket of human hands covering my body. I wanted to run, but I had to stay the course.

"Give this child the Holy Ghost and let her tongue flow with your word."

I forced a syllable salad from my lips. I blathered like a baby. I swept my bangs from my forehead, pushed up my welfare glasses, and forced a smile. Everyone rejoiced. I'd done it. I spoke in tongues.

Slinking back to my seat, I felt no different. Only relief that it was over.

After that, I too, put my hands in the air during prayer, and called out praises to Jesus. Still, the memory of the preacher collecting tithes for a new Cadillac gnawed at me. That was the beginning of my moral confusion.

Mom had quit drinking and smoking. She stayed home studying the Bible on her nights off — that is, when she wasn't downtown preaching on the street. Her look changed too—her mascara lighter and her lipstick paler. She'd gained a few pounds and let her gray roots grow in, and she dressed more conservatively. I didn't think the changes in Mom were bad, especially her decision to quit smoking. Deb and I had begged her to do that for years. But the transformation seemed so drastic and sudden.

Because of how often we went to church, my social life was limited. It was like a tornado had swept up my life and spit it out with missing pieces. Church swallowed my weekends. I stopped running around town with friends, and since we went to church on Saturday nights, no more sleepovers. I clung to what I still had: seeing my friends at school, talking on the phone, and Friday nights at the roller rink. I'd count down the days, fantasizing about peeling around the rink to "Keep on Truckin" or "Funky Stuff," flirting with boys before kicking their butts at air hockey, accompanying cute boys to the twilight skate. Thank God there was no church on Fridays. I was used to change but this felt different. The little I did have of Mom, was slipping away. And, just when I thought it couldn't get any worse…

***

Buddy, a silver-haired man with a southern accent, showed up at church one night a couple of months after Mom's conversion. His face was pleasant, but he wore a chronic, sneaky smirk that rubbed me the wrong way. Mom spent all her free time with him, going with him to church, studying the Bible, and street-corner preaching. We saw Mom seldom as it was, and some slick, fast-talking conman stole the little time we did get with her. It didn't take long for me to grow to hate him.

After school one day, Mom called Deb and me into the living room—she had something to tell us. Looking pensive, she pulled a chair in from the dining room and sat in front of us. Buddy sat next to her, wearing his usual leer. He crossed his legs, ran his hand through his pompadour, then leaned back and folded his arms. The last time Mom sat us down like that was when we sold everything and moved to California.

Mom looked over at Buddy like she was waiting for his cue. He kept his arms folded and his gaze fixed on Deb and me.

44

"Girls. I have something to tell youse." She smiled and looked over at Buddy. "We got married last night."

Stunned, Deb and I exploded with questions. When? Where? Why without us? Is Buddy going to live here?"

"We went to Las Vegas last night when youse were sleeping," Mom said. "And yes, Buddy's gonna live here. Now, no more questions." Her face turned serious, but Buddy's smug grin stayed stitched on his face. My stomach twisted.

The thought of Buddy living with us gave me the willies. He didn't have a job, and Mom barely knew him, and that smirk… Something wasn't right.

Buddy became our disciplinarian. He made us read the Bible daily, inspected chores and homework. He'd grill us after school: Who were we with? Did we do something we shouldn't have? We didn't fear him like we feared Mom. We weren't going to let some mooch come in and take over. I mouthed off, slammed doors, and burned holes in him with my dagger eyes. "You can't tell me what to do," I'd scream. "You're not my dad." He'd laugh and snicker, then make me write, "I won't yell at Buddy" hundreds of times. I'd sit at the dining room table, scribbled the sentences, fuming.

Deb and I united against Buddy. We'd sit in our room commiserating about how much we hated him, how we didn't believe they *actually* got married, how he was using Mom. We wanted to tell Mom he was mean to us when she wasn't around, even laughed at us, but she told us God sent him to us. She wouldn't listen. We knew telling her was futile. She was hooked.

One day I cracked. After he punished me again, I took a razor blade, sat on the edge of the clawfoot tub, rage coursing my veins, and carved I HATE BUDDY into my forearm. My adrenaline was so high that it didn't hurt. I wanted Mom to see it.

Afterwards, I sat down at the dining room table and opened my Bible. I had purposely worn short sleeves. The cuts hadn't bled much, but they were red and raised. I paid them no mind. Buddy walked in, then stopped in his tracks.

Wearing his usual snicker, he said, "Wait till your mom sees your arm."

"So…I don't care. I hope she does." I went back to fake reading the Bible.

When Mom walked in, Buddy had me show her my arm.

"What'd you do?" She asked, eyes wide.

Buddy sat at the table, droning on about how my body was the temple of God and I'd defiled it. "I know you don't hate me," he said, chortling. "You're mad I'm disciplining you."

Mom agreed with everything he said.

I wanted to stand up and shout, "I hate Buddy because he's using you and he's fake!"

I didn't like it when Mom punished me, but she was my mom—it made sense. Buddy was some guy, fifteen years her senior, who was bilking us for what little we had. Mom sent me to my room for the rest of the night. After I stomped off, Buddy made me come back and walk normally.

A few weeks later, Mom and Buddy announced that we were moving. I was devastated but said nothing to Buddy. Silence was my only safe posture, but my insides crumbled. I'd finally found friends, a house, a rhythm. I told Mom how I felt but it didn't matter. She said we had no choice.

By eleven years old, I'd lived in twelve homes. But this goodbye hurt most.

***

We turned onto our new street that summer day. The sun beamed over the cookie-cutter houses, all spaced perfectly apart and painted bright colors. Ours was peach. Some yards were pristinely groomed with round bushes and lawns like putting greens. Others were severely in need of mowing and littered with kids' toys. Children of all colors were everywhere, riding their bikes up and down the street. Little girls jumped rope and sang jingles, their beaded braids bouncing.

When we pulled into the carport, my heart did jumping jacks. We lived in apartments, duplexes, with friends, even above the firehouse in Mom's hometown. But we'd never had an entire house to ourselves. We were going through an FHA program (a government loan for low-income families), which made sense because we were hard up, as far as I knew.

It felt odd stepping inside, like we were intruders in another family's house.

"This whole house is *ours*?" I asked.

"Yep. I told you you'd like it, Peggy," Mom said.

Grief instantly lifted. Three bedrooms, two baths, a huge backyard, and the best part: a living room long enough for tumbling.

I got a running start. "Watch Mom," I stretched my arms tautly above my head, then did two cartwheels and my signature roundoff at the end. I practiced that thing more times than I had hairs on my head. I'd pour all my energy into a combination, repeating it over and over until it was perfect. I wanted to be a gymnast, but Mom didn't have that kind of money. From gym class, I learned the

pommel horse, the balance beam, uneven parallel bars, the trampoline, and tumbling—my favorite. I could do it anywhere, and I did: sidewalks, driveways, parking lots, any open space. But in our new house, I had a built-in tumbling floor
that had my name on it.

I still missed my friends, but I focused on what I had rather than what I'd lost.
I'd crank up the radio, put on shorts and a t-shirt, and dance across the floor,
stopping periodically to do a few Rockette-style kicks or my well-practiced tumbling routines. Mom often told the story of how I'd hold myself up by the rail of
the playpen before I was even one, dancing to American Bandstand, volume up.
"Peggy danced before she walked," she'd say. When I danced, I didn't *listen* to
music; I *felt* it. The lyrics didn't matter. If I caught the groove, I'd move to any
lyrics until sweat ran down my back. And if the hooks were catchy, I'd sing. When
I was around eight or so, my friends and I played on the swings and sang Chuck
Berry's "My Ding A Ling." *My Ding-A-Ling. My Ding-A-Ling. I want you to play with
My Ding-A-Ling;* we'd sing, swinging high in the air, clueless about the meaning
of the lyrics.

Mom loved to dance too. Back in Pennsylvania, she'd play records while she
cooked, and Deb and I, along with our friends, jumped around to the music.
Mom would sashay into the den with a big gummy grin. She'd grab one of our
hands and twirl. "I'm dancing the boy part so youse'll know what to do when a
boy asks you to dance," she'd say. Then, we kids would practice what she'd taught
us, twirling with each other, taking turns being the lead. Deb and I were often
rivals, but while dancing with Mom, we put our differences aside.

Our new house was a dream, but Buddy made it a nightmare. He had a hold
on Mom. He didn't have a job; he didn't cook or clean or do anything to contribute. Yet Mom let him take over. "Never let a man take over your life," she'd
taught us. But it seemed like that was precisely what *she* was doing.

Buddy spent days pacing with an open Bible in his palm, rehearsing sermons
aloud. Or he'd lay on the couch, barking out orders at Deb and me. And, except
when Mom was present, he always wore that smirk. Deb and I hoped they hadn't
actually gotten married and that Mom would see him for who he was—a user—
and kick him out.

I was trying to keep faith in Mom. We'd been through so much. Deb and I
clung to the hope that she would come through for us again. We'd landed on our
feet many times: fatherless, homeless, poverty, Mom giving up our baby brother,
escaping Tiny.

We'd stopped going to that Pentecostal church with the rock band and the preacher who wanted a new Cadillac. Mom said he crossed a line when he met with her privately and said she shouldn't date. "No so-called man of God is going to tell me what to do with my love life," she said. Instead of joining a new church, we church hopped on Sundays. I was glad we were only going once a week, but as soon as I got a taste of church surfing, I wanted to return to the old church, even if it *was* three times a week. I'd gotten used to speaking in tongues, the dance trains, the women fainting.

At first, I didn't understand why we went to different churches each Sunday, but then I noticed a pattern.

One Sunday, we went to an outdoor conservative Pentecostal church. We were greeted with handshakes from women in floor-length dresses and hair nearly to the floor, and bearded men in dark suits. Under an enormous canopy, enclosed by soaring fragrant honeysuckle bushes, the congregation sat in metal folding chairs. No rock and roll band, no moms sitting on the floor swaying with their babies, no hippies with bare feet.

We sat near the back. My mind jumped from thought to thought, my stomach tight. I knew what was coming.

The organ player led us in a few boring hymns, then the sermon began. The Pastor, a thick, middle-aged woman with steely tresses down to her knees, put one hand in the air and held a mic with the other. She bowed her head and led a prayer. Then she stood square and spoke into the mic. "Today I want to talk to you about what's expected of women of God. The book of Titus tells us that women should be sober…be keepers at home…and obey their husbands."

Mom's bottom lip tightened. Her glare was fixed on the Pastor. Buddy crossed his arms against his chest.

Uh oh. Here we go. The Pastor pulled up her reading glasses on a chain and perched them on the edge of her nose, then flipped open her Bible. As her preaching intensified, she bustled up and down the rows, stopping to look into people's eyes. I would die if she came over to me.

Buddy sat, one knee shaking. Mom was straight-backed, fingers interlocked, rubbing her thumbs together. It was like Mom and Buddy were bank robbers waiting for the perfect moment to draw their guns.

Finally, Mom leaped to her feet, holding her Bible in the air, and shouted, "Jesus don't care if women wear pants. Or makeup. Or cut their hair. He cares about what's in their hearts." Mom remained on her feet.

I wanted to slither into a hole.

The Pastor fired back, "The Lord wants us to follow his commands." She puffed out her chest. "Who are we to question His intent?"

"Our Lord don't want women bowing down to men. We must serve God first, not a husband."

The Pastor shot back, "Deuteronomy says a woman shall not wear a man's garment, nor shall a man put on a woman's cloak, for whoever does these things is an abomination to the—"

"That's from the Old Testament. The book of Matthew says, judge not, lest you be judged." The veins in Mom's neck bulged. "Blessed are the pure in heart, for they shall see God. Is your heart pure?"

The Pastor ignored her question, pivoted, and returned to preaching to the congregation.

Mom breathed heavily, and her eyes bulged. Still holding up her Bible, she shouted, "Your teachings are wrong. You're preaching bondage, not salvation."

The Pastor didn't concede. She and Mom continued to blast each other with scripture, their volume increasing with each exchange. Buddy stayed silent, which was a first. Deb and I shrank in our seats.

Finally, the pastor said, "You need to leave." She motioned to a couple of guys to usher us out. The men gestured for us to come with them.

"We don't need no escort," Mom said, nose in the air.

We filed out. When we got to the parking lot, Buddy adopted his usual sneer. Mom was still worked up, breathing shallow, and beads of sweat above her lip.

From the driver's seat, Buddy swiveled to face Mom. "Satan's in the pulpit, and people need to know. We'll go to every church in this city if we must." He grinned and patted her shoulder. "Your Mom and me are training for battle." Mom nodded in agreement.

Looking back, it was an initiation. Mom had lost her church-preaching virginity. She was hungry for purpose. Buddy fed her appetite.

***

Deb and I started our new school. Me in seventh grade; she in eighth. I clung to normalcy like a life raft. I still hated church-surfing but after a few weeks, I got used to it.

I figured I needed to keep my head down to survive Buddy. I did my chores

49

when expected, came home on time, stopped talking back, and read the Bible without Buddy's prompting. Then, he shifted his attention over to Deb. Once his focus was on her, I became invisible. She'd backtalk, roll her eyes, walk away. He'd take away her books as punishment, something he knew would cripple her.

Then Deb broke her leg at school. Instead of taking her to the ER, Buddy convinced Mom to take her home. "It's just a sprain," he said. I didn't understand why he insisted on *not* taking her to the ER. His religious brand didn't forbid it.

The next day, while Mom was at work, Deb lay on the couch, her inflamed and swollen leg propped up with pillows. I was tumbling across the living room floor, fine-tuning my roundoff, when Buddy got home. Deb had been moaning in pain on and off, but she was trying to read a book. Buddy's hair was slicked back flatter than usual from sweat, and he wore his typical short-sleeved button-down and shabby dress shoes. But that day, he was also wearing a wide brown tie. He'd returned from trying to sell encyclopedias door to door. He stacked his sample book and briefcase on the breakfast bar, then wiped his brow.

"Nobody was buying today," he said, plopping into the chair.

That was the first time I'd seen him work. The idea that he had a job gave me a titch of hope.

Deb's voice cracked. "Buddy, I need to go to the hospital."

I caught my breath. "Yeah, Buddy. Her leg is bad. Look at it."

"Oh, it's just a sprain," he said with that smirk. "Sprains look worse than they are."

"Can we go to the hospital to see?" Deb cried.

"It'll be better in a couple days." He flipped off his shoes. "You just need to ice it."

Deb removed her glasses and dabbed her eyes. "Please Buddy. What if it's broken?"

He shook his head. "It's a sprain. I told you. Y'all need to settle down. I had a hard day.

I wanted to scream.

I can't remember exactly how long Deb laid there. It was three days when she told the story, but a day and a half when Mom told it. Either way, too long. Deb's leg swelled even more, and her pain didn't stop. Finally, Mom took her to the ER when Buddy was out. She came home in a cast.

I laid my books on the coffee table and sat on the edge of the couch. "Deb, it's 'cause of Buddy that Mom didn't take you to the hospital, you know."

"I know." Deb said. "I hate his guts."

"Me too. Our life was good before him. Did you notice, we ain't got no food?"

"Yeah, I know. Good thing we can eat at school."

"Yeah, but what about the rest of the time?"

"Mom will figure something out," Deb said.

A couple of weeks after moving into the house, Mom got fired from Rosemount Grill, one of the most stable jobs she'd ever had. The tips were good, and she worked days. "They fired me 'cause I spent my breaks reading my Bible instead of gossiping with the girls. Jesus was persecuted too, ya know."

We didn't get our monthly food stamps because of some mix-up with the paperwork. With each day passing, the food dwindled until the fridge was empty. Luckily, we'd picked a bunch of oranges from the backyard of our place on L Street, and we had a jumbo box of Quaker Oats. Our diet for about a week was an orange for breakfast and oatmeal for supper.

When the food stamps finally came, it was pure elation. Since Mom wasn't working, she cooked full suppers every night and baked all our favorite desserts.

I had faith in Mom. We'd landed on our feet before. But I had zero confidence in Buddy. He was evil, and we needed Mom to open her eyes.

One day I finally got my chance when Buddy was out selling encyclopedias. Mom was in the kitchen, drying dishes and putting them in the cupboards. I stood in the doorway, shuffling my feet and chewing the inside of my lip. "Mom, Buddy's mean."

"What do you mean?"

"He acts different when you ain't around."

"When you *aren't*. *Ain't* isn't a word."

"Okay, when you *aren't* around."

"Different how?"

"He acts all nice when you're around, but when you ain't—sorry, I mean aren't—he's mean to us. He laughs at us and makes fun of us."

"Laughs at youse? I never seen him laugh at youse."

"When Deb was in the bathroom the other day, he moved her crutches. And when she came out, he made her crawl across the floor for them. She begged him, but he laughed and said she was faking. How could she fake a broken leg?"

"Well, I'm sure he didn't mean *that*."

"Yes, he did Mom. He hates us."

"No, he don't hate youse. He has a different way than me. He's a man of God,

Peggy.”

I rolled my eyes and walked away. “A man of God, my ass,” I said under my breath.

“Don’t take that tone with me, young lady.”

I never brought it up again.

***

Tension grew thick in the house. Mom and Buddy stopped talking when we walked in the room. They weren’t going out preaching as much, and Mom looked tired. Drawn. Less vibrant.

Deb and I did our own things: school, homework, chores. Deb devoured books. I talked on the phone every night. I wasn’t sure what had changed, but Mom *and Buddy* were off my back about my phone marathons. I talked to Pam and Nancy, my friends from my old school, but over time the calls dwindled, until eventually, they stopped altogether. The chapter of my life back on L street had officially closed.

My phone conversations became exclusively with Peter, my new boyfriend. Peter was my savior. He rescued me from my grief. We only saw each other at school, but our long phone conversations accelerated our relationship. He was like me. We both believed school was for socializing. We didn’t give two shits about grades, though we were both still middling students, though never getting Ds or Fs. I think you’re cute, he’d say. I think *you’re* cute, I’d say. I’d pop my gum in his ear. He didn’t mind. We talked as late as our parents allowed. Sometimes they’d forget about us, and we’d stay up later than we should’ve.

I rose every school day with a flutter in my stomach and a giddy-up in my step. I ended every night with a blown-through-the-phone kiss and a sweet “Goodnight.” Utter bliss. But then one night, Mom announced that we had to move back to Pennsylvania.

My heart sank. “What? *Why?*”

“What happened?” Deb asked.

“I can’t find a job, and the bank’s gonna take the house.”

Deb and I gave each other that familiar here-we-go-again look.

“What about Buddy? He’s been going out selling encyclopedias.”

“But Peggy, he don’t ever sell none.”

My chin quivered and a lump formed in my throat. “But I’ll *never* see Peter

52

again." Tears wormed down my cheeks.

Deb, dry-eyed, asked, "Where are we going to live in Pennsylvania?"

"With Mammy and Pappy. Just 'til we get on our feet."

Deb crossed her arms and lifted her chin. "What about school?"

"Youse'll go to Tarville, where I went. To finish the year. I don't know after that. We're not staying in Tarville. A lot of terrible things happened to me in that town. Remember, I told youse."

I laced my fingers into a prayer position. "I want to stay. Pleeeease."

"I racked my brain, but this is the only solution. Sorry, girls."

Deb tucked hair behind one ear. "Is Buddy coming?"

With that tone that said, *don't ask any more questions*, Mom answered, "No."

Deb's lips curled a bit. "Are you guys breaking up?"

"I don't know. Now, no more questions."

We had a yard sale and sold everything but the essentials. Our frequent moves taught us how to pack efficiently. I said my goodbyes to Peter on my last day of school, and to Nancy and Pam over the phone. I grieved Pam and Nancy all over again.

Mom and Buddy shared a butt-out hug and a cool peck that final day when he dropped us off at the airport. Good riddance.

I'd won the window seat in a coin toss with Deb. Cars, houses, and buildings shrank as we ascended into the billowy clouds, and so did my life in Sacramento. Just like that, Sacramento became another place I used to belong.

CHAPTER FOUR
Tarville, Pennsylvania, 1974

With Buddy out of the picture, I hoped Mom would forget about all that religious stuff. I told myself once we left California and Buddy, the demon stuff and the Bible wars would stay there too. Part of me was even looking forward to moving back to where my early childhood roots were. Frolicking up and down the street with my neighborhood pals, sledding down the dike, teaching myself how to ride a bike without training wheels. I was elated about seeing my uncles and eating Pennsylvania food: Hoagies, hot pretzels, and the best summer sausage in the world. My mouth watered just thinking about it. But another part of me was dreading the move to Tarville—population three thousand. The town where Mom was molested by dirty old men, where she was taken up into the strippings (mountains mined for coal) and sexually assaulted. Tarville, where Mammy buried Mom's late-term miscarried baby in the backyard. Tarville, where my dad still lived but showed zero interest in Deb or me.

I clung to the good memories like a kid holding onto the corners of a blanket in a windstorm. I wondered: Would Uncle Jim call me silly names, like Squirrel, the way he used to? Would Uncle Bob chase me, give me a whisker rub, and sing his limericks? Would Pappy—covered head to toe in coal dust from the mines—still chase me around the house for a hug and kiss? Would I get to know my dad? Did I even care? I told myself I didn't, but that was a lie. A useful lie.

Uncle Jim picked us up from Harrisburg airport in his white van with a bed in the back. The last time I'd seen him, he was thirteen—shaggy hair, acne, and Buddy Holly glasses. Six years later, he was a muscular man with a mustache and receding hairline. Mom always said, "I practically raised Jim," as if he was more her son than brother.

"Can you turn down that music?" Mom asked after we settled in the van.

Jim complied, then took off his cap and wiped his brow. "San, it's good to see ya."

Mom's eyes glossed over. She put her hand on his shoulder. "You've grown into quite a man. Got a girlfriend?"

"Oh, I see a couple gals here and there."

Mom chuckled. "A couple?"

He told us about his construction job and how he'd bought the van himself, how he lived at home to save for his own place. He held a black belt in Tae Kwon Do and had lots of friends. I was thrilled at the prospect of having a relationship with him. Someone I could count on.

As we descended the mountain a familiar feeling saturated. From way up, Tarville—nestled in the basin of the mountains—looked like a picturesque storybook town. House-speckled streets with tall evergreens and a few moving cars, a brick school, a church steeple. As the town came into view, it was far from picture perfect. Rows of dilapidated houses that hadn't been painted in decades mottled the side of the mountain in that last mile down, with their slanted porches, broken fences, scrawny dogs, and grimy kids running around half naked. Old folks waved and smiled, some with no teeth, as we drove by. Rusty kitchen appliances, and cars on cinder blocks littered the front lawns. Some yards looked like they'd never seen a mower; the grass was tamped flat by kids playing and dogs taking their afternoon naps.

At the mountain's base, Jim pulled into Mammy and Pappy's driveway. The fresh scent of pine trees made it feel like no time had passed. When I was little, we'd drive down that mountain every Easter, Thanksgiving, Christmas, and for Sunday dinners. Time had marched on, but the place hadn't kept up.

The massive old tree that canopied the driveway was still thriving, thick branches shading the gravel like an umbrella. The garage paint was as scant as I remembered. I dashed to the garage, swiped a thick layer of grime from the window, and peered in to see if the old piano was still there. It was in the same spot, surrounded by junk with a half inch of crud. Mom played by ear. The two songs she knew best were "Tammy's in Love" by Debbie Reynolds and "Donna" by Ritchie Valens. Deb and I, sitting on either side of her, would sing while her long fingers glided across the yellowed keys. Those were rare moments when the world felt gentle.

The backyard brought up memories of Uncle Bob telling us stories about how the Boogie Man only came out at night. I made sure to always come in before dark. I was scared shitless of the Boogie Man.

On the screened-in porch, shoes and boots were piled in the corner just like I'd remembered, and a couple of fishing poles leaned against the wall with a tackle box beneath. The tattered linoleum in the kitchen was curled up and peeling at the edges, so worn in places that you could no longer make out the pattern. The long farm table transported me back to holiday dinners. We weren't allowed to lean on our elbows. We couldn't leave the table until we cleaned our plates, except when Mammy made baked potatoes—she didn't want us eating the skin "because it was in the dirt." When she wasn't looking, I'd sneak a bite. I could've lived on potato skins with butter and sour cream.

There was always uneasiness at the Sunday dinner table. Sometimes the tension was between Mammy and Pappy, but they'd often tag team against Mom. I can't remember what they'd argue about, but often we would end up leaving, Mom in a huff, her hurt trailing like a cape.

Mammy had been in her forties when we left Pennsylvania and her fifties when we returned but looked identical: a sleeveless button-down floral shirt with Bermuda shorts pulled high over her belly and dingy Keds with gaping holes for her bunions. Her short, Fanta-colored, beehive hairdo looked indistinguishable from our last visit. If a photo of her had been taken when I was six years old and then again when I returned at twelve, I wouldn't've been able to tell them apart.

Mammy was always crabby, chasing us kids out of the kitchen with a fly swatter, always yelling at Pappy. Though, when Mammy passed gas, it would lighten the mood. She'd pace around the kitchen, rubbing her belly and saying "ooh, ooh, ooh," until finally she'd back into a corner and let it rip. We'd hold our noses and giggle.

"Hiya, girls," Mammy said when we walked in, her voice akin to Granny from the Beverly Hillbillies. She opened her gangly arms, and we took turns hugging her. Then she stepped back and looked at us up and down. "Youse got big." We smiled awkwardly. "Youse hungry?"

Mammy wasn't the cook Mom was, but I liked most of her food. I could have done without her leathery liver and stringy roast beef.

Pappy moseyed into the kitchen but kept his distance. "Hiya, girls."

Deb and I slid onto the bench, where kids were expected to sit. Pappy, in his white t-shirt tucked into high-waisted pleated dress pants, pulled out a chair, and sat at the head. He was a small man, with a little round belly and only a few strands of hair. What he did have, he greased back.

Mom sat at the corner next to him. I'd never seen her so enthused about seeing him.

"Pappy and I are gonna start a church together when we get back," she'd said.

Pappy had been a preacher wannabe for as long as Mom could remember. For years, he'd talked about the Rapture and starting a church in the garage, but nothing ever came of it.

"We're having ham potpie," Mammy said.

Ham potpie was one of my favorites. Square egg noodles in a thick broth with tender potatoes, carrots and celery, and chunks of ham. Mouthgasm.

Mammy carried over a stainless-steel pot, sat it in the middle of the table, then ladled the stew into our bowls.

"Mom, the girls can dish up their own. Peggy's twelve and Debbie's thirteen."

She ignored her.

Mom sighed, seeming to say, *okay, here we go*. But she let it go and returned to talking with Pappy. She told him about how she'd been spreading the gospel.

"God brought you back, San," he said, "now's the time to start God's church. He ordained me, and now you're ordained."

Mom beamed. Pappy led us in grace.

I'm certain I stuffed a big spoonful of pot pie in my mouth before everyone said Amen and opened their eyes.

"Them kids down the street are looking forward to seeing youse," Mammy said. "They been talking about it for days. When youse are done eating, youse can head down there and see 'em. Maybe they'll take youse uptown."

Uptown? *What's* uptown?

"So…what grade youse girls in now?" Pappy asked, looking over his glasses, hunched over his food. He took a hefty bite of potpie and gummed it in his toothless mouth.

The last time I saw him, he had teeth. It was hard not to stare. We told him our grades.

"What's *uptown?*" I asked.

"Oh, it's nothing special. It's just where the kids go."

I was even more intrigued.

"Youse gotta watch out." Mammy wagged her finger. "With your age and all, there's gonna be boys after youse. We can't be having that around here."

"Mom. Don't worry about them," Mom said. "They're good girls." She scooped another helping onto her plate.

"You think you need another helping, San?"

Mom raised her eyebrows and tilted her head back, as she often did when she was angry. "Don't start with me."

"Alright. Just trying to help. That's all."

"Well, it don't help me." Mom folded her arms. "So, stop."

"You don't need to get all worked up about it, San."

"Lydia, leave the girl alone," Pappy said. "She just got here. Let her eat her food."

"I'm not all worked up," Mom said. "You can't help yourself. You always gotta find a way to put me down." She pushed her plate away. "I lost my appetite."

Mammy got up and started clearing the table.

Mom motioned to us. "Girls, let's carry our things upstairs, then youse can go see your friends."

Lugging my bag up the mahogany staircase, I caught a whiff of Mammy's bedroom, a hodgepodge of mothballs, cigarettes, and Jean Naté. Mammy followed behind me.

"Peggy, you'll sleep with me, and your Mom and Debbie will sleep in the guest room. Your Pappy moved to the attic to make room for youse."

Her room was frozen in time. A jewelry box and perfume bottles sat atop white doilies that adorned her glass dresser top, and her bed donned a crocheted gold Afghan folded at the bottom. The air tasted like perfume filtered through cigarettes.

Mammy straightened one of the doilies and stubbed her cigarette in the ashtray. "Did you get your period yet?"

"Uhhh...yeah, last year." I actually hadn't started my period yet, but I didn't want to appear like a little kid.

"Well, I'm gonna have to put plastic under the sheets. I don't want no blood stains on my mattress."

I turned and rolled my eyes.

"And don't think about taking none of my things. The jewelry stays right here. I'm gonna check it every day to make sure you ain't took nothing."

"I don't wear stuff like that."

"Well, I'll still be checking."

She was still the cut-to-the-chase, icy grandmother I remembered.

Walking to the neighbor kids' house, Deb and I talked about how everything was identical to before, except dwarfed. As usual, Deb had an explanation. "We're taller now, so we're looking from a different perspective."

The closer we came to their house, the more familiar it felt. The giant, two-story with barely a fleck of paint and a balcony that looked unsafe was unchanged from six years prior. The family had several kids. I couldn't remember their names—thankfully, they re-introduced themselves. We'd barely arrived when a couple of the sisters suggested we walk "uptown" to Al's, a neighborhood convenience store with a soda fountain and a jukebox.

The screen door whapped behind us, as we walked into Al's. Every head turned. Elton John's "Daniel" played on the jukebox. Kids sipped sodas and smoked cigarettes in booths; others clustered around the jukebox chatting it up. I couldn't believe Al allowed kids to smoke.

One of the sisters walked us to a group of kids by the jukebox and told them we were from California. They shot questions at us like we were celebrities: Had we ever been to the beach? Had we been to Disney Land? Did we have "colored" friends? Was it warm every day like they'd heard?

Deb was beaming, a stark contrast to her demeanor in California. She stood more erect, smiling, a lilt in her voice. I'd never seen her so confident. She'd walk alone in the school hallways back in California, shoulders slumped, hair in her face. She annoyed me ninety percent of the time, but I didn't like seeing her lonely. Tarville was a fresh start. A chance to be viewed differently.

Moving back had its advantages. We reconnected with family and old friends. We got away from crazy Buddy. I assumed Mom wouldn't be standing on the streets of Tarville waving her Bible and preaching or dragging us out church surfing. I assumed that part of our lives was over.

After a few weeks of school, summer arrived. Deb and I spent most of our days at the town pool, chlorinated water smoothing out our rough edges. Sometimes we'd walk home in our swimsuits with shorts pulled over them. Mammy would drive by and shout out the window, "Youse better cover up! Youse look like whores." We'd ignore her. We went by Mom's rules. She never complained about how we dressed. Mom insisted that we were good girls and would tell Mammy to mind her own business.

Inside the house, Mammy and Pappy had a shell of a marriage: they hadn't slept together in years, avoided eating together, and didn't speak to each other unless it was snarky or transactional.

Mammy made supper, ate alone in the kitchen, then went into the parlor for a cigarette. Afterward, Pappy would roll himself out of the sunken couch that stank like farts, shuffle into the kitchen, and eat alone. He'd put his dirty dishes in the sink, then go back to watching TV. When he was done, Mammy returned to do the dishes. It was like watching two ghosts haunt the same house on different shifts.

***

Pappy was thrilled that Mom had gotten saved. On our first night there, they stayed up until the wee hours talking about their start-up church. They could spend their days planning sermons and their nights saving souls. A holy partnership. But they soon discovered there were glaring differences in their fundamental beliefs. Pappy believed smoking, drinking, and sex before marriage were sins— Mom didn't. She believed women should be equal to men; Pappy believed men should have dominion. They'd debate nearly every night until one or two a.m., then slept late. Pappy collected disability for Black Lung Disease from working in the coal mines, and Mom hadn't found a job yet.

"San! Melvin!" Mammy would yell down the stairs. "Some of us work for a living around here! Shut up and go to bed!"

They'd lower their voices for a few minutes, then it would escalate again. Mammy would yell two, three, four times, increasing the intensity each time, before they'd finally heed her call.

Pappy's enthusiasm about their partnership fizzled fast. One minute they were cozied up with their Bibles, and the next, they were slinging scripture like weapons. Mom would sit at the table, Bible open. Pappy would pace, yelling and waving his arms wildly. I didn't have an opinion about who was right and wrong; I just wanted to sleep.

Uncle Jim had been out of high school for about a year. The neighborhood kids were fascinated by him. They bombarded me with questions and comments. He's so handsome. Does he have a girlfriend? He's got a van *and* a motorcycle?

Is he really a black belt? I was proud to be his niece. I'd fantasized about him taking me out for ice cream on the back of his motorcycle, and to Knoebels Amusement Park where we'd ride the rollercoaster and throw darts to win a stuffed bear. Every weekend, he'd wash his prized van. Around town, they called it "the meat wagon," assuming he was getting laid a lot, I presumed. I never saw him with a girl, so I didn't understand that label. Sometimes he'd ask me to help him wash his van. I jumped at the chance. We'd rock out to Zeppelin while scrubbing and rinsing. I wasn't a rock fan, but I didn't care; I was spending time with my Uncle Jim.

Aside from the tension in the house and the nightly arguments, I felt hopeful. I focused on friends, flirting with boys, and starting school in the Fall. But my hope that Mom would abandon her conquest to save souls was short-lived.

One afternoon, I ran home for a snack. Whap! The screen door flapped behind me. The sun-flooded windows filled the parlor with light.

"Don't slam the door," Mom said, whisper-talking like she was trying not to wake someone.

"Sorry," I said, slowing down.

In my cut-off jean shorts, bikini top, and flip-flops, I headed to the kitchen, ignoring the scene in the parlor: Jim kneeling on the floor. Mom crouched beside him with a hand on his back. I wanted to turn around and go back out the door, but I was famished.

Before I made it to the kitchen, Mom called out, "Come over here and pray over your Uncle Jim."

I gaped out the screen door, heart pounding, worried someone might see.

"Stop worrying about what people think. Come over here."

I knelt on the other side of Jim and placed a hand on his back. Mom spoke in tongues. I murmured in tongues as softly as I could utter. I was terrified someone would see and it would get all over town that we were crazy.

Mom summoned the Holy Ghost, "Lord Jesus, we call upon you." Mom alternated speaking in tongues and praying that the Holy Ghost would enter his body. Soon Jim babbled. She looked up, her hands in the air. "Hallelujah. Hallelujah. Praise Jesus. We love you, Lord."

Jim pulled out his hanky, sat back on his heels, and blew.

Finally.

He wrapped his arms around Mom and wept. I'd never seen him cry. Mom pulled back and held him by his shoulders, then looked into his eyes, her gaze shifting back and forth, giving each eye equal attention. "You're saved now, Jim. All your sins are washed away. You have eternal life now."

Jim hung his head and wept even harder.

A week later, I came home to a similar situation. But this time it was in the garage, and it was Jim's Tae Kwon Do teacher, Ron, kneeling at the piano bench, snot streaming from his nose.

I hadn't considered that Jim getting saved would affect my life. But that day in the parlor set into motion events that would impact my entire future. Mom's respite from her ministry was over. She had two new converts. She was on fire.

It's no surprise that Jim fell prey to Mom's spell. He wasn't close to Mammy and Pappy. Pappy had drilled into him that the rapture was coming. When Mom—his sister—showed up with "the way to the Kingdom of Heaven," it must have felt like confirmation.

***

I stayed away from the house as much as possible. But I had to eat and sleep. One balmy day, I stopped at home for a cold drink. I flung open the screen door and headed for the kitchen. I stopped in my tracks when I saw Mom in the parlor, hair in a blue bandana, hands in the air, dancing and singing to "My Sweet Lord," by George Harrison. Sadly, she sounded like an out-of-key old man. "I had a bee-you-tee-ful voice when I was a young girl," she'd say. "I ruined it with smoking." I didn't buy it. Smoking or not, she couldn't sing in key to save her life.

She saw me before I could ricochet out the door.

"Peg. Come dance for the Lord." She turned up the music.

"I'm just here for a drink."

She dropped her arms and stopped dancing. Her smile went slack. "Get over here and dance."

I looked out the screen door and the windows, biting the inside of my lip. What if people see me? They'll think I'm a freak. "I don't feel like dancing."

"Get over here and dance for Jesus…right now."

"Mom, don't make me…please."

"You heard me, young lady. Get your butt over here and dance." She put her hands in the air, closed her eyes, and furrowed her brows.

I swayed my body, so I was moving but not enough to look like I was dancing. I turned and looked out at the screen door again.

"Stop looking out that door. Are you ashamed of Jesus?"

"No. I ain't ashamed of Him."

"It's, I'm *not* ashamed. *Ain't* isn't a word."

"Okay then, I'm *not* ashamed to dance for Jesus. I wanna go hang out with my friends."

"You're not going no place until you dance for Jesus."

I sighed and rolled my eyes.

"Don't you roll those eyes. Dance right now."

I bobbed my head along with my sway.

"Peggy Louise, I said dance!"

"I *am.*"

"Don't sass me. I know what your dancing looks like. Now dance for Jesus."

When she called me Peggy Louise, she meant business. I did a step tap, and prayed to myself, please don't let anyone see me. Pleeeeeease…

"My sweet lord…mmmm, my lord," Mom sang. "Peggy, put your hands in the air."

I put my hands up halfway.

"Put those arms up higher." She reached over and pushed my arms up with the elbows.

I continued the step tap, wishing I could vanish. Whenever she looked away, I'd immediately check the windows and the screen door. The music was blaring. I was sure the whole neighborhood could hear.

"Jesus hung on that cross for you. The least you can do is dance for him."

She'd dash over to the console each time the song was over and move the needle back to replay it. Then she'd grab my hand and step-tap with me, beaming.

"C'mon, Peggy, sing."

"I don't feel like singing."

"Peggy Louise, sing for Jesus, this minute."

I sang in a whisper and looked back at the screen door.

"Stop looking out there," she commanded. "By the time I'm done with you, you won't be ashamed of Jesus no more."

After an hour or so and countless repeats of "My Sweet Lord," Mom finally let me go.

Every day after work, Jim studied the Bible with Mom instead of going out with his friends. They sat at the kitchen table, reading, writing, and discussing scripture. Mom had a pupil. That breathed life into her. She cooked supper every night, baked cookies and pies, and packed Jim's lunches. Mammy said Mom was bribing him. Mom said Mammy was jealous.

Mom's attention shifted away from Pappy. Their late-night arguments stopped, replaced with silence. Pappy stormed around the kitchen, nose in the air, while Mom and Jim did Bible study. Mom said he couldn't stand that Jim was following her and not him. Mammy didn't like it either. "My Jimmy loves *me*," she'd say to Mom. "*I'm* his mother, not you." Mammy and Pappy's jealousy only pumped energy into Mom. She was being persecuted like Jesus, she said.

Mom still craved Mammy's love and approval. For a while, she got it. Mammy had some sort of stomach infection and needed an operation. On the day of the surgery, despite their strained relationship, Mom went to the hospital to pray for her. She said Mammy looked helpless. Mammy actually turned to Mom for help.

This is how I imagined it, piecing together what Mom had said over the years.

Mom walked into the hospital room, dark, drawn drapes, Mammy in bed with fear in her eyes. Mom rushed to her side, grabbed her bony hand, and held it against her cheek.

"I want you to save me, San," Mammy said.

Mom placed her hand on Mammy's shoulder and bowed her head, furrowing her brows. Mammy wept and asked Jesus to forgive her. She asked the Lord to spare her from dying on the operating table. Mom asked the Lord to forgive her, and for her to receive the Holy Ghost. Then Mammy spoke in tongues.

Mom visited her daily, reading the Bible and praying with her. I'd never seen Mom so buoyant. She'd longed for Mammy's love her whole life. For a moment, it seemed like she had it. I remember nights when Mom sobbed for Mammy. Deb and I tried to comfort her, telling her we loved her and that it would be okay, but our words never touched the deep place her grief lived. Sometimes she'd get drunk and call Mammy, demanding to know why she didn't love her. Whatever Mammy said only made Mom more depressed.

I was happy for Mom, but I didn't trust their newfound closeness. I didn't see how a lifetime of coldness could just melt. For Mom's sake, though, I hoped it was genuine.

Mammy came home from the hospital a non-smoker, Bible in hand. Pappy said Mom wasn't ordained to save her, and Mammy was faking. Unfortunately for Mom, Pappy was right. Days after her discharge, Mammy iced Mom out. No more Bible study, no more praying together, no more love and acceptance. Mom said Mammy's heart hardened again after God got her through the surgery.

After Mom and Mammy's brief mother-daughter reunion had ended, Mammy and Pappy formed a coalition. They huddled in the kitchen, whispering about how Mom was brainwashing Jim. Jim would come home from work to the three of them yelling and wagging their fingers at each other.

I didn't care about doctrinal wars. I was twelve. I woke up thinking about what outfit I could wear and how I might do my hair, or if I got to sit next to Barry, my crush. I shoved my home life in a vault and drew a hard line between the milieu inside the house and out. Mammy forbade us from bringing friends home, but I wouldn't have anyway. Our house was a freak show.

Sometimes, though, the worlds collided.

***

When I was home sick one day with a cough, Mom asked if I wanted to go with her to Sunbury, a town over the mountain, to run errands. I felt like crap, but I knew a cheese steak hoagie would be my reward, so I agreed.

Mom sang along to every oldie song, tapping her rings on the steering wheel of Pappy's old station wagon. As we ascended the mountain, passing the dilapidated houses carved into steep cliffs, I tried singing along too, but that only triggered coughing fits.

"Stop that coughing, Peggy. Every time you cough, you're giving in to the Demon of Sickness."

I swallowed several times, sucked in my stomach, and held my hand over my mouth, but they were unrelenting. I let out a string of deep hacks.

"Peggy! Stop that coughing, I said!"

"I can't help it. I'm trying."

"I don't want no excuses. You're giving into the Demon of Sickness."

I tried to focus on the music. But the only rhythm I felt was the beast rattling in my chest.

Mom turned off the radio and looked at me with brooding eyes. "The Lord rebuke you, Demon of Sickness!"

I hacked and hacked.

"You don't wanna get better, I guess," Mom said.

"I *do*, Mom. I *do*. I wanna get better. I can't help it."

"You can *too* help it. The Lord rebuke you, Demon of Sickness!"

The more I tried to stifle the coughs, the more violent my hacking spells became. Mom rebuked the demon and me the whole time. Her efforts were futile. I coughed all the way there and back.

***

Another time Mom took me to a tiny church out in the boonies. Surrounded by woods, it would have been invisible if not for the lights that were on inside. The night was hazy. An earthy pine fragrance tickled my nose as Mom parked the station wagon. The service was underway when we arrived. The congregation, of about twenty-five, was singing a hymn. The preacher wore jeans and a t-shirt.

"Welcome, sisters," he said as we entered. It was the kind of church Mom liked: unassuming, warm, with a liberal dress code. We slid into a pew, picked up hymn books, and sang along. The man next to Mom gave her a two-hand shake.

Soon, we knelt at our pew, foreheads pressed against our palms, praying and speaking in tongues. Having knelt for some time with my eyes pressed against my hands, I stood to go to the bathroom and wobbled from lightheadedness.

"You okay, Peggy?"

"Yeah, but I'm seeing black spots and I'm kinda dizzy."

Before I could utter another word, Mom waved the elders over. "The Demon of Blindness is trying to get my Peggy!"

Elders swarmed me like a hornet's nest, placing their hands all over my body.

"Get thee behind me, Satan!" Mom commanded.

"Leave this minute. You're not welcome here," a man demanded. Part of me wanted to run, another part liked the attention.

"Can you see yet," Mom asked.

"Yeah, I can see."

"Halleluiah. She's healed!" one of the elders called out. Everyone put their hands in the air and called out praises to the Lord. Thanking Him for saving my sight.

Later, that became one of Mom's favorite stories to tell potential converts. Of course, I knew I hadn't gone blind, but I didn't contradict her. Too scared.

66

Meanwhile, back in Tarville, my day-to-day life had settled. My social life was thriving, *and* I had a boyfriend. In that part of my life, I was content.

Walking home from school one afternoon, with my step a bit nimbler and wearing a shit-eating grin, I sang, "Barry loves me, and I love him…Barry loves me, and I love him."

He was wispy, freckles across his nose, and with dirty-blonde shaggy hair. He'd take long strides with his scrawny legs, revealing his white socks. Plaid pants, a short-sleeved button-down, and brown laced dress shoes were his usual attire. Instead of using his fingers to move his long bangs from his eyes, he'd flit his head. He was the only boy who wore dress pants and dress shoes to school. I liked that about him. He introduced himself on my first day of school. After that, we became inseparable. We ate lunch together and walked through the halls holding hands. We'd meet after school to talk and make out. Sometimes we'd go to Al's to slow dance to the jukebox. And we'd kiss, and kiss, and kiss. He hadn't met my family, and I intended on keeping it that way. I was sure he'd never seen our brand of crazy.

Half a block from Mammy and Pappy's house, I heard yelling, but that wasn't rare. I walked around the side of the house to see what the ruckus was.

"Get the hell out of my house!" Mammy yelled. "We took youse in to help youse, and you take my Jimmy from me."

Things were flying out the upstairs bathroom window. I wasn't wearing my glasses, so I had to squint to make out what the items were. Once I got close enough, I could see the items were our clothes. My mind raced. My stomach knotted. I rushed through the back door, then stood for a second, trying to get my bearings. Pappy was pacing the kitchen, his hands clasped behind his back. I walked through the kitchen. He paid me no mind. Then I walked up the rigid staircase, carefully placing each step so I wouldn't be heard. At the top, I peered into the bathroom at the end of the hall. Mammy was bent over, hurling clothes out the window, hangers, and all.

"I've had it. I ain't takin' this shit no more. We want you outta here. Today! And take your bratty girls with you. We don't want youse here no more!"

"Mom. Stop." She grabbed Mammy's arm. "We don't have nowhere to go."

"Take your hands offa me!" Mammy yanked her arm away. "Ain't my problem. You made your bed. Now lay in it."

Mom sat on the toilet, her head in her hands. "How can you kick out your own grandchildren?"

Mammy bent over and got in her face. "What you did to my Jimmy is wrong. You brainwashed him and now he don't even talk to me. He tells me I'm the devil. Why couldn't you leave well enough alone?"

"Mom, you asked me to save you and I did. The Lord spared you on that operating table, and now you're against Him."

"I ain't against Him. It's you."

Mom's face tightened. "Fine. We'll go."

I stood in the hall, frozen, my world spinning.

"Vengeance is Mine sayeth the Lord!" Mom said, walking off, red-faced.

Mammy followed her down the hall, yelling. "You took my Jimmy from me!"

I wrung my hands so hard my knuckles ached.

"C'mon Peg." Mom's voice snapped me loose. I followed her into her room. She pulled our suitcases out from under the bed. "Your Mammy and Pappy are kicking us out."

"Why?"

"Don't ask questions. Go pack." She shoved a suitcase in my hand.

Deb arrived a minute later. She tried to question Mom, but Mom told her the same thing.

When we were just about packed, Jim called out, "San—" having just arrived, "what's going on?"

Mom went to the top of the stairs and yelled down, "Jim, Mom's kicking us out."

By then, Mammy had gone downstairs and joined Pappy in the kitchen. They took turns yelling up at Mom. They said she'd blown her chance by taking Jim from them and they could never forgive her.

Jim went downstairs and tried to reason with them. Pappy hollered, "Don't listen to her, son. She's the devil, I'm tellin' ya."

"No, she ain't Dad. She ain't doing nothin' wrong."

"She ain't doing nothing *wrong*? She turned you against us. You ain't the same since she got here."

"Jimmy. I'm your mom. I love you. Don't listen to her. Please," Mammy pleaded.

"Mom. Dad. Don't do this," Jim begged.

"She did this to herself," Pappy said.

"And she's trying to take you from me," Mammy said.

"I'm a grown man. I can make my own decisions."

"Fine then," Mammy said. "If you're gonna believe her, then you can go too."

From upstairs Mom hollered, "Jim, it's no use. Come up and get packed."

"I wash my hands of youse both," Pappy said.

Jim called Ron, his Tae Kwon Do teacher and friend. He agreed to let us stay with him. We loaded our things in Jim's van. Mammy and Pappy stood by the back door, side by side, arms folded, eyes cold.

Pappy shouted, "The Lord's gonna getcha. You'll see."

"You can rot in hell," Mammy yelled.

Finally, we got everything loaded, including Snowball, Jim's white German Shephard. We made our final pass by Mammy and Pappy.

"*Vengeance is Mine sayeth the Lord,*" Mom said, searing them with her glare.

Mammy stuck her head out the door and yelled, "You'll be back, San. With your tail between your legs…like ya always do."

Mom didn't look back.

We piled in and headed over the mountain to Sunbury. Deb and I sat on the bed in the back, quiet, with our hands in our laps, chins quivering. My heart—again—heavy with grief. My head—again—unsure of what would come next. I ran different scenarios through my mind: We'd end up living in Sunbury, return to California, or maybe somewhere new. I wasn't worried about being homeless—Mom always figured something out—but I was worried about never seeing my friends again, and Barry, I didn't even get to say goodbye.

"Jim, Mom and Dad let Satan in their heart," Mom said, sitting in the passenger's seat with her back straight. "I tried to save them, but they're too far gone."

Jim pulled the damp bandana from his back pocket and blew his nose, honking. "I know, San. I don't get it. I don't know why they always been against you. You ain't done nothing to them."

"Jim, all I ever wanted was for them to love me. But instead, they have hate in their hearts. I wash my hands of them. The Lord wants you to wash your hands of them too."

Jim adjusted his sitting position. "What do you mean?"

Mom's gaze stayed affixed to him. "Jesus said, for whosoever forsaketh his mother, father, sister, brother, for His name's sake shall inherit everlasting life. Do you want everlasting life?"

"Well…sure San, but give them up completely?"

"Jim. Don't allow the Demon of Doubt in your heart."

"That seems extreme."

"Jim, everything's predestined. This is what was supposed to happen. Trust in the Lord."

"Alright, San." Jim shook his head like he was bracing for impact.

Deb's nostrils flared. "*Mom*. Why can't we stay in Tarville? We could find a house or something."

"Debbie, we can't stay in Tarville. We don't have nowhere to live."

"But Mom, that was the first time I had friends. I was actually popular."

"I know Debbie. There's nothing else we can do. I don't have no money for rent or a car."

Deb's face slackened. So did mine. I felt what she felt: the pain of leaving behind a life with a foundation that had started to form but disintegrated beneath us. Deb's chin quivered and tears ran down her cheeks. "But Mom, I don't want to leave?"

"We're staying in Sunbury. Youse like Sunbury. Remember all the stuff youse liked about it?"

She was right. I remembered the Squeeze-In Hamburger joint, the ham and cheese Hoagies from Marvin's, the dentist who I thought looked like my dad (but apparently looked nothing like him), the dike that I thought led to China, and playing with my friends on the street.

"Can we go see the old house?"

Mom agreed we could.

***

We schlepped our bags up the steep staircase of Ron's two-bedroom apartment.

"C'mon up, guys," Ron hollered.

The waft of dirty diapers filled the hallway as I slogged up the dark staircase, with bags slung over both shoulders. Diane's toddler, Jill, ran to the top of the stairs, wearing a drooping diaper and a shirt dotted with food stains. Diane stayed seated, hands folded over her long legs, apologizing for how messy the apartment was. She had a sweet demeanor and dressed comfortably: A T-shirt, mid-length shorts, and Keds with no socks. Her short, golden hair framed her pretty face that seemed tired.

Afternoon sunlight beamed through the window of the micro living room, punctuating the brightly colored toys strewn across the floor. After introductions, Mom directed Deb and me to tidy the apartment. "You gotta earn your keep when you're a guest," Mom reminded us. Then she claimed her stake in the kitchen, cleaning and organizing it to her standards.

After supper, we sat around listening to Mom preach late into the night. Ron had already gotten saved, so Mom had her sights on Diane.

"For whosoever shall save his life, shall lose it…and whosoever shall lose his life, for my name's sake, shall save it." Mom paused. Tears filled her eyes. "I've had so much pain in my life." She placed her hand over her heart. "Then I found Jesus. He healed me."

Diane listened intently, while Jill slept on her lap.

The further Mom got into her preaching, the more animated her hand gestures became. Mom was magnetic and tireless when she had an audience. "If you follow Jesus and forsake all others, in return he'll give you everlasting life. For what does a man gain if he owns the whole world, and loses his soul?"

Everything Mom preached circled back to eternal life. She loved the idea of living forever in heaven at the seat of God.

Finally, we went to bed. Deb and I slept in Jill's room on the floor, Mom slept on the couch, and Jim on the living room floor. It was fine. I'd grown used to sleeping in all kinds of situations—hard floors, church pews, metal chairs, noise, no noise.

The next day, Mom and Jim went looking for a place to rent. Deb and I stayed back to deep clean the apartment and help Diane with Jill. At twelve and thirteen, we could manage it. We'd had plenty of experience babysitting and could clean circles around most adults.

The next night, Diane told us about her domineering father and distant mother. She was adopted, an only child, and raised Catholic. She'd married a controlling man she didn't love, but her parents approved of. They had Jill, got divorced after a couple of years. Then she met Ron.

Mom opened her Bible. "Jesus said in Matthew Chapter Ten, whosoever loves father or mother more than me is not worthy of me, and whosoever loves son or daughter more than me is not worthy of me. And whosoever does not take his cross and follow me is not worthy of me."

Diane furrowed her brow. "You mean, if I get saved, I'll never see my parents again."

Mom flipped to another passage. "Luke Chapter Fourteen says, So, therefore, any one of you who does not renounce all that he has, cannot be my disciple."

Ron testified. So did Jim. Each telling the story of their salvation. After a couple more nights, Diane agreed to give up her parents and stop allowing her ex to have visitation with Jill. She repented and got saved.

***

We only stayed with Diane and Ron for a couple of weeks, but during that time, Mom took over disciplining Jill.

Jill's flaxen ringlets framed her plump cheeks, and expressive eyes. She was precocious, a firecracker—full of energy and defiance. Mom didn't like that. She was determined to break her. Diane still fed, bathed, and dressed Jill, but if Jill misbehaved, Mom handled it.

"I had youse girls out of diapers at nine months," Mom said. She'd set Jill on the potty chair for long periods. "Up?" Jill would repeatedly ask, the corners of her lips turned down. "Not until you go potty," Mom would say. After a long while, Jill would stand without permission. Mom would spank her. If she had an accident in her pants, Mom would spank her. If she didn't go in the potty, Mom would spank her. On the first day, Jill's bottom and thighs turned all shades of red and blue. Every scream stabbed my heart. I wanted to rush to her aid and be a human shield over her tense little body. With the apartment being so small, there was no escape. I tried cleaning to distract myself, but the cries sliced right through the sound of running water and clattering dishes.

When the spankings didn't work, Mom stood her in the closet with the door shut. "Out. Out," she'd cry. Tiny fists pounding. Mom ignored her.

I wanted to scream, Stop! This is child abuse! I was going out of my mind. I'm sure Deb felt the same, though we didn't discuss it. We'd sometimes give each other wide-eyed, open-mouthed looks, then we'd go about our business. When Mom sensed our pity, she'd tell us to stop feeling sorry for Jill because "that makes the demon stronger." I learned to avoid looking in her direction.

Mom said Jill had a Demon of Stubbornness, manifesting in her refusal to go on the potty. So, in addition to the spankings and isolation in the closet, she tried casting the demon out. "Leave her! Leave her, Demon of Stubbornness!" she'd holler, her hands on Jill's head. The rest of us spoke in tongues and laid our hands on Jill's hot, sweaty body. It didn't matter; Mom's efforts were futile. Jill would cross her arms and jut out her bottom lip. "Don't you give me that attitude," Mom would say, shaking her finger. Then she'd spank her.

Mom worked on that demon daily, but Jill stood her ground. After hours of

72

crying, her face would swell and turn flame red, her shoulders shaking with each whimper. Her cheeks stayed puffy and soaked with tears. Her nose ran constantly but Mom didn't wipe it.

After a few days, Jill's bottom turned black and lumpy. My gut was a twisted mess. I didn't know what to do with the rage, the fear, the shame of watching it happen and doing nothing. We'd dropped an entire family into Diane's lap. Then, a woman she'd known less than a week, claiming to be sent by God, convinced her to give up her parents and took custody of her daughter.

I couldn't believe what I was seeing. I'd gotten used to the speaking in tongues thing, even casting out demons, but I would never get used to watching Mom beat a baby until her bottom was the color of coal. Mom whooped Deb and me, sometimes with the belt, but she never did it repeatedly in the same day. I was only twelve, and even *I* knew it was wrong to show up and take over Diane and Ron's apartment when they so graciously allowed us to stay. She said it was God's will. I was no expert on potty training, but I knew spanking a toddler repeatedly and standing her in a closet wasn't the way to do it.

Witnessing Mom's treatment of Jill shoved Barry and my friends right out of my head. I lived in a constant state of panic. I wanted to stop it, but how? Mom wouldn't've listened to me. Besides, that's not the kind of relationship we had. Yeah, I'd done sneaky things—dumb adolescent stuff: smoked (lots), drank (once), shoplifted (caught once), but I didn't stand up to Mom—ever.

I was on the verge of imploding, carrying the weight of Mom's crimes, while feeling powerless to intervene. Alone and withered, I shoved the pain in my heart into the depths of my gut, hoping it would stay there. It didn't.

CHAPTER FIVE
New Columbia, 1974

Mom and Jim had found a big farmhouse. Mom said she wanted a place large enough to house all her newly saved souls.

Pulling up to the picturesque farmhouse outside New Columbia, tiny town near Lewisburg, Pennsylvania, home of Bucknell University. I felt something rare: hope. A new school. New friends. I'd bounced back before. And we had Uncle Jim with us. He had a steady job and a van. If Jim was around, I was certain we'd never be poor again.

We spilled out of the van. Snowball tore across the yard, nose down, tail up, peeing on everything in sight. Open fields stretched for miles in every direction. Clusters of tall trees sheltered brown and white cows that looked half-asleep in the afternoon sun. The air was the cleanest I'd ever breathed.

Mom convinced Ron and Diane to leave Sunbury and move into the farmhouse with us. I had mixed feelings. I adored tickling Jill, playing peekaboo, and styling her hair with those tiny pink barrettes. But watching how Mom treated her made something inside me twist.

It didn't take long for Mom to make the place her own. She bought tasteful, second-hand furniture, hung plants in knotted macramé holders, and lined the walls with mismatched artwork. Every night she cooked huge meals, Diane, Deb, and me working beside her. Mom was in bliss: family and converts gathered around the table, breathing in her sermons and eating the foods she'd denied herself her entire life, because of dieting.

Since the Lord had told Mom to give up her worldliness, she'd stopped "caring about her appearance." The glamorous, image-conscious mother I'd once known slowly transformed into a stout woman with cascading straight hair and gray roots she didn't bother covering. Though, she didn't let go entirely, she still wore mascara and was rarely without lipstick. "Do I need lipstick?" she'd ask several times a day. Deb and I always told her the truth. Even with the extra weight and gray roots, she maintained her beauty and grace.

Starting eighth grade didn't scare me. I'd been the new kid more times than I could count. Being new even had perks. I was a tiny bit famous for a day or two. Their eyes got big when I told them I'd seen The Jackson 5. I'd begged Mom for tickets when they played in Sacramento. To my shock, she said yes. Even from the nosebleed seats, it was the most exciting day of my life.

Before long, I fell in with a group of friends. No crush yet, but I knew myself—boy crazy, like Mom always said. I loved the fluttery maybe-he'll-sit-next-to-me feeling more than the crush itself.

But I couldn't fully fit in at school. I was living a double life. At home, I was the daughter of a fanatical preacher. At school, I was a normal twelve-year-old who just wanted friends and decent grades. At school I could breathe. At home, I folded in on myself again. It was exhausting shifting between two versions of me.

One night at supper, Mom announced that the Lord told her she was one of the two witnesses from the book of Revelation, charged with saving as many souls as possible. She said she'd be killed in the streets by nonbelievers, which would signal the beginning of the End. It would all unfold in three and a half years, she said.

I didn't believe any of it. It was wrong to take converts' paychecks, wrong to ask them to leave their families, wrong to discipline their children. And Mom lied, she claimed she healed people and raised men from the dead. I knew the truth.

Mom was unpredictable. You never knew where you stood. You could fall out of her graces over nothing—a look, a tone, not wanting seconds of something she cooked, working too slow, being "off in your own world," or, worst of all, disagreeing. I dreaded supper because it so often turned into hours of Mom wringing confessions out of us.

Every night was the same: the women cooking and the men doing odd jobs Mom assigned. Men weren't expected to cook, except grilling, but they had to wash dishes. After cleanup came dessert. Meals were hearty—spaghetti and meatballs, pot roast with carrots and potatoes—and always ice cream sundaes. All the women gained weight. The men didn't. They worked construction all day and did Tae Kwon Do before supper.

Mom prayed before every meal, long, gut-wrenching prayers pulled from the pit of her soul. Never memorized, never repeated. Sometimes she wept.

During the meal she'd go around the table, expecting each of us to testify— who we'd witnessed to that day. My stomach dropped when my turn came. Thankfully, I'd learned to invent stories on the spot. I'd say I talked to a classmate about Jesus or testified to someone on the bus. She never suspected a thing, despite her supposed "mind-reading abilities." It only confirmed what I already suspected: Mom was a fake.

So, I learned to play the game. I acted like the perfect convert—read my Bible, worked from sunup to sundown, never opposed her.

Sometimes we had guests. Friends of Ron, Diane, or Jim, or people Mom met on the street. Even old childhood friends. With her friends, she never preached. Not once. She never explained why. Nobody asked. Still, she never ran out of new converts. Someone new showed up almost every week, though just as many left. It was a revolving door.

Some nights we preached downtown in Lewisburg. Mom paired us off and told us to say, "Jesus is coming. Are you ready?" If someone bit, we'd testify and try to get them to the farmhouse for supper. Faking was harder on those nights. I was always on high alert for kids from school. My worlds were too close, separated by nothing more than a bus route. I'd do just enough to appear obedient, then sit on the curb when no one was watching. If paired with Deb, I was safe— Mom would tell her to focus on the beam in her own eye instead of the mote in mine. We didn't rat each other out. The threat of being the next target kept us loyal to each other.

I couldn't decide what was worse: street preaching or Mom's interrogations. She was like an Army sergeant, tearing people down, humiliating them until they broke into repentance. "One of youse is back. We're getting together after dinner," she'd say, usually mid-meal. Our eyes would dim. The corners of her mouth curled as if she enjoyed our discomfort. We ate silently, hoping to be invisible.

After dishes, we carried coffee and dessert to the living room. Mom would target someone, firing questions about their thoughts, accusing them of sins she was certain they'd committed. If they confessed and showed proper humility, they were forgiven. If not, we'd be up until one, two, sometimes three in the morning. Mom recruited elders—converts she liked—to assist her interrogations. If someone doubted, argued, or refused to repent, she kicked them out. I wanted to believe being her daughter protected me, but deep down I wasn't sure. So, I obeyed.

One night at supper, Ron confessed during repentance that he'd had oral sex with Diane. Mom had taught us oral sex was a sin. We were still sitting around the table, pot-roast aroma hanging in the air, when Mom accused him of letting in the Demon of Lust. She said he'd been licking his lips—a sure sign of lust, she claimed.

Ron crossed his arms. "I don't see how licking my lips proves I have a demon."

Mom pushed her plate away. "Those without natural affection who commit such sins are worthy of death."

He rolled his eyes, saying what he did in the bedroom was none of her business.

Hours later, Mom exiled him to the garage.

The garage was huge, big enough for tractors. No heat. No soft surfaces. Mom gave him a blanket and pillow. I felt sorry for him. It was fall—cold at night.

Several days later, after returning from seeing *Enter the Dragon*, we smelled something awful. Jim tightened the back-porch bulb until it flickered on, revealing poop smeared across the glass.

Ron crawled out from near Snowball's pen, on all fours.

Diane gasped. "What've you done?"

Ron slithered forward, Snowball's feces smeared across his face and bare torso.

Mom handed Jill to Diane. "Take her inside."

I knew exactly what Ron was doing. It was the story of Job. Mom loved telling it. How Job lost everything, lived among swine, covered in dung, yet stayed devoted. Because he stayed loyal, God restored everything tenfold.

Ron was showing shame, begging his way back into the house.

Streams of snot dripped from his nose as he begged for forgiveness. I pitied him—and hated Mom for driving him to it.

Mom told us all to go inside. Ron came back into the house later that night.

But it wasn't his last time in the hot seat. He kept arguing with Mom until she finally kicked him out for good. He tried to get Diane to come, but she said she had to stay to serve Jesus.

Mom moved on quickly, hunting for the next convert. Diane cried for a few days, but Mom assured her God would send another man.

Mom never mentioned Ron again, except in sermons: "He put on a show to fool Jesus, but he got found out." He became a cautionary tale.

***

John, a new convert, couldn't pee anywhere but his own house. Mom met him while street preaching. He had a tiny jockey's build, oversized feet, facial tics, and a high-pitched voice. Without facial hair, he could've passed for a ten-year-old. Mom said the Demon of Fear lived inside him and she would cast it out.

One night she lined us up in the living room and had John kneel at her feet. Earl, a friend of Jim's who'd converted was a tall Hawaiian man with curly hair and a pockmarked face. He leaned against the couch and spoke in tongues. Mom cleansed John of his sins, then started in on the demon.

"Lord Jesus, free John of the Demon of Fear," she cried, face flushed. "Leave him! Leave him, Demon of Fear!"

We chimed in, yelling commands. Suddenly Mom's body contorted. She thrashed, speaking in a deep, demonic voice. "I won't leave! I'll stay as long as I want!"

She jerked backward, laughed wildly, banged her head on the floor. We circled her, shouting louder. "Get thee behind us, Demon of Fear!"

After twenty-five or thirty minutes, she went limp. We assumed the demon had left. Jim helped Mom up. She preached some more. The night ended around two a.m. Deb, and I had to catch the bus at six-thirty.

John returned the next night, and the next, and the next. Mom cast the demon out every time, but he still couldn't pee. Sometimes he drove home just to use the bathroom. Mom sent me with him once—he had to sit on two phone books to drive.

I was terrified someone would find out I was a fake. Everyone else seemed to want to serve God. I didn't. I just didn't want to end up in the garage.

One night during deliverance, I threw myself to the floor and mimicked Mom's convulsions. I thrashed, growled, screamed. Diane held a spoon between my teeth while everyone prayed over me. Eventually I went limp, exactly like

Mom. "Thank you, Lord Jesus," Mom said, beaming. Jim helped me up. My throat burned.

I wasn't sure why I'd done it—fear, survival, wanting to be noticed. Maybe all three.

John still couldn't pee, but my performance earned me praise. Mom boasted that I was willing to be the Lord's vessel—that I was a warrior for Jesus. I soaked up the attention, though it didn't last long.

***

One afternoon, curtains drawn, Mom lay pale and clammy in her bed. The bare room, her limp body under blankets—it looked like a scene from an old black and white movie. Deb, Diane, and I tended to her, spooning soup into her mouth, placing cold rags on her forehead, rubbing her back. I didn't mind. When I was sick as a child, she'd make chicken broth with toasted Chinese noodles and rub Vicks on my chest. I lived for those moments.

On the third day, she told Jim to gather us. We filed into her bedroom. Sunlight leaked around the curtains. Mom struggled to sit up.

Jim's eyes were wet. "San has something she needs to tell youse."

Mom raised her eyelids. "I'm very, very sick. It's time. I'm gonna die soon."

Deb's face drained of color. My stomach dropped.

"I don't want none of youse to intervene," she said. "Don't take me to the hospital. When I die... that'll be the sign Jesus is coming for us. Bad things will happen. Famine. Storms. The sky turning black. War. Disease. But don't youse worry. Jesus'll take all of youse to heaven. You're the last chosen ones."

She'd told us not to intervene if someone tried to kill her, because that would start the End Times. But she'd never mentioned illness. If everything she said was true, I was doomed. I wasn't perfect. Not even close. She'd taught us that only the perfect and pure entered heaven.

We kneeled at her bedside, praying in tongues. Diane wept over Mom's hand. Jim wiped tears. "San, I'm not ready. It's too soon."

My mind ricocheted everywhere at once: What will happen to Deb and me? Will Jim take care of us? Will we go back to Tarville with Mammy and Pappy? Stay in New Columbia? Will Jim run The Kingdom?

For the first time in years, I prayed for real. I didn't want her to die. I'd already lost my father and my brother. I couldn't lose my mother too.

For days, I barely slept. The tension lived under my skin.

But within a week, Mom recovered. "It's not time yet," she said.

CHAPTER SIX

I-80, 1975

A few weeks after Mom recovered, she dropped two bombs at supper one night. Bomb number one: "It's the Lord's will for us to go back to California to be with Buddy," she said. The Lord had revealed to her that he was the other witness. She reminded us that the Bible says there are two witnesses: one from the east, and one from the west, California being the west and Pennsylvania the east.

Bomb number two: "You girls won't be going back to school. Youse don't need school no more. The end of the world is coming soon."

Deb teared up. "You mean, we're never going back?"

"Youse got all you need. The three Rs—readin,' writin,' and 'rithmatic."

Deb pushed up her glasses. "I'll never finish high school?"

"No, Debbie. I didn't graduate from high school neither. Besides, school's one of the heads of the Beast."

"But won't we get in trouble?" I said, tying my hair back with a rubber band.

"Don't play with your hair at the table. We'll have to say youse are sixteen and seventeen. It's legal to drop out of school at sixteen—I did. Youse are so mature, nobody's even gonna think twice. If anybody does ask you, say, 'None of your business.'"

Mom had taught us that the school system was corrupt because they taught evolution. She said the earth was seven thousand years old and that dinosaurs roamed the earth back then, but God wiped them out when he flooded the planet because they were unclean.

The two other heads were government and religion. Mom didn't consider herself religious. In fact, she bristled at the sound of any insinuation that she was anything but a woman of God. Her disdain for religion ran particularly deep with the Catholic Church. "The Catholic Church is the richest and most powerful. They don't care nothin' about the poor and needy."

Mom always championed the downtrodden. She believed Jesus was physically present on the earth, incognito: a wino, a derelict, a prostitute. "Jesus don't make himself known. He comes in hiding to test us," she'd say. "And most people fail by ignoring or scorning them."

At first, I loved the idea of not going to school: no more tests, homework. Plus, we were moving, so I wasn't going to see my friends again anyway. But then it hit me. Without school, I no longer had an escape. School was my anchor, my sanity. Now I'd have to be around Mom all the time. I lived in constant fear of being discovered for the fraud that I was.

I'd ruminate on what could happen. What if it's true? What if the end really is coming in three and a half years? What's gonna happen to me? I'm a liar. A fraud. I finally decided to believe Mom—just in case it was true. I shoved all doubts from my mind and replaced them with all that Mom had taught me.

I later learned this is called Pascal's Wager. Developed in the 17th century by Blaise Pascal. He asserted that betting on God's existence was the only rational choice. Because reason cannot prove or disprove His existence.

While I questioned some of Mom's claims, I did believe in heaven and hell. I knew God's teachings. We'd been to church enough times, even before Mom's calling. Deb and I would get up early Sunday mornings and tiptoe around so as not to wake Mom. She'd leave us some coins for tithe. Sometimes, we'd veer off the path walking to church to buy candy. Deb was a goody-two-shoes in all other situations, but that was the one crime she'd commit with me. We justified our actions by saying we deserved to treat ourselves, because other kids got to stay home and watch Sunday morning shows.

Renting a U-Haul was too expensive, so Mom had Jim build a trailer. Jim doubted he could build it, but Mom assured him he had the skills needed and the Lord would guide him. He just needed to have faith. She was right. He did have the skills. He built a fine trailer out of plywood and a metal hitch and frame. We had a garage sale and sold everything that wouldn't fit. Mom bought two bean bag chairs for additional seating in the back of the van, which, by that point, would be enough seating for all of us. Paul, one of the converts, decided he wasn't cut out for the commune life. And Mom had kicked Earl out after I'd told her he put his tongue in my mouth.

Mom had everyone kiss on the lips upon greeting and saying goodnight. She taught us that pure love isn't unseemly and that men should be able to kiss men and women should be able to kiss women. But I guess it never occurred to her that this made Deb and me vulnerable.

One night during our bedtime kisses, I leaned up to give Earl a peck, and he slipped his tongue in my mouth. I pulled back, wiped my lips with the back of my hand, and escaped into the bathroom to splash water in my mouth. Before bed that night, I told Mom what he'd done.

The following day, she called everyone to the kitchen. She had that familiar look: pursed lips, eyes shifting back and forth like she knew a secret. Once everyone got settled in their seats, Mom fixed on Earl. He didn't notice—but I did.

"Earl, Peggy said you put your tongue in her mouth last night."

Earl's face turned the color of hell. "Is that what she told you?"

"My daughter don't lie, if that's what you're saying."

Earl squirmed. "I'm not saying she lied."

"Then what are you saying?"

"Okay. I'm sorry," he said, throwing up his hands. "I didn't mean to. It just happened."

"Are you saying it was an accident?"

"Yeah! No! I don't know!"

Mom made her lips into a tight circle and wagged her finger. "There's no room in this house for lust. Pack your bags." She pointed at the door. "And get out."

Earl wiped the sweat from his brow, then held his hands in praying position. "No, please. I won't do it again. I'm repenting."

Mom turned away. "It's too late for that."

"All right, fine! I'll leave then!" He stood up so hastily his chair toppled. He grabbed it and slammed it back into place. Jim rose, crossed his arms, and widened his stance. Earl softened. He was much taller than Jim, but you'd never know it by how he backed down. He went upstairs, got his things, then marched out without a word. Earl's trial and conviction were swift. I felt protected. We never spoke of Earl again. Without explanation, Mom stopped requiring the kisses.

I didn't know what Mom's plan was. I don't think she did either. All I knew was we were heading back to California so Mom could join Buddy. In the past, I would've moaned and groaned, but no complaints came from me. I saw Mom berate people who complained. Besides, I wasn't thinking much about Buddy. I was thinking about all the lies I'd been telling and how I'd faked casting out John's demon. I was riddled with guilt and terrified of my fate. I needed to confess, but when? How?

Somewhere amid the move, Mom had lost her glasses, so she wore mine. Without them, everything was hazy. I felt alone, saturated in self-condemnation. Everyone else had truly repented. I was the sinner among them who hadn't.

After being on the road for a day, I thought I might implode. My body shuddered at the images in my mind of people in The Lake of Fire, wailing, burning, clawing. My chest and throat tightened. Everything around me seemed amplified. Jill asking questions, Christian rock playing on the 8-track. Everyone clapping and singing along.

Finally, I couldn't take it anymore. I slid out of the bean bag chair and scooted on my knees to the front. Meekly, I poked my head between the bucket seats. Jim was driving, and Mom was in the passenger seat.

I cleared my throat. "Mom, I… I need to talk to you about something. I have something… I have to tell you. I've been lying to you."

Mom turned toward me and folded her arms. "What'd you lie about?"

I swallowed the lump in my throat. "I lied about everything. About testifying. About believing. And I faked casting out the demon that time." Tears streamed down my cheeks.

Mom turned off the music and motioned for Jim to pull over.

As he pulled the van over, I began to feel relief.

"Come on, everyone, let's pray over Peggy." Everyone placed their hands on me and spoke in tongues. Mom pressed her hand on my forehead. It felt like it was a hundred degrees in that van.

"Peggy, ask Jesus Christ for forgiveness."

I continued to weep uncontrollably, barely able to speak. "P-p-p-please forgive me for everything I did wrong. I'm so sorry for lying. I'll never lie again. I promise. I will only serve you, Jesus."

Mom was waiting for me to speak in tongues, so she would know the Holy Ghost was inside me. I worried it wouldn't come because before I just spoke gibberish, not real tongues. I concentrated on feeling the Lord in my heart, using remorse as the vehicle. I began speaking in tongues. This time, it felt real. I was no longer an imposter. I was an actual member of The Kingdom. Everyone rejoiced and hugged me.

"Okay, Jim, let's hit the road," Mom said.

I didn't lie to Mom again. I believed everything she said and no longer questioned the Lord's will. Given the opportunity, I would gladly have testified. I fought off doubtful thoughts and held onto only the pure ones. I vowed to be perfect, as Jesus commanded. Fear of The Lake of Fire drove a wedge between my emotions and my mind. I stuffed my real feelings deep into the pit of my stomach. I broke.

After that day, keeping my thoughts pure was an interminable battle. I'd notice a doubtful thought, then push it out as fast as possible. And when Mom twisted the truth or rewrote history, I told myself it was for the greater good and that sometimes she needed to exaggerate stories to save souls. Every night before falling asleep, I'd audit my behavior and thoughts for that day, praying to God to forgive my sins. Mom drilled it into us: "For the wages of sin is death."

***

On our second day of travel, the wind picked up while we were driving through Utah, heading down a steep slope on the interstate. Gusts howled. Our ears popped. We became more alert; our bodies stiffened. Even Snowball's ears were back. The trailer swayed and made a knocking sound.

Mom looked in her rearview mirror and screamed, "It's rocking! The trailer's rocking! It's gonna snap off! Jim, what should I do?!"

"San, keep it steady and lightly tap the brakes to slow it down."

Mom clutched the steering wheel. "It's not working! It's still rocking! Jim, I don't know what to do!"

"San, stay calm. Keep holding it steady and tapping the brakes."

"I don't know, Jim. It's gonna snap off. If it does, it could throw us off the road."

Deb was in one of the bean bag chairs, her mouth open, fear in her eyes. Diane clung to sleeping Jill on her lap. I sat on the bed biting my nails.

"Lord Jesus, we need your help," Mom pleaded. "Please intervene. Please make the trailer stop." She turned to us. "Everybody, pray."

We spoke in tongues.

Jim wiped his brow, then adjusted his baseball cap. "San, you're doing good.

Eventually, the hill leveled off, and the trailer stopped rocking.

Mom pulled over, then closed her eyes. "It's a miracle. Thank you, Jesus. We praise you, Lord."

The rest of us chimed in. I was overcome with disbelief. Was it the Lord, or was it just that the road leveled out? But I pushed those questions aside, telling myself the Lord stopped the rocking because of our prayers.

***

On the third day, after several hours of driving, Mom put on a Christian rock 8-track, singing, and clapping to the music. She'd played that 8-track so many times we knew the words by heart. Same with Paul McCartney's "Band on the Run." It wasn't religious music, but Mom loved that album. We always followed Mom's lead. If she sang, we sang. If she danced, we danced. If she clapped, we clapped.

We all sang along and clapped, except for two-and-a-half-year-old Jill. Mom swiveled around and, in a high-pitched voice, said, "Jill, look. Clap like this."

Jill put her head down and kept her hands in her lap. "C'mon, honey," Diane said, trying to cajole her. "You can do it. Like this." She demonstrated.

My chest tightened. Here we go again. I pushed out that thought and replaced it with: Mom is trying to teach her.

Mom crawled into the back beside Diane, grabbed Jill by the wrists, forcibly clapping her hands together. "C'mon, Jill, clap your hands!" Jill looked at her vacantly, then wailed. "Stop that crying and clap those hands," Mom said. She placed her hand on Jill's head. "Get out of her, Demon of Stubbornness. Leave this child!"

Jill whimpered. Diane's face was soaked with tears.

"Wipe those tears and stop that crying. If the demon knows you're weak, he'll get to Jill through you."

Diane took a few deep breaths to stifle her tears.

She's her kid. Who are you to tell her? Oh no! Another sinful thought. I pushed it away, drowning out the sound of Jill's whimpering by saying Praise Jesus repeatedly to myself. This can't be right. How can this be holy? Praise Jesus. Praise Jesus. Help me, Jesus. Help me get rid of these thoughts. My body screamed, Grab Jill and run! Every cell was filled with rage. But I didn't know what would happen if I intervened. Would Mom damn me to The Lake of Fire or leave me on the side of the road?

After two hours of Mom alternating between yelling at Jill, slapping her hands together, and commanding the demon to leave, Jill finally lifted her swollen, red hands and clapped softly.

Mom smiled "Good girl. See now, that's not so hard, is it?" She turned to Diane. "The demon's gone."

Mom pulled a white hanky from her bra, wiped Jill's face, hugged her, then lay her on the bed. Jill fell right to sleep, her body still shuddering with whimpers.

The tension in my body released. My thoughts settled.

Then:

"Diane, don't ever undermine me like that again," Mom said, her brows furrowed.

Diane's chin trembled.

"If Satan senses one of us is weak, the demon won't leave."

"I'm sorry." Diane held her face in her hands and sobbed.

"Okay…well, stop crying. The demon left Jill. This is a time to rejoice."

Diane wiped her face and forced a smile. Mom hugged her.

In the days that followed, I was overcome with guilt for not helping Jill. I was her ally, but only in my core. My soul belonged to a God who could condemn me to eternal burning. My mind got evicted. Terror was the new tenant. I pushed the incident into the recesses of my mind. The prerecorded sound bites that made me feel like I was in God's grace again played in a loop.

CHAPTER SEVEN

Sacramento, 1975

Mom had arranged for us to meet Buddy at his son David's house in Sacramento. She didn't share much about the deal she'd made with him, just the headline: Buddy was the witness from the west, she was the witness from the east. It was the Lord's will for the two of them to be together. Then, they would be killed by nonbelievers. Their deaths would trigger the beginning of the End of Times. Mom instructed us not to intervene. To let them be killed. Intervening would be interfering with the Lord's plan.

We pulled into a gravel driveway shaded by a canopy of tangled branches. David, tall and angular with a full, dark beard, stepped from his little bungalow. Beside him stood his wife, Sharon, her long blonde hair spilling down her back, his arm protectively encircling her pregnant belly.

The aroma of beef stew greeted us at the door, thick and rich. We'd been living on Velveeta or peanut butter sandwiches—things that were cheap and didn't need refrigeration—so the smell of real food hit me like a warm hand on my back.

I carried my bowl of steaming hot stew into the living room and sat on the lumpy couch. The paneled walls were dinged up, grease stains streaked down the side of the stove, and a few ceiling tiles sagged like they were thinking about giving up altogether. The gold shag carpet was matted and bald in spots, worn thin by too many feet and not enough money. David rushed to clear a pile of laundry off a chair, motioning for Diane and Jill to sit.

After the meal, Mom saved David and Sharon. David's experience was emotional, much like Jim and Ron's, but Sharon's was subdued. New converts who were truly humble—something Mom revered—shed tears. Most were able to cry, but inevitably there'd be one person who couldn't squeeze out a tear. Mom would keep us up for hours trying to get that one convert to break. "God resisteth the proud, but giveth grace unto the humble," she'd quote. To my surprise, this time she didn't press Sharon to cry. She let Sharon's dry eyes stand, like a test she wasn't grading that night.

Later that day, Maryanne plodded through the door, diaper bag slung over one arm, baby in the other. Her shaggy, ash-blonde hair was mussed. Her bell bottoms were tattered at the hem. I was thrilled to see her and even more excited to learn she'd had a baby named Melissa, who she called Lissa. Lissa's skin was sun-kissed. Her curls were the color of the night sky. She had heart-shaped pink lips and long curly lashes. She was the most gorgeous baby I'd ever seen, like someone who had taken all the sweetness the world had left and poured it into one small body.

Maryanne and I had gotten close while Mom and Buddy were together. Only a few years older than me, she understood me in a way that made me feel less strange. Leaving her when we moved back to Pennsylvania had felt like losing a sister. I'd figured I'd never see her again.

While Sharon rested in her bedroom, Mom, Deb, Diane, and Maryanne straightened up the house and prepared supper. My job was to hold the baby on the couch. I didn't complain. Cradling Lissa felt like being entrusted with something holy and breakable.

We heard a knock, and there he was. Buddy: that silver-haired, pompous ass with his perma-smirk. Buddy, the man who convinced Mom she had a "calling." Disdain for him leeched into my body and mind, a slow poison. Praise Jesus, praise Jesus. Get out of here, doubtful thoughts, I told myself. Mom greeted him with a hug and a closed-mouth grin. The tension between them was palpable, buzzing in the air like a fluorescent light about to blow, but I had no idea why.

After exchanging pleasantries, we each got a plate of food, found a place to sit in the living room, and waited for Mom or Buddy to say grace.

Buddy sat on a kitchen chair at the head of the room, leaned back, and folded his arms. "We come to you, Lord... as your humble servants..."

I was tempted to open an eye to see Mom's face, but I kept both shut, holding my breath like that would keep the room from tipping.

Buddy not only said grace but also dominated the preaching the whole night. In the past, he'd shared the stage with Mom. In some cases, he'd let her do all the preaching.

Buddy leaned forward. "Jesus came to me in the night. I saw him through the keyhole in my bedroom door. He was wearing a white robe. He said I'm the chosen one."

Mom's face was inscrutable. Everyone else shifted and stared at the floor, like the linoleum might offer an escape route. Buddy kept touting the miracles he'd performed and the souls he'd saved—much like Mom had, but with a dose of extra crazy. He talked about prophecies delivered through visions, and traveling to other dimensions. He didn't mention Mom or the part she'd played in his ministry, like she'd been edited out of his story.

Mom stayed expressionless all night. Finally, around two a.m., Buddy left, planning to return the following night. The minute the door shut behind him, Mom gathered us. She said Buddy had done LSD in the past. She was certain his keyhole experience was him tripping. She said Buddy was of the devil and that we needed to leave the next day.

David leaned back in his chair and rubbed his beard. "What do you mean, he's of the devil, Sandy?"

"David, something's not right about your dad. I think he gave in to a demon. He don't talk right. He's talking about going to other dimensions. That don't sound right."

"Yeah, but he's always talked like that."

"I think he might be on something."

Jim adjusted his cap. "Yeah, San, I wasn't gonna say nothing. But I was thinking the same thing."

Mom rubbed her forehead, like she could smooth out the whole mess with her fingertips. "We need to be gone tomorrow before Buddy gets here."

Maryanne, who was sitting at Mom's feet, said, "Can I come with you? I don't want to go back to Sam."

Mom opened her arms. Maryanne rested her head on Mom's thigh, and Mom wrapped her arms around her. "Yes, Maryanne. You're coming with us. The world's coming to an end. You're one of God's chosen. There was a reason we came back out here. It wasn't for Buddy; it was for you kids."

Sharon rubbed her swollen belly. "Where are you going?"

"The Lord will guide us."

Sharon scraped her hair into a ponytail and cleared her throat. "I don't know. Just leave? So fast?"

David put his arm on her shoulder. "Come on, Babe. This is our chance to be saved and to serve Jesus. And I think she might be right about the end of the world. Look at the way the world is. Everything's messed up."

"I know, but what about the baby?"

David put his hand on her belly. "The Lord'll take care of us and the baby. Don't worry. I trust Sandra."

Mom adjusted her glasses. "Sharon, the end is coming. Youse need to get ready." She sat taller, her voice husky with emotion, and read from Revelation, "Behold, I stand at the door and knock, if any man hears my voice, I will come to him. He's here knocking right now, Sharon."

By night's end, David and Sharon had vowed to come with us. The plan was simple and impossible: wake early, help David and his wife pack, take Maryanne home to pick up things for the baby, and then let God lead the way.

The following day, Sharon left to go and say goodbye to her family. Mom was reluctant but allowed it, saying she needed to be quick. She instructed Jim to un-hitch the trailer from the van and drive Maryanne to San Francisco to get her things—she sent me along to help. Time was of the essence. It was a ninety-minute drive, one way. If we were going to get on the road that day, we had to hurry. Maryanne left Lissa in Mom's care.

***

We stopped in front of Maryanne's duplex. The sun bounced off the cars lining the steep street. Maryanne chewed her lip—her signature telltale sign when she was nervous. "Okay," she said, taking a deep breath, "I'm going to run in and grab a few things." She flung open the door and jumped out.

Jim darted his head around. "Peg, you go with her, and I'll stay here n' watch out."

We went through the side door into the kitchen. The counters were littered with dirty dishes, cans of food, and baby bottles. The place reeked of rancid trash. We filled a couple of garbage bags with Lissa's things, jumped back in the van, and drove away unnoticed.

On the drive back, Maryanne described the abuse she'd endured. She said she'd been wanting to leave Sam but was too scared and didn't have money or anywhere to go. Her words came out flat, like she'd told the story too many times in her head already.

Jim adjusted himself in his seat. "Well, that guy ain't gonna hurt you no more, I'll see to that."

Maryanne blushed.

Once back at David and Sharon's place, we started loading their things into the trailer when we heard the roar of a vehicle pulling up. "It's Sharon's family," David said, squinting out the window. "It doesn't look good." We all ran to the window. Walking toward us was a craggy woman carrying a shotgun. Behind her two younger, lanky guys with wild hair: one a little hunched and the other pigeon-toed—also carrying guns.

"Let me talk to them," David said, holding out his arms protectively. "I'll see what's going on."

Before we knew it, they'd pushed their way through the door with their long guns. We instinctively formed a human wall—even Mom, with sleeping Lissa in her arms. The three of them faced us, smirking. The woman stood square and pointed her shotgun at Mom. One of the guys leveled his gun at Jim and the other at David. I'd watched scenes in movies where people were held at gunpoint and everyone fell apart—hysterical women, men jutting their chins out trying to hide their fear. I didn't feel hysterical or even like crying. My emotions were suspended, hanging like a held breath, waiting to see what would happen next.

The woman leaned toward Mom. "We ain't letting you take Sharon from us. C'mon David, tell this woman to get the hell out."

David puffed out his chest. "Nope. I'm not making them leave. Where's Sharon?"

The woman bared her teeth. "Don't you worry none where she is. She's where she belongs." She peered around at us. "She don't want nothing to do with these crazy people."

"That's not true," David said. "She got saved last night."

"My niece don't wanna do this. She told me about it an hour ago. These people are trying to brainwash her. And you too, David. Even if she did wanna go, hell would freeze before we'd allow it."

David's face tightened. "She's, my wife. This is our house."

"So, you're saying you wanna be one of these crazy-ass people, David."

"They're not crazy. God sent them."

The aunt roared with laughter. "God sent them… what a joke. I ain't no God-fearin' woman, but even I know God don't split up families."

"Well, all I know is, this woman speaks the truth and I'm following her. If Sharon doesn't want to be saved, I guess that's her choice."

"You got that right. Sharon's with us. David, can't you see this woman has taken over your mind?"

"I can think for myself."

"David, you ain't gonna never see Sharon and that baby if you go with them. You okay with that?"

David adjusted his pants. "I guess I have to be. If she chooses damnation, I can't do anything about that."

"Well, okay. Sounds like you made your choice. Then, you need to leave with these crazy people. Right now." She aimed the gun at David's stomach.

David stood tall and looked her dead in the eyes. "This is my house. You need to leave."

The aunt sneered. "Last I checked, we got the guns." The scraggly guys giggled. Inching closer, she elongated her neck, making her pointy cheeks more prominent. "You. Need. To. Leave."

Mom stood still as a statue, cradling Lissa. Jim's nostrils flared and he crossed his arms over his inflated chest.

Mom, clenching her jaw and speaking through her teeth, said, "Get thee behind me, Satan." Her gaze could've burned a hole straight through the woman.

The woman cackled, then let loose a couple of smoker coughs.

The veins in Mom's neck bulged. "Don't mock me."

"I can mock you all day. I got the gun."

She moved closer to Mom, handed her shotgun to the man on her right, then got in Mom's face. "I don't know who you think you are. You can't come in here and take people from their lives."

Mom didn't blink. "The Lord rebuke you, Satan."

The woman narrowed her eyes and pointed at the door. "Get the hell outta here."

Mom didn't move.

Then:

The woman wrapped her hands around Mom's neck and squeezed. Mom didn't resist. Her face turned purple and the veins in her forehead bulged. From the minuscule bit of air that remained in her voice box, she commanded Satan to leave.

My eyes darted around the room. Nobody was moving. Mom's eyes rolled back in her head.

Without thinking, I jumped at the woman, growling in a high pitch, "Get your hands off my mom!" I clawed and tore at her like a feral cat. I pulled her hair and peeled her hands from Mom's throat. Then I shoved her to the floor. Complete mayhem ensued. Maryanne took Lissa from Mom's arms just before she collapsed.

"The police are coming!" Diane yelled.

The two guys held back the woman from lunging. After she regained her composure, she pointed the gun in Mom's face.

Strands of her salt and pepper hair were in my fist.

"Let's get outta here," one of the guys yelled.

The woman leaned in. "Alright. We're leavin.' But when we come back… y'all better be gone."

Mom stood, wordless. The woman pulled back her gun and backed out the door. She and the two guys scuttled out and sped off in their rusty pickup, leaving a cloud of dust in their wake.

I figured I was in massive trouble. I'd completely lost control. Even fear of The Lake of Fire didn't stop the animal I became in that moment. But Mom didn't say a word. No reprisal. No "thank you." Not that I wanted or expected a thank you, but the silence sat heavy. Later I learned Mom had been so out of it, she didn't realize I was the one who intervened.

The police took statements, asked if we had guns, and when we were leaving. They didn't like that Jim had hunting guns, but they couldn't do anything about it because they were registered. Mom was pissed that they were more interested in when we were leaving town than how she'd been attacked. After they left, Mom instructed Jim to get the guns from the van. "We're not gonna be sitting ducks if they come back."

They never returned, but another confrontation was just around the corner.

***

We'd finished getting David's things together when we heard the screech of cars pulling up.

Jim sniffed loudly—as he often did when he was worked up—then peeled the curtain back. "San, we got more trouble."

She ran to the window. "Okay, Satan's not stopping. It's more enemies."

"We here for the baby!" a male voice yelled. "Send her out and nobody gets hurt."

"Don't say a word," Mom said. "We're not letting them in this house. Jim. David—" Mom said, nervously rubbing her hands together "—sneak out back and check out the situation."

Jim and David slipped out the back door, then slithered on their bellies under the bushes to get a look.

"Give us baby Lissa! Then, we'll go on our way! We ain't leaving 'til you send her out. We got guns."

I was still reeling from tearing that woman off Mom's neck. And there we were, threatened with guns again, like the whole world had decided to aim itself at us.

"There's eight or ten cars out there, San. We're surrounded," Jim said, as he cracked his knuckles.

Mom scooted to the edge of the couch. "You guys need to be ready to fight. You're warriors for the Lord."

They nodded.

"Now, gird up your loins and get ready."

Jim loosened his belt and hiked up his pants, then cinched it two notches in so he could stretch his legs. He got into a wide squat and stretched from side to side. David stretched too. By some dumb luck, David was also a black belt. They practiced their front snap kicks and roundhouses together. They air punched: double punched, and solar plex punched—Jim's favorite. Jim wasn't a tall guy, but he was powerful. He had huge, callused knuckles, thick legs, and not an ounce of fat. He was fast and limber—he could kick a leaf off a high-hanging branch. David was tall, lean, and equally strong.

The last golden hour of the day drained away. The sky turned purple, then black. We thought we heard the cars pull away. Mom sent Jim and David out to evaluate the situation again.

They army-crawled on their bellies. The rest of us sat in the living room, waiting, biting our nails, twisting our hair, listening for sounds that might mean everything was about to explode again.

Jim and David slipped through the back door; their knees covered in dirt and leaves clinging to their clothes.

Jim, out of breath, slicked back his hair. "It's all clear, San. They must've left."

"Alright, guys. Let's get outta here."

As we approached our van, a bunch of cars swarmed us and flipped on their headlights. We rushed back into the house and locked the door.

"Call the cops again, Diane," Mom hollered. "Jim, tell 'em we called the police."

Dashing over to the window, he bellowed, "We called the cops. They're on their way."

Within seconds, the cars dispersed, like cockroaches when the lights come on.

Not long after that, the same cops we'd seen earlier showed up. This time, they didn't take statements. Mom told them Maryanne was leaving her abusive husband, and his family was trying to take the baby.

The cop tipped back his hat. "You folks need to get out of town as soon as possible. That's how this is going to be resolved."

Mom backed away. "Wait a minute. Aren't you gonna do nothing? Aren't you gonna arrest those people? That woman from before tried to kill me. Look at my neck. And those other people held us captive in this house."

"I think it's best if you folks leave town. You seem to have pissed off a lot of people. And maybe with good reason."

"We're just a family that wants to be together. Maryanne's like a daughter to me. Her husband's been beating her. That don't mean nothing? And this is David's house. He should be able to choose who he wants here."

It didn't matter what Mom argued; they said we needed to leave. They stayed until we loaded the van and drove off; the whole time, Mom ranted about the injustice of how we were peaceful people, not hurting anyone, yet we were the ones being run out of town.

Driving away, Mom talked about Sharon and Lissa's family non-stop. They were interfering with the Lord's work. God's wrath would take care of them in the end.

I felt good about Maryanne leaving Sam, but I wondered how David felt about leaving pregnant Sharon. I pushed those questions down and told myself Sharon had let the devil into her heart and David had made the right choice. I reminded myself of what Jesus said in the book of Matthew: to forsake all and follow Him. I told myself that he who has forsaken his sister, father, mother, child will inherit everlasting life.

With eight of us, plus Snowball, sleeping in the van was impossible. I trusted Mom and Jim would figure something out. We used one of the bean bag chairs as a crib for Lissa. The rest of us piled on the bed or sat cross-legged on the floor. Jim drove as the cops escorted us to the interstate. Mom said the Lord would give us a sign for where we should stop.

We bought a bag of diapers and a few cans of condensed milk for Lissa, while the rest of us went back to eating Velveeta and peanut butter. We only had enough money for gas, so we'd need to find free places to sleep.

I figured once we got on the road, Mom would confront me about interfering with her attempted murder, but she never did. Maybe it was predestined for me to save her, and everything happened as it was supposed to.

We never saw Buddy again. Not much more was said about him, except that he did drugs, was crazy, and wasn't the other witness after all.

We drove all night—Mom, Jim, and David taking turns. While driving in the dark through Utah, the wind kicked up. Jim's knuckles whitened, and he hunched over the wheel. When we hit a hilly stretch, the wind picked up even more. There were no rest stops, billboards, streetlights, or other cars, so we kept going. We drudged up the hills at a glacial pace, gas pedal to the floor, then wrestled the wind all the way down. We were clocking fifteen or twenty miles an hour and nearing empty on gas. Mom prayed, begging Jesus for help. We spoke in tongues, pleading with Jesus to slow down the wind and put more gas in the tank.

After driving and praying for a while, we finally saw a billboard advertising a new hotel that would be opening soon. We didn't have money to pay for a room, but Mom said since it wasn't open yet, they might allow us to stay for free.

We'd run out of water hours before. When I swallowed, my tongue stuck to the roof of my mouth. We pulled into the parking lot, lit by a single Coca-Cola vending machine. I could imagine the wet bubbles on my tongue and that sweet liquid magic swirling down my throat. To my chagrin, Mom said we'd drink water once we got in the hotel room because we couldn't waste money on soda.

We waited in the van while Mom and Jim went to the hotel office. It was closed, but the manager lived in the room above. Mom and Jim came back with two hotel keys. The girls took one room and the guys the other.

Walking toward our room, I pictured how the cool water would feel as I slurped it from the bathroom faucet. I flung open the door and ran to the sink. I turned the handle. Not a drop. It hadn't been hooked up yet. I cranked the tub faucet. Water came out, but it was yellowish.

"Peg, don't drink that. It's sulfur," Jim warned. "It ain't safe."

"Wasn't planning on it. Smells nasty."

Simultaneously we all let out a sigh of disappointment. Then Mom reached into her smock pockets and pulled out a couple of cans of Coke, along with a mason jar of water, to mix milk for Lissa and Jill. We sat on the beds, passing the Cokes around, making sure to sip only a little so there'd be enough for everyone.

Jim said the water wasn't safe to drink, but we could bathe in it. During my bath, I washed with one hand and held my nose with the other.

After eating peanut butter sandwiches the next day, we set out for the town up the road. The plan was that we'd look for work so we could continue funding our trip.

Looking back, it's a haze how they found us work. Perhaps a temp agency, or maybe they approached the owner—but Mom and Jim landed short-term work cleaning new mobile homes at a sales lot. We'd be staying a few days to earn enough to get back on the road, but we couldn't waste our earnings on motels; we had to find a church that would take us in.

After clocking as many hours as we could that first day, we drove around looking for a church. Finally, we came upon one that Mom said looked promising—Methodist, I think. The building's façade was modest, and a house was attached to the back. The lights were on. We pulled up to the front. A bald man with a friendly face appeared. Mom appealed our case and he was sympathetic.

He led us into the kitchen to make some sandwiches and warm some milk for the babies. I crossed my fingers behind my back that there wouldn't be peanut butter or Velveeta. To my delight, there were ham slices in the fridge. After we ate, we made beds on the church floor with pillows and blankets.

The next morning, Mom instructed us to fast because everyone had doubtful thoughts. She could feel it in her body, she said. Fasting for three days would rid us of our doubts. "When hunger pangs come, pray and they'll go away," she said.

I'd gone without meals before, but never entire days at a time. During my fast, I constantly monitored my thoughts, weeding out and discarding doubts. Maybe we should've stayed in New Columbia—doubtful thought. What's gonna happen to us? —doubtful thought. Shouldn't we have more of a plan? —doubtful thought.

At the end of our workday, we sat around on the floor, our stomachs gurgling, singing in tongues, praying, and listening to Mom preach. In one sermon, she taught us that babies are born sin-free, but then demons try to get into them. And when they do, they become sinners like everyone else. "Lissa don't have no demons yet," she said.

After three days, we got back on the interstate. Mom treated us to a meal at a roadside restaurant to break the fast. I don't remember what I had, but I do remember that food never tasted so good. Knowing we were returning to peanut butter and Velveeta made me savor every bite.

It was indisputable that David and Diane had taken a liking to each other. Diane blushed when she talked to him and her eyes twinkled. They'd hold hands on the bed in the van. Diane would nap on his shoulder. Mom was elated. She announced that they were married from that day on.

CHAPTER EIGHT
Kansas City, 1975

I'd been sleeping in the back corner of the bed in the van; my body molded onto the thin mattress like it was trying to disappear. When my eyes blinked open and I peered out the rear window, I saw we'd stopped. City lights bled into the darkness. Sirens wailed, horns bleated, and motorcycles growled past in uneven bursts. A thick cocktail of fuel, fried food, and factory output crawled up my nostrils. Men in slicked-back hair and briefcases hurried along the sidewalks while grimy street people shuffled past with vacant eyes.

"Where are we, Mom?"

"We're in Kansas City. This is where we're supposed to stay. I can feel it."

I suspected her "feeling" had less to do with the Lord and more to do with an empty wallet, but I shoved that doubt down where all the other dangerous thoughts lived. Mom and Jim headed into an office across the street and came back with a slip of paper—the address of a halfway house. They'd called ahead to let them know we were coming, as if we were some odd little group of disciples instead of a family with nowhere else to go.

A shingle hanging from the top of the porch read, HOLY FAMILY HOUSE. A tall woman with a sunny disposition stood on the porch, flannel shirt tucked into high-waisted jeans. I'd expected robes and a habit, like the nuns on TV. The word "Holy" made my stomach tighten. I was worried about the woman being a nun because of how Mom hated the Catholic church.

She held out her hand. "Hello, I'm Kay. Welcome to The Holy Family House."

Uh oh, this place is called the Holy Family House. I knew that name would be put under a microscope. If you dared call yourself holy around Mom, you'd better be spotless. The house would've had to be damn near perfect to live up to that sign.

We stepped through a thick, creaking door with a brass handle. Something was cooking inside, but I couldn't place it. I didn't care what it was—as long as it wasn't peanut butter or Velveeta.

"The agency said you'd be needing a meal, so we prepared some sandwiches."

Saliva rushed into my mouth. I pictured turkey and cheese, or salami with a giant pickle on the side. I would've even settled for bologna, and I hated bologna.

"I hope nobody's allergic to peanuts," Kay commented, pulling out a chair.

Peanut butter. I can't eat no more peanut butter.

"Uh, you got anything different?" Mom asked. "We been eating peanut butter for days. We need meat."

"Sorry, peanut butter is what I can do right now. We'll have soup later. Do you still want the sandwiches?"

"Yeah, I guess. We're starved."

I ate every bite of that peanut butter and jelly on wheat and drained the milk, even though I didn't like milk. Mom taught us it was a sin to refuse what was given. Somehow, that sandwich tasted like mercy. The jam was bright and sweet, and the bread was homemade and still warm, like it had just been pulled from a kind grandmother's oven.

I told Kay that whatever she was cooking smelled good. She said it was vegetable soup and that this was a vegetarian house.

Uh oh, that's gonna be a problem.

Mom's face fell, her mouth tightening. I could see the argument rising in her, then sinking again. She swallowed it—for the moment.

All day, the soup's smell snaked through the halls. It seeped into the corners of the living room, weaving around the tenants gathered in front of the TV. When we walked in, they all turned and stared, their faces devoid of expression.

After we settled into our rooms, I went back downstairs. A stick-thin elderly woman with wavy silver hair fixed her gaze on me. I flashed a thin-lipped smile, and she answered with an ear-to-ear grin. I tried to ignore her constant staring, but it was like trying not to notice a flickering lightbulb. Eventually, I understood—watching me was her entertainment. Maybe I reminded her of someone she'd lost. Maybe she used to have red hair. Either way, I accepted it the way you accept a drafty window—you don't like it, but you live around it.

Most everyone in the room was elderly, except a man who looked about forty and spoke like a little boy. "When's I Love Lucy on?" he asked, flapping his hands with excitement. Everyone ignored him, like he was just another sound in the room, a cuckoo clock, the TV.

In the corner sat a man with sunken eyes and no teeth, slumped in his chair. The cuckoo clock ticked behind him. As soon as it struck five, the forty-year-old guy jumped up and hollered, "Time for dinner."

I sprang from my chair and then forced myself to move slower. I didn't want to look desperate. We filed into the kitchen and sat at a long table tucked into a nook.

I was ready for that soup I'd been smelling all day. Mom wore a sour expression like a badge. I knew why. "Vegetarians think they're better than us," she'd say. "People are meant to eat meat."

Mom tasted the soup, then set her spoon down carefully, lifted her chin, and folded her arms. "You don't have no meat at all?"

Kay, still handing out bowls, smiled awkwardly. "Like I said, this is a vegetarian house."

"Well, we need to eat meat. We been traveling for days. Beans aren't gonna cut it."

"I understand, ma'am. I'm sorry. We don't serve meat." She kept serving, smiling briefly at each diner, like she was passing out tiny apologies with every bowl.

"The Bible says we're supposed to eat the animals that are put on the earth."

"I'm sorry," she repeated, and walked into the kitchen.

Kay stayed there and ate her soup at the counter, one wall away, as if distance could protect her from Mom's disapproval. Mom sat with her nose in the air; disdain wrapped around her like a shawl. Eventually, though, she picked up the spoon and ate.

The next day, we discovered our van had been ransacked. Our eight-track player and CB radio were gone, sliced out of our lives like they'd never existed.

"I wouldn't get your hopes up," the cop said. "We rarely recover stolen goods from car robberies."

After he took the report, Mom and Jim left to "take care of some business." They put in a change of address so Jim could get his unemployment checks and Mom applied for food stamps.

I wandered toward the commons area. The sweet aroma of baked bread wrapped around me as I came down the stairs. Everyone was gathered in the living room. The old woman's eyes snapped to me like a magnet finding metal.

"Young lady," she called out. "Come here."

I glanced behind me, half-hoping she meant someone else.

"Yes, you. Please come over here. I have something I want to ask you."

I ambled over.

She lifted her bony fingers and handed me a brush with pale pink roses painted on the porcelain handle. It looked like it had lived an entire life on a dresser somewhere before ending up here. "Will you brush my hair?"

"Uh," I looked around the room, "Sure."

Mom had taught us to do what was asked of us, whether we wanted to or not.

The old woman straightened herself in her chair. I stepped behind her and ran the brush through her hair. The strands were greasy, like they hadn't been washed in weeks, maybe months, and they smelled musty, like old closets and forgotten coats. I reminded myself of what Mom taught me: care for the poor and needy gleefully, be selfless. After a few strokes, it wasn't so bad. She talked as I brushed—the way her life had been when she was a young girl, her husband who had passed. I gathered she never had children, though she never said it outright.

"I used to have long, pretty hair like yours. My husband loved my hair. Now it's all white. It used to be red."

"It's still pretty," I said.

After ten minutes, I handed her the brush. I figured that was enough.

She looked up at me with crystal blue, liquid eyes. "Will you brush my hair again sometime?"

I agreed. She didn't ask my name. I didn't ask hers. Later, I learned her name was Pearl. Back then, I didn't appreciate the beauty of her name. But now, when I hear the name Pearl, I marvel at the time it takes for a tiny grain of sand to work its way into the mollusk, eventually becoming a lustrous, breathtaking little sphere.

I brushed Pearl's hair every afternoon. At first, it felt like a chore—another thing on the endless list of duties. But as the days passed, I started to look forward to it, the way you look forward to a quiet corner in a noisy house.

As the days dragged on, I wondered how long we'd be living at the Holy Family House. Jim and Mom left most mornings to look for housing and jobs. Maryanne, David, and Diane went along, chasing work too. Deb and I stayed behind with Jill and Lissa.

While the babies napped, Deb and I read magazines or watched TV. Deb was better at the waiting game. She could crawl into a book or a show and disappear for hours. Before Mom started The Kingdom, Deb had read night and day and loved singing. Then Mom decided that reading and singing made Deb "go into her own world," and that world was off-limits. Deb was only allowed to sing religious songs when we all sang together, and she could only read the Bible. (Later, though, when Deb was fifteen, Mom loosened her grip. She even allowed her to take singing lessons.)

I'd lost all sense of time. Without school, days blurred together. I didn't know what Mom told people about why Deb and I weren't enrolled—maybe she said we'd be registered once we found a house, or that we were home-schooled. Every day repeated like a scratched record. Get up and help with Lissa and Jill. Eat breakfast, wash dishes. Find something to clean and help with Jill and Lissa. Eat lunch, wash dishes. Clean more, help more. Watch TV while the babies nap. Eat supper, wash dishes again. Watch more TV. Go to bed. Repeat. Lissa and Jill were in Deb's and my care—except discipline. Mom kept that for herself.

One afternoon, I was downstairs brushing Pearl's hair when I heard Mom yelling upstairs. I couldn't make out the words, just the sharp edges of her voice. I dropped the brush and ran to the bottom of the stairs.

"When—I—tell—you—to—go—in—the—potty—I—mean—it!"

Oh no! Mom's giving Jill a lickin'?

I darted up the stairs. In the bedroom, Mom sat on the edge of the bed with Jill sprawled across her lap, belly down, pants pulled down. Mom's hand came down repeatedly on Jill's tiny bottom.

"You—are—not—supposed—to—poop—in—your—pants… You—are— supposed—to—go—in—the—potty."

What if they call the cops? They're not gonna understand. They're gonna think Mom's abusing her.

I knew this "casting out demons" by spanking was ridiculous. I knew she had no right. But I shoved that knowing down, the way I always did. I told myself Mom was doing the Lord's will.

"Sandra!" Kay called from the bottom of the stairs. "What are you doing? You can't do that."

Mom stopped. "Oh yes, I can. There's no law against spanking a child."

"But Sandra. We have to think of everyone who lives here. That sort of thing can bother some people. If you don't stop, I'll have to call the police."

Mom lifted Jill into her arms and patted her back. "Go ahead. Call the police. I'm not doing nothing wrong."

Kay backed away, shrinking like a shadow at dusk.

"People need to mind their own business," Mom said.

But Mom wasn't much for minding her own business. One afternoon, she snooped in the deep freezer and discovered a frozen turkey. From that moment on, getting that turkey cooked became her mission.

***

We were all sitting at the kitchen table eating lentil soup and warm bread for lunch. Mom set her spoon down.

"So, I seen there's a turkey in the deep freeze."

"We're saving that for Thanksgiving," Kay said, lips stiff, eyes avoiding Mom's.

"There's people here now who need to eat that turkey. Thanksgiving's months away. We don't even know if the world will be here come Thanksgiving."

"I understand how you feel, but that turkey was donated to us. We're saving it for Thanksgiving. I'm sorry. That's just how it is." Kay stood and began clearing dishes from the table.

Hunched over his soup, a thirty-something blond volunteer said, "Yeah, we get one every year."

Mom narrowed her eyes. "I thought this was a vegetarian house?"

Kay walked into the kitchen, turned on the faucet, and squirted detergent into the sink. "Well, we splurge on Thanksgiving."

The guy nodded.

Mom leaned back and pushed her bowl forward. "Come on, let's go upstairs."

Kay kept her back to us, washing dishes as we passed. We usually stayed to clean up, but not that night.

Mom ranted about that turkey for days, as if the bird itself symbolized everything wrong with Holy Family House.

When Jim's unemployment checks finally came through, we moved out. Our stay lasted a month. On our final day, I said goodbye to Pearl. Her eyes filled, and I had the urge to promise I'd come back and visit, but we both knew that would never happen. I hugged her, and her hair brushed my hands. The oily feel and musty smell were suddenly comforting. It was what we shared.

***

We turned down the street to our new rental. My heart stayed flat in my chest. I knew the house, the city, the whole setup was just another chapter in Mom's End Times book—one that would close in a year or two, when all but 144,000 people would be cast into the Lake of Fire. I desperately wanted to be one of the 144,000. I also knew that to make the cut, I had to be perfect. Staying pure and free of sin was my get-out-of-hell card.

"Well, this is it," Mom said as we parked behind the house.

It was a tired Victorian with a stained-glass attic window. The front porch tilted forward, slanting just enough to look like it wanted to slide off the house. The wood swing creaked on its chain. The grass stood over a foot tall. Thick, jungly foliage clung to the property like it was trying to reclaim it. Mom loved a fixer upper. Most houses we lived in started out odious. After Mom worked her magic, they were scrubbed, disciplined, and respectable—just like she wanted us to be.

The neighborhood seemed decent enough. Mom did point out that we were only a few blocks from a street filled with pushers, pimps, and prostitutes. Instead of worrying, she brightened. She loved the idea of living near "the humble."

Walking through the ornate door with its glass-faceted knob, I felt a small, unexpected awe. Soaring ceilings, blood-red carpet, a curved white staircase—like we'd walked onto the set of a movie where rich people lived. The massive living room held an elegant gas-powered fireplace that Mom said would be perfect for raising bread dough. (While she would never admit it, she was inspired by the homemade bread back at the Holy Family House).

Snowball raced laps in the backyard. He'd been chained behind Holy Family House for a month and before that, cooped up in the van. I loved that dog. He was the only dog I'd ever felt truly safe around since a dog had nearly torn off my earlobe when I was four.

Our days were filled with work: cleaning, yard work, baking bread, tending to

106

Jill and Lissa, working odd jobs Mom scrounged up. For a steady paycheck, Jim took a job at Stereo Town doing technology installations. Maryanne and Diane landed waitress jobs. Before they started their jobs, Mom trained them on how to earn fat tips. Like refilling water glasses, keeping ashtrays emptied, and lighting cigarettes for the smokers. She taught them how to balance multiple plates on each arm. She was proud of her knowledge and called herself "a professional waitress." I sat on the sidelines but stored everything she taught them, assuming I'd be waitressing one day.

After Diane and Maryanne started working, I became Lissa's full-time caregiver. Even when Maryanne was home, I kept the job. It wasn't that she was shirking her responsibility—Mom decided who did what. Eventually, Lissa started calling me Mama. I never called myself that. It felt strange at first, like I was wearing someone else's coat. But I grew to love it. Lissa was the best part of my life.

I bathed her and sang, Scrub-a-dub-dub three men in a tub. I played This Little Piggie Went to Market with her toes. I fed her and rocked her to sleep, pressing my cheek to hers, breathing in that intoxicating baby scent that made everything else—the demons, the rules, The Lake of Fire—fade for a moment.

Mom helped with the babies too, mostly Jill. She remained determined to cast out the Demon of Stubbornness, so the spankings continued. Jill's bottom was always black and blue. Mom eventually started spanking Lissa too, though not as often. As Lissa got older, Mom instructed me to smack her on the inside of her thighs to keep her still during diaper changes. I tapped her lightly—just enough to get her attention. When Mom wasn't looking, I didn't do it at all. Mom also told me to pop them on the mouth if they stuck out their tongues. "Don't want the Demon of Lust to get in," she'd say.

It broke my heart. I loved Jill and Lissa so much. I knew deep down it was wrong. But I fought that knowing with everything I had. Going against Mom meant going to The Lake of Fire.

We were often reminded of that threat through her accusations and interrogations.

***

One afternoon, Mom called us to the circle. Her command dropped into the house like a stone in water. We all stopped what we were doing and filed into the living room. My chest tightened, throat constricted. I grabbed a paper towel in the kitchen to dab my damp face and sat on the couch next to Maryanne, who was biting her lip and shaking her foot. Jim and David came in from the yard; faces streaked with grime.

Jim removed his cap. "What's up, San?"

Sitting on the couch with her hands laced across her plump belly, Mom said, "Well, Debbie found this washrag that somebody blew their nose in." Thin-lipped, brow wrinkled, she held up the washrag between her thumb and index finger like it was evidence in a trial. "Who did it?" We all looked at each other.

She waved her hand. "Better sit down. We might be here a while."

Jim and David sat on the floor, cross-legged.

"I'm gonna ask again. Who blew their nose in this?"

Dead silence.

"We'll be here all day if we have to. One of youse did it. C'mon, if you did it, just say so."

Did I do it? I knew I didn't, but I second-guessed myself anyway. Doubt lived in me like a parasite by then.

Mom set the rag on the coffee table and folded her arms. "Who used the bathroom last?"

I don't remember who answered. I just remember her gaze landing on Maryanne.

"Wipe that smile off your face," she said to her.

Maryanne always smiled when she was under pressure. Sometimes she muttered under her breath. Both drove Mom crazy.

I fought the usual doubtful thoughts and tried to resist feeling compassion for Maryanne. Compassion was disloyalty.

After hours of interrogation, Maryanne, wearing that nervous smile, finally said, "if you say I did, I must have."

Because her confession wasn't tearful, Mom decided she wasn't humble before the Lord. She rejected the repentance and told her to come back and repent again when she could be humble.

I didn't think Maryanne had done it. I figured she took one for the team.

∗∗∗

Most nights, Mom was worked up, convinced someone was backslidden. When

108

no one confessed, she grew more frustrated, like a preacher whose congregation refused to sing.

One night, she announced, "Since none of youse can seem to keep from sinning, I guess youse need some stripes."

We lined up after supper, one by one, bent over for five or six swats across our backsides. "A few stripes are nothing compared to what Jesus went through," she said. After a few nights, our rears and thighs were black and blue, raised lumps like small, dark islands under our skin. Eventually, my bum went numb.

I could handle my own whippings—they weren't the worst we'd ever had. It was the watching that nearly broke me. My legs would wobble, not from fear of my own licks, but from having to witness everyone else's. I wanted to run, but my feet felt super-glued to the carpet. Doubt crashed into me. Mom's gone off her rocker. She's beating us when we didn't do nothing wrong. This can't be right. I fought hard. I repeated praises to Jesus until they wrapped around my thoughts like barbed wire. I told myself Mom was the chosen one. Who was I to question God's methods?

Mom wasn't getting the results she wanted, so the whippings stopped after a couple of weeks. But not before Jim got it over his bare back.

Maryanne had been crazy about Jim for a long time and had told Mom back when we were still on the road. Mom had decided Jim and Maryanne were to be married. When she said married, she didn't mean licenses, vows, and cake. "You don't need no piece of paper to be married," she'd say.

Jim wasn't attracted to Maryanne. That didn't matter. Mom whipped him to humble him, so he'd comply with the Lord's will—though she never spelled it out that way. I just knew. He knelt on the floor, head lowered. Mom brought the belt down across his bare back five or six times. One of the licks cut his abdomen and left a scar that would outlive that house.

Eventually, Mom allowed Jim to stop sleeping with Maryanne until he could give in to the Lord's will and marry her "gleefully." Maryanne was still married to Sam, but Mom didn't recognize that marriage as legitimate. She planned to marry Jim and Maryanne by proclamation alone.

In the meantime, to break Jim down, she had him fast and isolate himself in his room, praying for days at a time. Maryanne knew Jim didn't want her, but Mom assured her it was the Lord's will for them to be together.

Jim's relationship with Mom was different from the rest of ours. He was her brother, her "right-hand man." As an elder and her blood, he had more leeway.

He could give his opinion, challenge her, even argue. Mom didn't drag his sins to the circle; she handled him privately—except for that beating.

She'd run out of ideas. Fasting hadn't worked. Isolation hadn't worked. Whipping hadn't worked. So, she decided to send him back to Pennsylvania. It wasn't a punishment, she said. It was a test—to see if he had truly forsaken all for the Lord. She believed he had unresolved issues with Mammy and Pappy that prevented him from fully committing himself to the Lord. She wanted him to realize his old life wasn't fulfilling. She expected him to swallow his pride and marry Maryanne willingly when he returned. I didn't understand how moving back in with Mammy and Pappy translated into accepting a marriage he didn't want.

Mom bought a used 250-horsepower motorcycle for the trip. Jim doubted such a small bike could make it, but Mom told him to put his trust in the Lord.

It was gray that day, the air was sharp against my cheeks. I stood with my hands shoved in my pockets, shifting my weight from foot to foot. Jim fastened a plastic crate to the back of the bike and filled it. He stuffed the rest of his things into his backpack.

Tears welled in his eyes. "Well, San," he said, standing by the bike in coveralls and work boots, "I'm ready."

Mom's glassy eyes locked onto his. "Jim, you know you gotta do this, right?"

"Yeah, I know, San," he said, pulling a hankie from his back pocket and blowing his nose.

The rest of us lined up to hug him goodbye. Maybe this is it. Maybe he won't come back. My heart was heavy as lead.

Jim was the only man in my life who hadn't left. He was the one who showed he cared. He taught me self-defense moves, took me rabbit hunting, danced with me to disco music. Once he joined us, there was always food in the house. A vehicle in the driveway. A solid roof overhead. That was about to rumble away on two skinny tires.

Jim swung his leg over the bike, kick-started it, and looked back at us.

Mom pulled her jacket tighter, folded her arms, tears sliding down her cheeks. "Just go. Just go."

We watched until he turned the corner. My heart dropped like a rock.

An hour later, Jim called from a phone booth to say the little Honda had died. Mom told him to abandon the bike and hitchhike. She said it was the Lord testing him.

He called a couple of days after that to let us know he'd made it. A trucker had picked him up and driven him all the way.

He called most nights. Afterward, at supper, Mom would give us little updates. At first, Mammy and Pappy were thrilled he was home. Mammy cooked his favorite meals, did his laundry, and spoke to him in a syrupy voice. Mom said it was Satan, using Mammy's kindness as bait.

Pappy tried to drag Jim into religious debates. Jim avoided it, keeping mostly to himself—reading the Bible, doing odd jobs around the house, practicing karate workouts in the backyard. After a few days, Mammy and Pappy started pressing him for answers. Why did he come back? Was he staying? Did he still believe his sister's crazy ideas?

He said he believed what Mom taught him. That infuriated them. Heated arguments followed. Finally, after a couple of weeks, Mom announced Jim had been "purified by fire" and could come home.

We celebrated his return with spaghetti and meatballs and garlic bread, his favorite. We listened to his stories about standing up to Mammy and Pappy. I didn't care much about the details. I was just glad he had kept his promise and came back.

***

While Tim had been gone, Mom's frustration with Maryanne had grown. She argued with her more, questioned her motives, and still hadn't cried the tears Mom wanted. Mom said the Demon of Stubbornness wouldn't let Maryanne cry.

One night, we gathered in the living room after supper. The fireplace warmed the room, and the smell of roast beef hung in the air. The babies were down for the night. Mom was angry that Maryanne hadn't cried when she repented. Maryanne sat with her leg crossed, wearing her usual nervous grin. The rest of us sat quietly, watching. I had a bad feeling.

Hours of interrogation had already passed. Mom had commanded her to cry and reminded her of her impending damnation to the Lake of Fire, but Maryanne still couldn't.

Mom straightened her back. "Go pick some grass from the yard and bring it back here," she said, then took a sip of tea.

I gnawed the inside of my cheek and held my breath.

Maryanne cleared her throat. "Why?"

Mom's face hardened into stone. "Just do it."

I glanced around the room. Everyone looked just as confused. Maryanne walked slowly toward the door, looking back several times, as if hoping Mom would call her off. She didn't. We waited in a silence that felt thick, like the air had been replaced with syrup.

When Maryanne returned with a handful of grass, Mom told her to put it on the floor. My insides boiled. I knew some bad shit was coming.

Maryanne dropped the grass in a little pile on the carpet and stood in front of Mom, waiting.

"Now, get on all fours and eat it. And don't use your hands."

I wanted to scream, STOP THIS MADNESS, but nothing came out. Fear pressed on me like a boot on my neck.

Maryanne looked at Mom, pleading with her eyes. Anger roared through me, the same way it had when Mom had spanked Jill over and over. Doubt flooded in. This is abuse. This is wrong. I tried to push the thoughts out, but they kept coming. It doesn't seem Godly. This can't be what Jesus would do. It's sadistic.

No! It ain't sadistic. She's trying to save Maryanne. Maryanne needs to cry, and Mom's helping her.

But how can this be right? Mom's treating her like an animal.

No! No! I can't think that. She's trying to help her. What about all the drastic stuff Jesus did? Like when he turned over the tables in the temple.

Get thee behind me, Satan. You're not gonna make me doubt.

Praise Jesus. Praise Jesus. Praise Jesus. Praise Jesus. Praise Jesus. Praise Jesus...

Maryanne got down on all fours, lowered her mouth to the grass, and ate.

Praise Jesus. Praise Jesus. Praise Jesus. Praise Jesus. Praise Jesus. Praise Jesus...

She chewed, staring at the floor, her eyes empty. When she finished, she started to stand, but Mom grabbed her arm and pointed.

"There's more."

Maryanne's eyes filled. "But there's hair in it."

Mom folded her arms. "Eat it all. Even the hair."

I stared at the carpet. Praise Jesus. Praise Jesus. Praise Jesus. Praise Jesus. Praise Jesus. Praise Jesus...

Maryanne crouched again, tears dripping onto the blood-red carpet. She ate the rest of the pile—including the hair. She coughed but kept going.

Everything slowed to a crawl. I felt wrung out from the war in my head and, at the same time, charged with emotion that had nowhere to go. Doubts punched through my wall of praises. This is wrong. This is crazy. How could Mom be so heartless?

I wanted to shove Mom aside, pull Maryanne up, and run. But where? I wanted to yell, Maryanne, you have a choice! You don't have to do this! But I wasn't brave like I'd been that day in Sacramento when I'd torn that woman off Mom's neck. My fear of The Lake of Fire sat on my chest like a cinder block. It stood between Maryanne and me. That, and the fear of having to eat grass off the floor myself.

Maryanne finished and sat back on her heels. Her shoulders shook as she wept. Mom pulled her up by the arms and hugged her. She cupped Maryanne's cheeks and looked into her eyes.

"You're humble now. The Lord forgives you."

We took turns hugging her and singing praises to Jesus.

I wish I could say we talked about that night afterward. I wish I could say we told each other how awful it was, that I pulled Maryanne aside and told her Mom was wrong. I wish I could say that was the last of the craziness.

David changed after that. He started questioning Mom, arguing with her. Finally, she kicked him out. David asked Diane to go with him, but she declined. Fearing that comforting her would be "giving into Satan," I stayed rigid when she cried. It took everything I had not to hold her and not to say, "I get it." Soon, it was as if David had never existed.

***

Mom decided Maryanne would grow more if she lived on her own. She didn't call it punishment—she called it a trial. Maryanne was to leave Lissa behind and have visitation on her days off. From the beginning, Mom had made Maryanne promise that if she ever left The Kingdom, she'd leave Lissa with us.

I knew it was wrong to keep Lissa from her mother. I pushed the feeling down and kicked out doubtful thoughts. I told myself Lissa would be spared The Lake of Fire if she stayed, that Mom was obeying the Lord's will. I worried that Child Welfare might show up over the bruises on Lissa's thighs and bottom. I'd overheard one of Maryanne's friends ask where they came from. Maryanne said her grandma (Mom) spanked her sometimes. That must've been enough because Child Welfare never came.

Maryanne seemed to like being on her own. She didn't object or even act bothered by Mom's insistence that we keep Lissa. It made sense—she was only nineteen. She made friends at work and started dating a guy. Mom didn't like him. "He looks shady," she told her. Mom always found something wrong with Maryanne: moving too slowly, a wrinkled uniform, not enough lipstick.

Like the rest of us, Maryanne desperately wanted to please Mom. Around her, she chewed the inside of her lip and chose every word like it might explode. When Mom wasn't there, she loosened up, got goofy. We'd dance and blow bubbles and talk about cute guys. She'd tell me work stories—rude customers, flirty guys who left big tips, the messes the night shift left behind. With her, I felt like a regular girl.

She'd been living on her own for a few weeks when she came over one day to get Lissa for a visit.

"Peg, get the door," Mom hollered from upstairs.

"Who is it?" I called.

"It's Maryanne."

I opened the door with Lissa on my hip. The corners of my mouth slid down when I saw Maryanne standing there, somber, next to a man. I'd never met Sam, but I knew it was him. Maybe he'd been looking for her. Maybe she'd called him. My memories of him are blurry now; all I see in my mind is a dark shape standing beside her—a man about to take something from me that was never really mine to keep.

Mom propped her broom and hurried down the stairs. "What's going on here?"

"I'm here for Melissa," Sam said.

"Let's talk," Mom said, pointing to the dining table in the next room.

"Nothing to talk about. Maryanne and Melissa are coming with me."

"Come in and sit and let's talk."

He sighed, tilted his head, then walked in and sat. Maryanne followed, long faced. I sat directly across from Sam, still holding Lissa, swallowing around the lump in my throat.

Mom cleaned her glasses with the edge of her apron. "I understand Maryanne going with you—that's her choice. But she made a promise to God that she'd never take Lissa from this family."

"Well, she's, my daughter. She's coming with me."

Mom's eyes filled. "If you take her, she'll die."

"Whatchu mean die?"

"She's one of the Lord's. Saved from damnation. Maryanne can go, but Lissa's gotta stay here."

"Well, that ain't go'n happen, crazy lady."

Mom looked at Maryanne, pleading. "Maryanne, you can't let him take her."

Maryanne hung her head. "Sorry, San."

Mom swallowed hard and pressed her lips together. "Peg, give him Lissa."

I walked around the table. I kissed Lissa's chubby cheek. "Bye, Lissa. I love you." I handed her to Maryanne. She mouthed, "I'm sorry," then, with Lissa on her hip, wrapped her free arm around my neck and held me for a couple of seconds. Grief shot through me like electricity.

"Well, you're not taking her stuff," Mom said.

Sam rolled his eyes. "Fine."

In that moment, I knew I'd never see Lissa or Maryanne again. It felt like someone had cut off a leg and expected me to keep walking.

***

From the outside, our life in Kansas City probably looked normal. We worked during the day, cooked and ate together at night, and when no one had backslidden, we watched TV. We were down to just the family: me, Deb, Jim, and Mom. Diane lived on her own with Jill. Like Maryanne, Mom had pushed her out so she could "learn to live independently" as a single mom.

Our evenings settled into a routine. After a late supper and dishes, we'd watch *Wild Wild West*, followed by *77 Sunset Strip*. They weren't shows I would've chosen, but I grew to love them. I was only thirteen, but Robert Conrad looked fine in his waist jacket and spandex pants.

Most nights in front of the TV were uneventful. We'd crank up the fireplace and glue ourselves to the set, gobbling ice cream sundaes. But when Mom sank into one of her moods, the living room turned into a minefield. If she went quiet, something was wrong. I'd sit straight-backed, jaw clenched, terrified of thinking or doing anything she might call a sin.

Mom said demons used TV as a vehicle. The Demon of Mockery could sneak in through comedies and slapstick scenes. The Demon of Lust hunted during nudity and sex.

She'd park herself at one end of the couch where she could watch all of us at once. During funny scenes, her eyes would move from face to face, her lips pinched in a grimace, an invisible word bubble floating above her: "I got my eye on you." Not so much as a giggle slipped from any of us. The tension itself was what made it so hard not to laugh, it was like being stuck in a staring contest. Seeing Mom fighting a smile made my own laughter want to rise, but I crushed it.

Sex scenes were tricky. Looking away could be seen as shame, but watching too closely was dangerous. I'd keep my eyes on the screen but focus on the furniture or the pictures in the background. And I made sure my tongue stayed in my mouth—licking lips could mean the Demon of Lust had slipped in.

One time back in New Columbia, Ron—the man who'd smeared poop all over himself—laughed when someone slipped on a banana peel. Mom kept us up for hours interrogating him. Ron argued it was a knee-jerk reaction. Mom insisted it was a choice, an act of free will. By the end of the night, Ron surrendered, and Mom cast the Demon of Mockery from him.

Still, our house wasn't humorless. Jim could make Mom laugh. When she laughed, she didn't hold back. Mouth wide open, head thrown back, she cackled from deep in her belly. She liked old comedies like The Lucy Show and Dick Van Dyke. She despised newer ones like *Laugh In* and *Love American Style*. Mom said those shows were lustful and not even funny. I disagreed. Deb and I used to crack up at them.

Over time, I learned how to keep the demons away, or at least how to avoid being accused of inviting them in. I listened. I followed the rules. If I was accused of something, I admitted it, even if I hadn't done it. Whenever I had doubtful thoughts, I told myself the Lord was testing me.

I convinced myself that Mom making Maryanne eat grass was God using her as a vessel to test the rest of us. I told myself to trust Mom, the chosen one.

My mind no longer wandered to friends, crushes, or skating on Friday nights. I hadn't done a cartwheel or danced (unless it was for the Lord) since leaving Tarville, P.A., when I was twelve. I hadn't hung out with anyone my age since the last day of eighth grade. I hadn't thought about my future—getting married, going to college, having kids—since that old version of myself had been evicted and a new tenant moved in.

The old Peggy was animated, talkative, sometimes rebellious. The new Peggy was careful, obedient, a people pleaser, trained to keep her eyes on The Lake of Fire and her mouth in line.

Jim's boss mentioned a transfer opportunity to St. Petersburg, Florida. Mom took it as a sign that we were meant to move. We had a yard sale and sold everything that wasn't "necessary." Mom redrew the line of what counted as necessary. The Lord told her it was time to get rid of anything worldly we felt attached to. She quoted John 12:25, "He who loves his life shall lose it, and he who hates his life in the world shall keep it for eternal life." I sold everything I liked—including my favorite jeans. I hesitated over the jeans for a second, but it didn't seem worth The Lake of Fire.

Converts had come and gone during our year in Kansas City. A few days, maybe a week, that's usually all it took for Mom to kick someone out. One convert stands out in my memory. He'd been coming every night for a few days, feasting on Mom's "revelations." Then, like most, he started arguing. A few hours after she kicked him out, the police showed up at the door with him in tow. They said they'd found him crawling backward down the street. He was a psych patient who had just been released. He told the police he was crawling backward to rewind time so he could return to The Kingdom. I don't remember what Mom did with him. That part is a blur.

By the time we were ready to leave Kansas City, every convert was gone, even Diane. She'd built a small life for herself and Jill—renting a little house with a flower garden, finding steady work, getting a new boyfriend. Mom said Diane was choosing death over eternal life and condemning her own daughter. The day we said goodbye, Diane was covered in poison ivy from working in her garden. God was punishing her, Mom said. Despite her condemnation, Mom gave her kitchenware, lawn tools, and our perishable food. She held Diane and Jill in a teary hug. Like everyone else who dared to step outside The Kingdom, Diane and Jill became a closed chapter. I knew I'd never see them again.

CHAPTER NINE

St. Petersburg, 1976

We rolled into St. Petersburg and, instead of palm trees and miracles, got hit with bad news: the Stereo Town job had fallen through. The promise that had dragged us across the country fizzled out in one sentence. Mom said not to worry—it was the Lord's will for us to be there anyway. God's plan, she said, just didn't always look the way we expected. To me, it mostly looked like we were broke again.

We rented a little bungalow on a dirt road, across from an old folks' trailer court. Our tiny slice of paradise sat on a big lot, a mix of scraggly and lush— mature pine trees holding court, with a few palm trees and tropical plants scattered around like they'd washed up there by accident. Mom walked the grounds like a doctor making rounds, surveying what looked healthy and what needed resuscitation. She had an affinity for green things I never fully understood. She'd prune a plant down to a stump, and just when it looked like it would never recover, it would sprout again, slow, and stubborn, then burst into life, as if it had finally learned how to please her.

I felt oddly optimistic about our new home. It was tiny—with two bedrooms and one micro-bathroom—but I was used to shoehorned spaces and back-breaking work. That part felt familiar.

We spent our days working the odd jobs Mom dug up, and Jim landed a bricklaying job for a steady paycheck. On his first day, he came home with his shoulders slumped, saying he'd be making less than he'd earned as a brick tender back in Pennsylvania. Mom blamed it on an employers' market—too many workers, not enough jobs, wages shaved thin. Even so, with our combined efforts, we got by. We hadn't won the lottery like Mom said we would, but we weren't starving either.

Mom knew how to stretch a shoestring until it looked like a rope. She also couldn't ignore anyone in need. If a poor person crossed her path, she'd do something, even if all she had to give was a few coins and a prayer.

One day, while we were out running errands, she picked up a homeless man.

Deb slid open the van door. The hunched man climbed in and plopped onto the beanbag chair. His frizzy silver hair was matted and crawling with bugs. Wiry whiskers covered his craggy face. Thick, unruly eyebrows shadowed his eyes. He wore a stained gray T-shirt and baggy wool pants with shredded hems. His big toes poked out of his shoes like they'd given up on being covered. He clutched a black trash bag that looked like it held everything he owned. My eyes burned from his stench of stale alcohol and body odor.

Mom turned around and smiled. "I'm Sandy and these are my girls Debbie and Peggy."

Slurring his words, he said it was nice to meet us. His name was Harry. I stared at his hair, worried his lice could jump on me. Bile rose in my throat. Deb, in the passenger seat, plugged her nose. It took everything I had not to scoot away and make a face, but I stayed put. For all I knew, he was Jesus in disguise, checking if we'd pass the test. I'd seen plenty of homeless men sleeping on park benches back in California, but I'd never sat this close to one. It dawned on me that he probably hadn't bathed in months, maybe years. I tried to imagine going that long without a shower and couldn't.

Mom tapped her rings against the steering wheel in time with the radio. "Whatcha hungry for?"

Harry scratched his head. "You're gonna to feed me?"

Mom said he could get whatever he wanted.

"Alright then. I'd like 'Tucky Fried Chicken." He licked his dry, cracked lips and made smacking sounds. "Can I get a ten-piece bucket?"

Mom cackled. "Sure." She pulled into the nearest Kentucky Fried Chicken.

Back in the van with the bucket, Harry tore into the chicken with long-nailed, grubby fingers, stripping every edible bit from the bones. Deb and I watched in stunned amazement, like we'd stumbled onto a nature documentary.

"You're really enjoying that chicken, aren't ya?" Mom said, then winked at us.

He looked at her for a second, then went back to devouring the chicken. His scraggly beard and mustache turned into a graveyard of crumbs and chicken bits. He let out a huge belly burp. Mom roared with laughter and asked if he wanted to have a shower.

He smiled, revealing gaps where teeth used to be. "You bet I would."

By the time we got home, the ten-piece bucket was empty.

"Mind if I use your restroom, ma'am?" he asked, stumbling through the door.

Our meager kitchen had a tiny bathroom right off it. Mom had had Jim replace the solid door with saloon-style doors because she said it got too steamed up when we showered. That fixed one problem and created another. You could see our lower legs and hear everything. We all knew what each other's bowel movements sounded and smelled like. When someone used the bathroom, we usually retreated to the screened-in porch. The smell, though—you had to step outside to fully escape that.

Harry wobbled through the saloon doors. Deb and I slipped out to the porch, but it was impossible to ignore the sound of his peeing. Not because it sounded different, but because of how long it lasted. He peed and peed, starting and stopping, starting again. It felt like ten or fifteen minutes.

"He should be in the Guinness Book of World Records," Deb whispered.

Jim slid some clothing under the saloon doors.

"Thanks, man," Harry said.

After his shower, he asked Mom to take him to where he wanted to go— maybe a homeless hangout, someplace his people were. He didn't want to stay for supper. Mom handed him five dollars and drove him to his destination, letting him disappear back into the world he came from.

***

A little over a year passed, and we still hadn't looked for new converts. I didn't ask why. The deadline for the end of the world was getting closer on Mom's mental calendar, but I barely thought about it. I had buried The Lake of Fire somewhere in the back of my mind and piled daily life on top of it.

I immersed myself in our new life in St. Pete, which, truth be told, wasn't so bad. We lived in a miniature paradise with the ocean all around us. Sure, we worked a lot, but there were rewards. We ate BBQ chicken and steaks off the grill nearly every night. We built ice cream sundaes in the living room and went to the movies. We saw Star Wars in the theater that year.

At home, we watched our favorite shows: Charlie's Angels, Kojak, and The Jeffersons. The best part was that Mom's obsession with saving souls had cooled to a simmer. She'd changed since Kansas City. There were no more late-night sermons that stretched past midnight, no more circles of interrogation, no more group punishments. I kept my head down, did what was expected, and allowed myself to savor the small pleasures when they came.

Deb got a job in the deli at Albertsons, coming home smelling like roasted chicken and sliced meats. I worked with Jim doing yard work for neighbors—hauling, trimming, raking other people's lives into neat piles. Life was simple. For the time being, I was content, tucked into that tiny bungalow at the edge of the world, worried that the worst was still coming and hoping, maybe, it wasn't.

CHAPTER TEN
Battle Creek, 1976

Mom said the Lord told her to find a mate. Suddenly her mind landed on Martin—her high-school boyfriend, the boy who "took her virginity," the one Mammy and Pappy had wished she'd married. He was intelligent. She knew he'd be successful, but back then she didn't think she could love him. She broke it off after a few months. Shortly after that, she started dating George, my father, and got pregnant. She talked about Martin like he'd been tucked away in a drawer labeled *the one who got away*. The acne, the coke-bottle glasses—none of that mattered then. God had spoken, which meant the rest of us had to fall in line.

Martin lived in Battle Creek, Michigan, in a big farmhouse with four teenage boys he was raising alone. He'd divorced, built a tractor sales business, and seemed—at least from Mom's tone—like a promise wrapped in a second chance. After a few phone calls, he invited her up "to try it out."

At supper, she broke the news like she was announcing a weather report. "I need to find out if he's the mate I'm supposed to be with. Peg, you'll go with me. I don't want Deb to lose her job at Albertson's."

Jim leaned back, chewing slowly. "Are you sure, San? It seems kinda quick."

"Jim…would I go if I didn't think it was the Lord's will?"

He swallowed hard. "Alright, San…if you think it's the right thing."

Deb's fork clinked on her plate. Tears rimmed her eyes. "For how long,

Mom?"

"I don't know Debbie. Not too long. If it works out, then youse'll move up there with us."

Deb tucked her hair behind her ear like she was bracing herself. "Okay, I guess if it's not too long."

I could hardly keep from bouncing in my seat with utter joy. "What should I bring?"

Mom sipped her Folgers. "We might end up staying there for good, so bring plenty of clothes."

Inside, I was doing the happy dance; outside, I was chill. Martin had four teenage sons. I hadn't been around kids my own age since eighth grade. And until Mom announced I'd be going with her, I hadn't realized how socially deprived I was.

***

When Mom and I stepped out of baggage claim, there he was, Martin, his white convertible idling, the top up. He hustled out to grab our bags. The acne was gone, but the pockmarks tugged at his skin like permanent shadows. His glasses magnified his eyes. His pigeon-toed stance made him look unsure in his own body.

He hugged Mom stiffly, then turned to me.

"And who do we have here?"

"This is Peggy, my youngest daughter."

"Hello, Peggy. Welcome to Michigan."

"Hi," I said, polite, reading him like an unopened book.

Driving through Battle Creek felt like stepping into a winter fairy tale—sun glinting off mountains of snow piled twenty feet high. Yet, despite the snow and frigid temperature, the city was bustling. Like a storybook illustration, people with their parkas and thick boots lined the streets. Kids hurled snowballs at each other.

My mind spun with questions: Would I go back to school? Would Martin's boys like me? Would Mom start preaching again? When would Deb and Jim follow?

Martin described his five-bedroom house. "Kind of like the Brady Bunch house," he said. "But since my wife left, the house has gone to hell. It just needs a woman's touch."

Mom perked up. "Well…don't worry. We'll fix the house right up. Won't we, Peg?"

"Yup," I said, watching the snowy countryside blur by. Hard work never scared me.

On the way to his country house, the fields were blanketed in snow, the sky a gunmetal gray. We passed through endless stretches of wooden fences, hilly roads, and scattered houses. Finally, Martin slowed down and turned into a drive.

Farm equipment littered the yard, buried in snow, steering wheels poking out. And there was more equipment behind the house, several rows deep. We pulled in and parked near the house. Martin wasn't wrong. It *did* look like the Brady Bunch house. But inside it was a different show. More like the Bedraggled Bunch house. Dirty dishes, stacks of papers, open cereal boxes, empty milk jugs, dirty laundry—just what you'd imagine a house with five males would be like. And it stunk like stale socks and rotten food. But none of it dimmed the spark in me. I was thirteen going on fourteen—boys my age was oxygen.

Mom peeled off her coat and dove into cleaning. "Martin, don't you have those boys do no chores?"

He shifted. "Well, since their mother left…it's been hard. I work so much."

She crossed her arms. "You gotta be able to take care of yourself. And them boys gotta learn how to take care of theirselves too. Otherwise, they're gonna end up like you. Relying on women."

He nodded, shrinking.

"C'mon, Peg, let's clean up this kitchen and make these boys some supper. I can't cook in a dirty kitchen."

Truth be told, I couldn't either. When I was younger, I couldn't play in a messy room. I'd have to clean it first. My friends thought I was a kook.

We cleaned for hours, scraping what food could be salvaged, tossing the rest, and simmering a pot of chicken corn soup.

The boys barreled in at different times, coats hitting the floor, heads shoved into the fridge.

The youngest, Marty, introduced himself. My stomach flipped. Wavy brown hair. Preppy clothes. Fourteen and adorable. I wasn't usually attracted to the preppy-types, but there was something about him.

"Your dad told youse we're staying for a while, right?" Mom asked.

"Uh, yeah. I guess." He stared into the fridge. "Where's all the food?"

Mom wiped her hands with a dish towel. "Most of that food was bad. We threw it out."

"Okay, well…something smells good."

"Chicken corn soup," Mom said. "It's an old family recipe."

I adjusted my bandana and fluttered my lashes. He didn't notice. Didn't matter. I was already imagining our wedding photos.

"So, can I have some of that soup?" he asked.

"We're gonna all sit at the table together tonight."

"I have plans with my friends, so I won't be here," Marty said.

I frowned.

Mom put her hands on her hips. "Okay well, just tonight. 'Cause we're gonna eat together from now on. Plan on being home at six every night."

Marty smiled awkwardly. "O…kay."

The next night, Mom laid out the house rules like a general delivering orders. She put her fork down. "Me and Peggy have spent the last two days deep cleaning this kitchen and I expect all of youse to keep up."

The boys hunched over their plates.

"Is that clear?"

"Yes," they mumbled.

But my mind drifted to bigger questions—like whether it was okay to date a potential stepbrother.

***

We cleaned the entire house the next day. There wasn't an inch that wasn't filthy. On my hands and knees, scrubbing floors and scraping dried feces from toilets, I daydreamed about my new life in Battle Creek: high school, friends, skating, football games, dating. Mom said she'd enroll me as soon as we finished. For the first time in years, something inside me felt like it was blooming.

My life was taking root in Battle Creek in an unconventional way. Mom and I showed up, like some mail-order wife and daughter. She took charge as the lady of the house. I became one of the siblings. But I was also kind of like a maid. I cooked and cleaned alongside Mom. Though, it wasn't so bad. I was used to that. In our house, the women cooked and cleaned, and the men took care of the yard, repairs, grilling, and errands. Though Mom did expect the men to help with cleanup after meals.

The highlight of my week was Friday night skating. My crush on Marty deepened, but it became clear he only saw me as a friend. Marty and I skated with easy rhythm, but he flirted with girls, which made me doubt Mom's theory that he had "the Demon of Unseemliness," her code for gay. Either way, I didn't care. He was fun. He was my age. I felt normal around him.

But Mom began complaining about Martin—his long hours, his mess, his lack of discipline with the boys, his lack of romance. I should've known tension was brewing.

One night, after Marty and I returned from skating, I bounded inside ready to gush to Mom.

"Mom?" No answer. Then I heard her voice upstairs, sharp, rising.

"I don't know who you think you are, Martin Lesher. You don't know who *I* am, do you?"

Martin didn't answer.

My heart sank. Every step felt like I was walking back into an old, familiar ending.

At the top of the stairs, I peeked down the hall. Mom stood in the bathroom doorway, one hand on her hip, the other gripping a belt. She swung it with every point she made. Oh no! I guess we'll be leaving. I inched closer to the bathroom, stood outside, then peeked around the corner.

Martin was naked in the bathtub, hunched over, absorbing the blows.

She turned and saw me. "Peg, pack up your stuff, we're getting out of here. Now."

My chin trembled. "Why, why are we leaving?"

"No questions. Go pack." She threw the belt down. "You're giving me money for a hotel tonight and I'm taking your car," she told Martin. "You brought us up here, now you're getting us back."

He said nothing.

I collapsed on the bed and sobbed. My new life—my tiny sprout of hope—crushed in one night.

Mom stormed in, dragging a suitcase from the closet. "Come on, get packing."

"What did he do?" I sobbed. "Why were you hitting him? Can't we give it more time? I have friends. You said school—"

"Martin don't want to serve God. I'm supposed to be with a man of God."

And that was that.

Driving into Battle Creek, Mom announced our new plan. "We'll stay here one night and then head for St. Pete in the morning."

My heart clawed for air. I adjusted my glasses. "Can we just look for a place here? Maybe it's the Lord's will for us to live here?"

"We don't have much money."

"But we can get jobs. You like it here, don't you?"

"Well yes, but we can't. Jim's only wiring enough money to get us back to St. Pete."

"We can have Jim send us more, can't we? Please, Mom. Please."

Shockingly, she agreed to look. We circled affordable apartments in the newspaper and called from a diner phone booth. Every landlord said the same thing: city ordinance forbade renting a one-bedroom to an adult and a child. We couldn't afford two bedrooms.

"You're my daughter. How could they think something so unseemly?" Mom snapped. "Must be a bunch of pedophiles on the city council."

I searched feverishly for something to change her mind, but her words stifled me. I knew Mom wouldn't want to stay in a town like that. She took it as a sign that we were supposed to head back to St. Pete.

I never got to say goodbye to Marty.

CHAPTER ELEVEN

Back to St. Pete, 1976

Life in St. Pete slipped back into place—work, eat, sleep—like beads sliding onto a familiar string. Since wages were low, Jim traded bricklaying for landscaping and built a small clientele. Deb and I became his crew. He mowed; we raked. He trimmed branches; we cut them into bundles that scraped our arms. When we weren't with him, Mom sent us across the street to clean trailers at the senior park for three dollars an hour.

The worst job she ever gave us was Alice's.

Mom arranged for us to meet Alice before starting the job. She said it wasn't a big one, just a one-bedroom mobile home. But the moment we stepped inside, the air hit us, thick and sour, like spoiled food trapped in a closed jar. Alice, a blind woman with white hair curling around her face, sat crooked in her wheelchair. Thin seams of sunlight slipped through the heavy curtains, tracing gold lines across her cheeks revealing just how frail she was.

Alice pointed her bony finger. "Can you turn that TV down for me?"

Deb twisted the dial. Mom introduced us.

"Nice to meet you girls. I'm so happy you're going to help me clean. Boy, you know it needs it."

"It's no trouble, Alice. We're here to help ya," Mom said.

"I know I got a few bugs. Can you help with that?"

Once my eyes adjusted, I saw what she meant. Cockroaches everywhere moving across the walls, the ceiling, the curtains. It felt like the whole trailer had a pulse. I perched on the couch beside Mom and Deb, itching everywhere but refusing to scratch.

"Yes, once the girls get the cleaning done, my brother Jim will spray. Don't worry, Alice, we're gonna take care of you."

I tried not to focus on the cockroaches, but that was impossible. Vomit came to the back of my throat, but I sat there forcing a smile. The woman told us Meals on Wheels brought her one meal a day, and she tossed the leftovers into the sink. Her son cleared them once a week. Until then, it was a smorgasbord for the roaches.

We woke up before sunrise the next morning, tying bandanas around our heads like we were gearing up for battle. Even so, nothing prepared us. Cockroaches fell from the ceiling onto our shoulders and slid into our shoes. Deb and I didn't scream. It felt like screaming would shatter whatever thin layer of courage we had left. We didn't want Alice to feel bad. We brushed off the bugs and kept going.

The stench made our eyes water. We started with the source—rotting food. We scooped the spoiled mess into black garbage bags. When we pulled dishes from the cupboards, the white plates looked black from the layers of insects. Lifting a cup felt like disturbing a small city. Even with masks and rubber gloves, we gagged repeatedly.

Each morning, Deb and I would tell each other our bug nightmares. My skin always itched, even after I showered. The back of my throat tasted like putrid food. My tongue tasted like bug spray. The odor was almost as unbearable as the spoiled food. It was distinct, not like any bug spray I'd ever smelled. It was like a combination of sulfur and Raid. Jim told us to spray every corner, crack, and deep surface, otherwise those nasty vermin would return.

By week's end—the longest week of my life—Deb and I threw away the clothes we'd worn. We didn't trust what might still be hiding in the seams.

Months later, whenever we cleaned Alice's place, I checked the cupboards and under the sink. I never saw another roach, but the dreams stayed with me.

***

A woman Mom cleaned for asked her to introduce me to her fifteen-year-old grandson. He'd gotten into trouble, and his parents sent him to Florida to get away from the "riffraff" in Indianapolis. Mom invited them for supper.

I wasn't nervous. I figured he'd be some troublemaking asshole or a dweeb I'd be stuck entertaining. But when I opened the door, Ricky stood there—olive-skinned, dimples, black wavy hair catching the light. Cowboy boots. A faint cloud of men's cologne. It felt like fresh air had pushed into a stale room.

"Hi," I said, twirling my hair.

"Hi," he said, smiling like he meant it.

Out back, Jim brushed BBQ sauce on chicken legs over the fire pit. Mom lit tiki torches. Deb set the picnic table. Colored lights strung along the bamboo fence reflected off the pool like glitter on water.

"Wow. You guys have an above-ground pool?" Ricky asked.

"Yeah… we can take a swim after supper if you want," I said, regretting it instantly. I wasn't overweight, but I thought my thighs were too thick.

All through supper, Ricky and I exchanged clandestine glances. I was aware of my every move, judging it as either cool or inelegant. After dessert, he asked if I wanted to play shuffleboard. Thank God he didn't bring up swimming. He ran his hand through his hair. "Nobody plays this time of night. We'd have the board to ourselves."

I asked, and Mom allowed it. My stomach did a somersault.

The moon hung low, bathing the dirt roads in amber light. Ricky's boots clomped as we walked. When his hand brushed against mine, I giggled. He shot me a closed-lipped smile, punctuating his dimples. Waves of joy rippled through my body, but I played it slick.

"Ever play before?" He asked, bending over to pick up the disc.

"No, but I'm a fast learner."

Despite playing for an hour, it seemed like two minutes. I didn't want to say goodnight, but his grandmother said to be home in an hour.

"Want to play again tomorrow?" he said, flashing his toothy smile.

I laced my hands behind my back and swayed. "I'll have to ask, but probably."

He walked me home and kissed my cheek. I floated through my own body until morning, no sleep, only thinking of him.

I thought the end of the workday would never come. I could've sworn the tangy scent of his cologne lingered. Though, except for our hands grazing and the peck on my cheek, we hadn't even touched.

That next night, I wore my best cutoffs, a lime-green halter, and yellow flip flops. As I walked through the gate leading to the shuffleboard court, I caught a glimpse of him at the end of the court, leaning on a shuffleboard cue. His eyes were crinkled at the corners. He wore a slightly seductive smile. His snug clothes accentuated his muscles.

"You ready to get beat?" I teased.

"You sound pretty confident for a girl who just learned."

"Like I said, I learn quick."

Soon shuffleboard turned into long walks. Mom kept saying yes, which surprised me. Maybe she thought God arranged it, or maybe she saw a soul ripe for saving. Since The Kingdom began, Mom hadn't encouraged friendships or dating. But something had changed in her. Thank goodness I liked him. I would've hated to be in a situation like Jim had been in with Maryanne.

On our first walk as soon as we rounded the corner, Ricky took my hand. Warmth spread through me. Our shoulders brushed as we walked. Every cell felt awake.

At a small wooden bridge over a creek, he slipped his arm around my waist, pulled me toward him, and kissed me. The world stilled—no sermons, no End of Time—just breath on skin, just possibility. We stood, kissing, and kissing, and kissing. I'd never been kissed like that. He ran his fingers through my hair and held the back of my neck. Sometimes he used a little suction, which gave me a twinge between my legs. Reality was suspended.

Walking back, a block before home, he looked down and asked, "Will you be my girlfriend?"

"Yes," I said, pretending calm.

"Woohoo!" he howled.

Then reality returned. I had to ask Mom.

"Uh… you're gonna need to ask my mom first. I can't go out with no one she don't approve of."

"I ain't worried about that. She's going to love me." He cupped my face. "Let's do it now."

Mom was sitting in the screened-in porch, sipping lemonade and fanning herself with a magazine. As hot as it was, Ricky still wore jeans and cowboy boots. He smelled like cologne and courage. The sleeves of his white button-down were rolled up, revealing his biceps and damp armpits. He opened the screen door, stepped aside, and allowed me to enter first.

"Hiya, kids."

"Hello, ma'am."

"Go get youse some lemonade from the fridge and come on out. It's not so hot once you get used to it."

My heart thudded. Everything depended on her answer. My life was dictated by Mom. If she disapproved, that would be it.

We sat on the white wicker couch sipping our lemonade. I held my glass with both hands to keep it still. Ricky seemed as calm as chimes on a still day. He smoothed his hair back then turned to Mom. "Ma'am. I have something to ask."

"I already know what it is," Mom said.

"You do?"

She leaned back in her chair, resting her glass on the arm. "Yep. You wanna date my daughter, don't ya?"

"Well… yeah."

She narrowed her eyes. "Just what are your intentions?"

I shrank.

He slid his arm around me. "Well, I like her… a lot… and I'd never hurt her. I'll be true to her, and I'll always treat her nice."

"Well, you sound sincere."

Ricky sat up a bit straighter. "I am most definitely sincere."

"Alright. You have my permission. But I'll have my eye on you."

He nodded. Fireworks exploded in me. I was over the moon. Before that moment, I'd assumed I'd never have a boyfriend. I'd adapted to not having friends and let go of any notion that my life would resemble a normal fifteen-year-old's. But meeting Ricky changed all that. Every brain cell was dedicated to thoughts of him. I'd smell my shirt to take in the sweet scent of his cologne after we'd part. I'd work extra hard during the day so the hours would pass quickly. I'd get my share of the cleaning out of the way as early as possible, giving me time to preen before he came over.

Soon he ate supper with us most nights. Afterward, he and I sat on the floor, hands laced, listening to Mom preach.

"Jesus died for your sins, so you don't have to die…"

Like most others who heard Mom preach, Ricky was enthralled, drinking in her recitation of scripture. I got jealous when he wanted to spend most of our time listening to her preach, but I slammed the brakes on those feelings. I told myself to be grateful that the Lord had sent Ricky, and to be content with the way things were.

Before long, almost all our time was spent with my family. I felt his attention lagging. Even when we were alone, he wanted to talk about how excited he was to be one of the 144,000. He was slipping away. Mom got in his bloodstream.

Ricky was so enthused about getting saved that he told his grandparents. They didn't take it well. His grandma called Mom and told her to stay away from him. She called her a loony and said she was teaching Ricky crazy things. She forbade him to see me too.

I threw myself on my bed and sobbed. "Mom, do you think his grandma might change her mind?"

"I don't know. Satan's in her heart."

"What if he goes back to Indianapolis and I never see him again? Am I supposed to just forget him?"

Then she said something I never expected.

"If they won't let you see him, we'll just have to get you pregnant… then they won't have no choice."

Pregnant. At fifteen.

"What? I haven't even had sex yet."

"Sit down on the bed. I'll give you a crash course."

I sat on the bed next to her. She turned and looked in my eyes. I turned away, feeling embarrassed.

"Here's what happens…" she said, explaining sex like she was giving directions, even mentioning her favorite position with my dad.

Heat climbed my neck. I liked kissing Ricky, but sex felt like stepping off a cliff. I tried to wrap my head around getting pregnant. Was it the Lord's will?

Around then, Mom said God wanted us to move. She'd read about Iowa farmers offering free housing in exchange for caretaking. That was the sign she'd been waiting for.

Ricky kept coming despite the ban. Mom asked if he wanted to move with us. He didn't hesitate.

"I'll marry youse, then youse can be together," she said.

Marriage felt impossible and inevitable, both at once.

We sold everything that couldn't fit in the trailer. Ricky's grandparents sent him back to Indianapolis, but Mom already had a plan.

I knew I was too young for marriage, but the end was coming. Why wouldn't I get married?

When we reached Indianapolis, Mom called Ricky from a phone booth. My stomach twisted with hope.

At dusk, we pulled into the alley behind his house. I sat on the bed in the van, fists tight in my lap. A black garbage bag flew over the fence. Then Ricky climbed after it. He scooped it up. I flung open the sliding door of the van and he jumped in. He kissed me and sat beside me, squeezing my hand. My whole body smiled.

At the time, I didn't realize it would be considered kidnapping—he was only fifteen.

CHAPTER TWELVE

Indianola, Iowa, 1978

When we reached Des Moines, Mom and Jim headed into a real estate office to ask about free-rent arrangements. The rest of us stayed in the van. Ricky slipped his arm around my waist. A quiver ran through me—small but electric, like a spark jumping a wire. I wanted him all to myself. And I wanted the kissing and whispering and the way his eyes softened when he said he loved me.

Before long, Mom and Jim came out smiling. Mom opened the door wide and said, "All right guys, we found a place. It's a big farmhouse in the country. The Lord answered our prayers. All we have to do is help on the dairy farm."

Ricky squeezed my waist. That was all I cared about.

We drove down a narrow, windy lane. Floodlights around a massive tin building lit the air thick with bugs. The smell of cow manure curled through the open windows, but it didn't bother me. Beneath my city-girl skin, a tomboy still lived. I imagined milking cows, petting calves, maybe riding a horse bareback. If not for The Kingdom, it might've felt like Ricky and I were living inside a Harlequin paperback—my arms around his waist as we galloped across clover fields, stopping only to kiss, like we had all the time in the world.

I knew in my gut it was wrong to take him from Indianapolis, but love made its own rules. When we kissed, the planet shrank to just the two of us.

The white farmhouse had a wraparound porch in desperate need of paint.

Mom loved porches. We spent evenings there, pointing out birds, moons, and sunsets that looked like watercolor drying on the sky.

The screen door creaked open when she pushed it. Inside, a long wooden farm table stretched across most of the dining room.

"Look at that table. It's perfect for us," Mom said, hands planted on her hips.

Faded floral wallpaper peeled from the walls in curling strips. High ceilings held water stains like bruises. No curtains. Windows cold with night air. The whole place felt abandoned midsentence.

We unloaded the trailer and set up beds. Mom announced we'd start work first thing in the morning: Jim and Ricky on the cows; Mom, Deb, and I on calves, cleaning, yard work, and cooking.

Then she did the unthinkable—assigned Ricky and me our own bedroom. A riot of feelings rushed me: thrilled, terrified, curious, shy. I wanted to have sex with him, but I worried I'd do it wrong, wondered if it would hurt, if he'd still look at me softly afterward.

I asked Mom when Ricky and I would get married. She said, "Youse are already married. The Lord does the marrying, not the government."

Before The Kingdom, I'd imagined a wedding—music, dancing, a chocolate cake so tall it needed dowels, a white dress swishing around my legs. But I shelved the dream and adopted hers instead.

That first night, I slipped into a cotton nightgown, dabbed on lip gloss, and let my hair fall loose. Ricky lay in bed shirtless, looking relaxed, as though we'd been married for years. I turned off the light. Moonlight pooled over the bed like warm honey. I slid under the covers.

"This is my first time too," he whispered.

"Really? You ain't just saying that?"

He insisted it was true. I nestled into him. His arm wrapped around me, steady and sure. A shudder ran through my whole body. When he kissed me, the room dropped away. We slid down together, his body warm against mine.

"I love you, Peggy," he breathed.

My heart felt too full for my ribs.

He eased a sleeve off my shoulder, and asked, "Is it okay if I touch you here?" and cupped my breast with such tenderness that something in me opened. When he entered me, pain shot through me like a wire pulled too tight—but beneath it, something else flickered. I swallowed every sound. His body pressed into mine, heat blooming all through me. When he finished, he pulled me close. We drifted into sleep without speaking.

A knock came at four a.m. Jim was waking Ricky for milking. Cows didn't care about sleeping or love—they needed work at five a.m. and again at five p.m., manure scraped after each shift.

Deb, Mom, and I woke early to make breakfast. Ricky gulped raw milk, leaving a foamy mustache that made me laugh. We ate with our knees touching while Mom rattled off chores: deep cleaning, stripping wallpaper, painting, mowing, fixing the porch. A whole world of work.

I kissed him before he headed back outside. All day, I thought of nothing but him. I could hardly wait for night. But at lunch, something had shifted. Ricky's shoulders sagged. His eyes were dull. He avoided looking at me as he passed me on the way to the bathroom.

Jim leaned toward Mom and whispered, "San, I don't think he likes working."

"What do you mean?"

"Well, he's slow, and I tell him something and he don't remember."

Mom waved him off. "Oh, he'll be alright. He'll get the hang of it."

"Okay, San. I hope you're right."

Ricky returned, grabbed his sandwich, and took a huge bite like a starving man.

"Join hands," Mom said for prayer.

"Oh, sorry." Ricky wiped his mouth and took Jim's hand and mine.

After lunch, they had a break before the five-p.m. milking, but Mom filled it with chores. She always found more work.

By evening, the truth settled like fog around my ankles—Ricky wasn't improving. "He's lazy, and he's got no work ethic," Mom said.

Every night, we gathered around the farm table for Mom's preaching. Ricky sat in the hot seat—accused of resentment, the Demon of Laziness, a stubborn mouth, the wrong posture, the wrong chew. She said she needed to break him down before building him back up. I wanted to scream, Stop! But fear tied my hands behind my back and stuffed a rag in my mouth.

Ricky questioned her. Why so many hours, why no time with me, and each question made her stiffen. Humility and obedience were the only traits she valued. Anything else smelled like rebellion.

At night, Ricky and I found refuge in each other. Skin to skin, breath to breath, shutting out the world. Even when it hurt, it was ours.

One afternoon, Mom resumed her assault at the lunch table. Ricky wasn't sitting straight. His mouth was wrong. His plate wasn't clean.

"Do you think you're too good to eat that part?" she asked.

"What? The gristle?"

A lump rose in my throat.

"Eat the gristle," she said.

Ricky flushed red. Everyone froze. He shoved a piece in his mouth, then another. The second he couldn't swallow. He glared at Mom, spat the gristle onto the plate, and said, "I'm outta here." His chair scraped hard against the floor. He looked at me—one last question in his eyes—then stormed upstairs.

"Mom," I whispered, begging.

"This is the choice he's making. Nothing I can do about it. He gave into the devil."

"Where's he gonna go?"

"I don't know, Peggy."

A moment later, Ricky came down with a black garbage bag over his shoulder. At the door, he turned and said, "I'm sorry Peggy, but I can't do this."

I wanted to run to him, wrap myself around his legs, beg him to stay. But I couldn't move.

I watched from the window as he walked down the lane. He looked back several times. I kept hoping he'd turn around. But he didn't. His body grew smaller, swallowed by distance.

"I guess he's gonna hitchhike," Jim said.

"I don't think his heart was in it," Mom added.

Tears broke loose.

"You'll be sad for a while, but he wasn't right for you," Mom said. "Now, wipe your tears and get going on the dishes."

I cried for days.

One afternoon, ironing clothes, tears dripping onto the board, and Mom said, "I been hurt worse than that. You'll get over it in time."

Her words felt like a fist to the chest. I didn't want to get over him. With Ricky, I'd tasted something close to normal. Close to freedom. All I had left was the promise ring—a tiny diamond chip, paid for by Mom because Ricky couldn't. I used to hold my hand out and admire it, daydreaming about our life together.

One morning, Mom said, "You might as well give it to me now." Matthew 5:40: Give your coat, then your cloak also. I slipped it from my finger and handed it over.

Without Ricky, my life returned to its previous state. Tears dried. Sadness lifted. Mom was right, I got over him. But I never forgot him.

A month later, Mom and Jim realized dairy work wasn't a fair trade for rent. Mom invited the farm owner and his son, Hank, for supper.

Hank—a big, burly man with a Marlboro stuck to his lip—said, "Mmmm, something smells good."

Mom set the roast on the table. Behind Hank stood his father, much smaller, face drawn tight. Jim took their coats. Deb and I brought in the rest of the food. The tension thickened the room like smoke. Mom laid out her proposal—wages for their labor—but the owner rejected it, shouting for us to get the hell out. He'd already shot and killed Snowball for supposedly eating the back end of a cow. He wasn't interested in fairness.

Hank stayed behind after his father stormed out. After a long, icy minute, he said he owned a house we could live in rent-free if we fixed it up. No water. No bathroom. Just a pump and an outhouse. But it was a lifeline.

Mom said, "Well, I lived in hard conditions plenty in my life. Didn't have no toilet as a kid. Lived in places with bare wood floors."

"You know what I'm talking 'bout, then," Hank said.

We packed quickly. We were experts at leaving by then. Except this time, Snowball wasn't with us.

Cross-legged in the van, I watched the farm shrink in the distance. It had been only three weeks since Ricky left, but it felt like years. The ache settled deep, stubborn as a knot.

It hurt. It hurt like hell.

CHAPTER THIRTEEN
Springbrook, 1978

The grass on either side of the lane rose nearly five feet high. The house at the end of the lane was tiny. Smaller than I'd imagined. More of a square block of concrete with a roof than a home. We parked in front, headlights left on to carve light into the dark. Just as Hank was cautioning us to watch our step, Deb's foot plunged through a floorboard.

"You, okay?" Hank asked, reaching out a hand.

Deb's cheeks flushed. "Yeah, I'm okay."

"I can fix that easy," Jim said. "Gonna need some two-by-fours and plywood."

Hank removed his cap, dragged a hand through his thinning hair, and nodded. "Alright. Get whatever you need. I'll reimburse you."

He and Jim shared a sturdy handshake; the kind men give when they want to prove they mean what they say.

Inside, the house held only three rooms, each one carrying a draft that felt older than the walls. Mom decided we girls would sleep in one room, another would serve as the kitchen—even though it had no stove or sink—and the third would be the living room. Jim would sleep on the couch.

A wood-burning stove was our only source of heat. Thankfully, someone had left a small stack of firewood for the night. When Deb and I went out to fetch water, we discovered the pump was broken. A shock of disappointment ran through me, but then we spotted a natural spring a few feet away, shining in the moonlight. Mom sent us down with a flashlight and a bucket to scoop enough for drinking.

The next morning, Mom and Jim bought a two-burner propane stove and supplies to fix the floor. Once the inside was somewhat livable—at least livable by our standards—we started on the outside.

The cement-colored stucco cabin sat crookedly on a couple of acres. Behind it stretched a field of overgrown hay that looked like it hadn't been touched since the war. Mom said that field would be a source of income one day.

Beyond the field ran a fast, muddy river. I didn't know it then, but that river would become our bathtub. For months, I was never truly clean. When I scratched my scalp, grit collected under my nails. Dirt seemed to live in the folds of my skin like it had claimed me. Once, Mom surprised us with a trip to Springbrook Park's beach house to shower. The water was freezing, but the shock of it felt holy. I stood under that spray until my body trembled. The water was freezing, but I didn't mind—I appreciated being clean for a change.

***

Come spring, Mom and Jim rented a tiller to carve out our vegetable garden. We planted every vegetable we could think of. Across the creek stretched a grove thick with apples, grapes, gooseberries, asparagus—things growing wild and half-feral. Mom sent Deb and me up to "whip it into shape." We sang while we worked, harmonizing with each other, and because Mom wasn't around, Deb let her voice out like she had nothing to lose.

I still missed Ricky, but working twelve-hour days left little room for longing. Each day barreled into the next—berry picking, jelly making, selling jars door-to-door to neighboring farms. We set up a vegetable stand at the top of the lane during harvest. Deb and I took turns sitting there for hours, waving at cars that rarely slowed down. We cut and baled the hay. We detasseled corn, walked beans, and worked for neighboring farmers who were always grateful for an extra pair of hands.

On one job at a hog farm, I worked the line preparing baby pigs to be weaned from their sow mothers. They received shots, had their tails cut off, and got branded. I couldn't handle the cutting or the branding, so I gave them shots. It still felt like participating in something bigger and harsher than I understood. It all seemed so cruel.

One day, as I worked, a deafening squeal pierced my ears. Three men were wrestling a huge pig to the ground. The pig kicked and thrashed, screeching so loud it vibrated my ribs. Two of the men lay flat on their backs on top of him, pinning him like wrestlers straining for a win. Once they had him still, they tied his legs. A man wearing long rubber gloves stepped in, squatted, and castrated him. That shriek was nothing I'd ever heard, and if I never heard it again, it would be too soon.

When fall arrived, the river turned too cold to bathe in. Mom brought home an aluminum tub, and we hauled buckets of creek water, heated them over the stove, and took turns bathing. Washing hair took forever, especially ours, long and tangled from months of wind and work.

After almost a year, Mom and Hank had a falling-out over money. Hank had agreed to pay Jim for building an addition on the house, but he backed out. Mom was angry but took it as a sign to move on. We figured the apple didn't fall far from the tree—his dad hadn't wanted to pay either. We packed quickly—nothing new there—and left behind an open cinderblock basement that often filled with standing water. The place felt unfinished, like it had never really wanted us.

To this day, I call our time living at Springbrook, "a year in the wilderness." Raw, relentless, and strangely alive. A place that stripped me down and toughened me in ways I didn't realize at the time.

CHAPTER FOURTEEN
Paledon, 1978

Mom had always talked about opening a restaurant, the way she talked about winning the lottery—half dream, half destiny. She carried her hoagie recipes like precious heirlooms. "We'll call it the Hoagie Shoppe. Shop with two p's," she said. "That's more original." Her voice was bright, almost girlish, as if she could already smell bread baking and the cash register being rung up.

When she stumbled onto an auction in nearby Paledon it was too good to pass up. A closed-down restaurant was liquidating everything. We ended up with nearly an entire place for pennies on the dollar: '50s-style chrome stools at three dollars each, a countertop for seven, a pizza oven, booths, coffee cups. The bones of someone else's dream repurposed for ours. And then a stroke of luck: a vacant, dirt-cheap storefront a few doors down.

Paledon looked like a toy town set out on a card table: population 1,200, one gas station, one bank, one tiny grocery store, two taverns, three churches, and a single restaurant: The West End. We tested their food one night. Mom chewed slowly, then whispered, "They won't be no competition for us. Wait 'till this town tastes my hoagies."

We moved into a farmhouse on the edge of town, a kind of place with wind-whipped fields and night skies filled with stars. To fund the Hoagie Shoppe, Jim hustled side jobs for farmers, and Mom got Deb and I hired at The West End.

Deb cooked and I waitressed. At barely sixteen, surrounded by adults carrying decades of life I hadn't lived yet, I felt out of place. My extroversion shriveled in adult company. "You don't go to work to make friends, you go to make money," Mom said. So, I ate my meals alone most days. The kitchen help occasionally invited me to sit with them.

Glyness—another waitress—kept her distance. She showed a polite lack of interest and coldness at the edges. She explained the seating system my first night: we alternated tables on slow days and used sections on weekends. Sounded fair.

But she bent rules like wet branches. If she recognized a customer—and she seemed to know half the county—she'd swipe the table. "They're my regulars," she'd say. She never compensated me by letting me take the next two turns. I'd been raised to respect adults, so I kept quiet until I couldn't anymore. I told Mom.

She cupped my cheeks in her hands, her stare locking onto mine like she was pinning down truth. "Next time she steals your table, you walk off the floor and call me. And don't say nothing. You wait 'till I get there."

I felt a wash of relief—Mom, fierce and righteous, ready to defend me again, like she had in the ER years earlier after that dog bite when the nurses strapped me to a table. But the confrontation that followed was nothing like what I anticipated.

It was a slow night when a family of four slid into a booth—my turn. Carrying a half-full coffee pot, Glyness zipped over, set it on their table, and chatted them up like old friends. I filled waters, walked over and waited for her to finish, but she ignored me.

"Excuse me, please." I nudged past her, set down the glasses, and greeted the family.

"This is my brother-in-law. I'm going to take them," she said, elbowing me aside.

I'm sure my face went pale. I turned on autopilot, went to the kitchen, and called Mom.

Minutes later, the swinging kitchen doors exploded open and Mom marched out, eyes blazing like flares.

"Where is she?"

I pointed.

Mom waited at the waitress station, gathering heat like a storm. Glyness walked back and clipped a ticket to the cook's wheel. Mom watched her like a raptor eyeing a massive fish. Then, hands on her hips, she asked, "Are you

Glyness?"

Glyness turned, her hair sprayed beehive unbudged. "Yeah. Who wants to know?"

"I'm Peggy's mother and I know what you been doing." Mom's face matched the color of her coral lipstick. "When you steal her tables, you're stealing food off our table. She's a young girl. You should be an example for her."

Glyness chortled and turned away.

"Turn around and look at me," Mom commanded. The veins in her neck strained. "Do you think this is funny?"

A scraggly man at the counter, wearing a greasy ball cap, chuckled.

Mom whirled toward him, pointed, and said, "don't you mock me! Get thee behind me, Satan!"

His smirk vanished.

I felt my stomach drop. I had convinced myself The Kingdom was dead and buried. Instead, it resurrected from the grave. It became clear that telling Mom about Glyness was a mistake. Sure, Glyness was wrong, but it wouldn't be long before the whole town would know about us.

"You don't know who you're dealing with, lady," Mom warned. "The Lord's wrath will come down on you. For the Lord giveth and the Lord taketh away."

Glyness kept walking, impervious to Mom's threat.

"Come on. We're leaving and you're not coming back," Mom said. In the kitchen she added, "Don't worry. We'll soon open the Hoagie Shoppe. You don't need this job."

A few days later, a rumor spread that Mom was a madam, Deb and I were ladies of the night, and Jim was the muscle. I wondered if Glyness' beehive had been buzzing with stories.

***

Preparing to open the Hoagie Shoppe became our full-time existence. Mom bought Deb and me navy-blue smocks with wide pockets for order pads, straws, and tips. We rehearsed taking orders like we were auditioning for a play.

Once we scrubbed the place top to bottom, it sparkled. The place was small, seated fifty, with an open kitchen. Mom said customers like to see their food prepared. We installed a jukebox stuffed with our favorites: Motown, oldies, disco. We chopped vegetables daily on the big slicer; our regulars cried with us when we sliced onions. Mom insisted on premium ingredients and generous portions. Coffee was strong and only ten cents to hook the locals—she planned to raise prices once they were addicted.

The Hoagie Shoppe was an overnight success. New restaurants in tiny towns were rarer than comets. Everyone wanted to know what a hoagie was. "Kind of like a submarine sandwich," I'd say, "but a lot better."

The work felt endless: slicing, scrubbing, degreasing, stocking, washing. Days blurred into each other. Grease, laughter, and exhaustion swirling together. Mom hadn't preached Kingdom doctrine for almost a year, except that blow-up with Glyness. She told us there were no more souls to save except for our future mates and children. We were to "occupy" until Jesus came. Blend in.

Her prophecies from the earlier years—three and a half years till the world ended—had fizzled. She never explained. She simply shifted the story: Jesus would now come like a thief in the night. We had to stay ready. Be perfect. Sometimes she tested us with drills. Like the night years earlier when she'd hollered, "He's here! He's here! Jesus is here!" We all came flying down the stairs, half dressed, with saucer-sized eyes. "I was testing youse to make sure youse have your oil lamps full," she said, referring to a Bible parable about five virgins who were left behind because their oil lamps weren't full when the bridegroom came.

In Paledon, under a new doctrine of permission, Mom decided we should smoke and drink. "Jesus hung out with sinners," she'd say, lighting up. I was conditioned to see Mom's will as God's will.

It had been difficult for Mom to give up those vices when she first got saved back in Sacramento. She said the Demon of Addiction had her. She often told the story of a cigarette butt on a public bathroom floor that spoke to her, telling her to pick it up. At that moment, she called out to Jesus for help to overcome the urge, and He did. She needed to prove her love and devotion to Him. "A man is not defiled by what goes into his mouth, but by what comes out," she'd quote. Since she'd proved her commitment and was perfect and pure in His eyes, he told her she could drink and smoke again. "Unto the pure, all things are pure," she'd say.

Mom gained attention almost immediately from the locals. They'd hang around in the afternoons drinking RC from red plastic glasses while Mom sat in the back booth smoking cigarettes, sipping coffee, and making entries in the ledger. She carried herself with aloof grace. She'd lost some of the pounds she'd gained, but not all. With her delicate wrists and narrow facial structure, the extra weight was well-hidden. She prided herself on using makeup to accentuate her full lips, high cheekbones, and alluring green eyes. She'd chat with male customers who made it known they were attracted to her. Sometimes she'd even flirt a bit. But that's as far as it went. She thought most guys were losers.

God had told her to find a mate—we were all supposed to find mates—but that endeavor was proving more difficult than expected. Mom wasn't picky about looks. She didn't mind if they were overweight or bald. But a guy with rugged hands and a solid work ethic earned big points.

Deb and I accompanied her to bars, both of us assumed to be over eighteen. At sixteen, I felt flattered and invisible at the same time. There were two taverns in town, each a couple of doors down from the Hoagie Shoppe. Mom preferred B&M's, a family-oriented tavern, during the day because she liked talking with the owners. She chose Fuzzy's at night because they were open later and had better men and music. But she was uncomfortable going to Fuzzy's alone. It could get a little rough sometimes, with fights breaking out on busy nights. To avoid that riffraff, we went out on weeknights. We'd close The Shoppe, freshen up in the bathroom, then head to Fuzzy's.

We'd sit in a booth, sipping beers, smoking cigarettes, dancing to Donna Summer or The Bee Gees—just the three of us, no men. Deb and I usually shot a few games of pool. Some nights, we'd play partners with guys who'd ask. Other nights we played one-on-ones. All the practice we'd got at B&M's on our afternoon breaks paid off. We both became excellent pool players.

Deb didn't like smoking, but Mom insisted. "I'm not gonna have you thinking you're better than the rest of us," she told her. Deb argued that smoking wasn't good for her and made her feel sick. Mom replied that she needed to smoke to stay humble. And refusing meant succumbing to the Demon of Stubbornness. After landing in the hot seat multiple times, Deb finally relented and became a smoker.

CHAPTER FIFTEEN

Des Moines, 1980

After Deb moved to Des Moines, I set my sights on doing the same. Stories about Deb's departure conflicted with each other. Mom claimed she was supportive of Deb and gave her furniture and financial help. Deb claimed that Mom kicked her out. My memory is fuzzy on why she moved out, but I recall shortly before, they'd fought over a guy.

One night after Mom and Deb had too much to drink, Deb left the bar with a guy they both had a crush on. Mom ran after her. They had an altercation in the alley. When Mom tried to stop her from getting in his truck, there was a scuffle. Deb's glasses broke. When Deb told the story, she said Mom beat her up. When Mom told the story, she said she only pulled Deb's arm to try to stop her from going with the guy, "because it wasn't safe."

At first, Mom was opposed to me moving out. She said seventeen was too young, but I convinced her I was mature enough. That I needed to learn how to live on my own, like Maryanne, Diane and Deb had. I knew how to take care of a home, hold a job, cook, balance a checkbook. I also got my driver's license, took out a bank loan, and bought an old rust bucket, the color of cooked spinach. But truthfully, it was my chance to get away from Mom's control.

Mom would need to hire someone to replace me, putting more strain on The Shoppe. Winter hit hard, tons of snow and frigid temperatures. Some days we'd barely take in fifty bucks. Plus, Mom had had an affair with a married man and word spread like a match to a long fuse. Business never picked up again after that. The farmer coffee clutches all but died, and our packed lunch crowd became a rare occurrence. I figured the wives in the town forbade their husbands from coming in.

Still, I felt compelled to move out, especially since I wouldn't be doing it on my own. I'd become friends with Brenda, a regular at The Shoppe. She too was ready to get out on her own after graduating high school. We found a one-bedroom apartment we could afford. I got a waitress job working days at The Doubletree, a 4-Star hotel restaurant. Brenda got a job as a nurse's aide working the graveyard shift. The one-bedroom worked because we slept at separate times.

We were two single girls ready to get out of hick-town Paledon and take on the world. I put The Kingdom out of my mind. I didn't realize until I'd moved out, just how liberated I felt.

Money was tight, but the first couple of months went alright. Brenda and I were complementary roommates. Because of our opposite shifts, we rarely saw each other, but when we did, we got along fine. Her boyfriend slept over a lot. I didn't mind; I was usually at work when he was there. He was nice enough, but Brenda could do better. He wasn't ambitious, laid around getting high all day. Not surprisingly, the relationship didn't last.

Soon after they split up, Brenda joined the Navy. I was happy for her but not thrilled that she'd left me with almost ten months remaining on a lease I couldn't afford. I could've found another roommate, but sharing a one-bedroom with a stranger was a hard sell.

I took a second waitress job, but it wasn't enough. So, when Pat, my new boyfriend, asked to move in, it felt like a saving grace. It was too soon for us to shack up: we'd only been dating a couple of weeks. But I needed financial help. Plus, I was captivated by him.

In his maintenance-man jumper, I noticed him my first day. His blonde, globe-shaped afro caught my attention first, then his dimples. Whenever we crossed paths, he smiled and held my gaze with his big, ocean-blue eyes. After a few days, he stopped to chat. Eventually, he asked me out. Well, not *out* exactly. He invited himself to my apartment. Mom's voice echoed in my head, her list of sexual sins recited like a catechism: no French kissing, no nipple sucking, no oral or anal sex. I carried those rules like invisible guardrails.

Despite my apprehension about moving so fast, I reminded myself everything was predestined. Like everyone else I'd dated, I asked myself if he could be my soul mate. His biggest drawback was his pot smoking. Mom wasn't keen on drugs of any kind. She said she'd only smoked once and ended up paralyzed on a bathroom floor. She didn't preach much about drugs; there was an implicit understanding that we were to stay away from them. I didn't know how I'd reconcile Pat's pot smoking with Mom, but I pushed that worry down the line.

I was filled with joy, living in the moment, shutting out thoughts about my family and The Kingdom. Mom hadn't made me testify to anyone since Ricky. In my mind, I had a tiny box where I locked away my desires. Inside it lived the hope that Mom would sustain her preaching hiatus and that I'd never have to testify again.

Since Mom was hyper-focused on The Shoppe and wasn't seeking new souls, the rest of us followed suit. Sometimes we didn't even pray before meals. Except for Mom retelling stories, like when Ron smeared poop on himself, or the guy who crawled backward down the street, it was as if The Kingdom had never existed.

Deb and I were living in Des Moines on our own. Jim was growing a handyman business, though he still worked at The Shoppe, and had gotten an apartment with his girlfriend, Bev.

I still believed the end was coming. I continued to thwart any doubtful thoughts about Mom. I thought a lot about predestination. How could we have free will if there was already a blueprint? Were we making choices? It sure seemed like we were. But maybe the choices were guided by the Lord. Trying to understand it hurt my brain, like pressing on a bruise that wouldn't heal.

So, I surrendered. I resigned myself to going along with whatever happened, accepting that everything was God's will. Following Mom's instructions, I forged ahead with every intention of finding my soul mate.

After a couple of months, it became clear Pat wasn't my soul mate. I broke up with him a few weeks before my eighteenth birthday after discovering he'd been cheating on me with his ex.

***

I wanted to celebrate my birthday, but all my friends were busy. A local bar had a pool hall in the basement with a good table. They had one-dollar margaritas on Thursday nights. I knew the bartender—Pat and I had been regulars. I'd never gone out alone, but I figured I'd chat with the bartender if all else failed.

So, I slid on my cutest pair of jeans and platform shoes, curled my hair into a Farah Fawcett flip, and applied a coat of red lipstick. I was going to have fun if it killed me.

My shoes clunked as I walked down the wooden stairs. I recognized a few faces. I knew I might see Pat, but I wasn't worried. I was still pissed and wouldn't give him the time of day.

Cigarette smoke swirled beneath green hanging lamps stamped with Budweiser insignias above each pool table. Styx's "Come Sail Away" drifted from the jukebox. I perched on a stool and lit a Marlboro Light. I told the bartender it was my birthday and that I was feeling a little blue. We chatted about my breakup.

Word traveled fast. Free drinks and pool challenges came at me like a birthday parade. A couple of guys asked for my number. I said I wasn't ready to date yet. They were sympathetic. Nobody had a kind word to say about Pat.

I'd eaten a hearty meal before leaving, but the tequila shots still caught up with me. Even water that last hour didn't help. I said my goodbyes, slid off the stool, and climbed the stairs, gripping the rail.

Walking to my car, two guys came up from behind and looped their arms through mine.

"Hey, little mama. Want some company?" one said.

"No thanks," I said, pulling my arms free.

Before I could protest further, they grabbed me and shoved me into the back of a car. The next thing I knew, I was flat on my back. One guy was on top of me, groping me, and trying to pull off my jeans. The other egged him on. I squirmed, clawed, kicked, and shrieked, "Get the hell off me! Help! Somebody help!"

Then a man's voice cut through the chaos: "Let'r go!"

The two guys backed away.

A short, schlubby, twenty-something with a loose ponytail and John Lennon–style glasses reached into the car and helped me up. He reminded me of one of those nice guys who got high and smiled a lot.

I straightened my clothes and headed for my car.

"C'mon, let me help you."

"I'm fine. I don't need help." I struggled to get the key into the door.

"You're in no shape to drive," he said. "Let me drive you home."

"I'm okay. It's just dark right here."

"Don't worry. You can trust me." He took my keys and unlocked the door. "Hey, I just saved you."

"Well, that's true. Man, I can't believe that happened. Thank you so much."

He flashed a reassuring smile. I climbed into the passenger seat.

When we got to my apartment, I gave him a pillow and blanket, showed him the couch, then passed out on my bed.

Sometime in the night, I awoke to him on top of me.

It took a moment to register. At first, I kissed him, maybe thinking I was dreaming, or that he was Pat. Once I was more lucid, I turned my face away. His whiskers sanded my cheek. All his weight pressed into me. He was inside me. My lungs felt like they might collapse. I tried pushing his shoulders away.

"It's okay. I'm almost done," he whispered, teeth clenched, body rigid.

Confused and numb, I lay there and let him finish.

He rolled off and fell asleep.

In the morning, he was gone. So was the cash I'd set aside for rent.

I was too ashamed to call the police. I figured they wouldn't believe me. I was drunk. I'd let a stranger into my apartment. They would've thought I was asking for it.

I chalked it up to a hard lesson learned.

I never told Mom. I didn't want her to think I was failing at living on my own. I shoved the entire night into the mental box where memories went to die.

***

I was already two months behind on rent when the eviction notice arrived. Mom was working herself ragged to keep The Shoppe afloat, but she was still the only person I could turn to. I didn't tell her about the assault; I didn't even have the language for rape back then. I carried the shame like it was proof I'd failed at being on my own. Plus, I didn't want to return to working at The Shoppe, The Kingdom life, and having nothing more than Fuzzy's for a social life. Even though living in Des Moines had been a disaster, most of the time I was just an ordinary girl, free to think for myself, make my own decisions, fall, and pull myself back up. Going back would mean admitting defeat and handing my life back to Mom. But with no other options, I called Mom for help.

Mom brought the money herself. She could've sent it, but she said she wanted to see me. Before she arrived, I scrubbed the apartment like it was an audition for adulthood—trying to erase any trace of chaos or weakness.

"Peg, you made a nice little place for yourself here. I like that chair," she said, pointing to the wicker queen's chair in the corner.

Whenever Mom said she liked something there was a tacit understanding that we were to give it to her. Maybe because I'd been gone for a while, or because I had bigger problems, I didn't offer her the chair. I still felt guilty, so I gave her a picture she'd also admired.

"So, your sister isn't giving you no rent money?"

Deb had been down on her luck, so I'd let her move in for fifty dollars a month.

"No, she didn't give me nothing yet."

"Well, that girl needs a talkin' to. I'm gonna stay 'till she gets home."

She sat on the couch, crossed her legs, and lit a cigarette. She talked mostly about The Shoppe, periodically spitting complaints about Deb. By the time Deb got home, Mom was primed.

With folded arms, leaning back, she said, "Your sister got an eviction notice. Why aren't you paying your share?"

Deb walked past her toward the kitchen. "Man Mom, I just got home from work. Leave me alone."

Mom followed. "Peggy's working two jobs, and all she asked for is fifty dollars a month. You need to pay her."

"I know, Mom. I'm trying hard too, you know. Why do you always take Peg's side?" She brushed past her.

Mom's face flushed. "Don't you walk away from me, young lady!"

Deb kept going. Mom grabbed her arm. Deb yanked it free. Mom lunged to slap her, but Deb caught her arm. They tumbled into the coffee table and broke it.

I stood frozen. Mom had overreacted, and I hated that she'd tried to hit Deb. But I also needed Deb to pay her share. I thought Deb was wrong to talk to Mom that way. Yet it impressed me that she'd stood up to her. Mom had slapped me a few times growing up, but I never saw it coming. Even if I had, I never would've fought back like Deb did. Ballsy!

Deb moved out a couple of weeks later.

Instead of using Mom's money to pay rent, I found a cheaper apartment. The apartment included a finished attic, which I figured would be perfect for a roommate. I forfeited my three-hundred-dollar deposit, but the lower rent was worth it. I posted flyers at Drake University and found a roommate within a week. She was quiet and tidy. Most nights, she slept at her boyfriend's. It was peaceful.

I slipped back into a routine: waitressing at JL's Fresh Bar by day, cocktailing at the Fox Three Lounge at night. On Fridays and Saturdays—my nights off— I went out with friends. But after the assault and robbery, I watched how much I drank and never went out alone again.

A work friend invited me to a house party one Friday night. The house was packed when we arrived. We pumped beers from the keg. Bob Seger's "Katmandu" came on, and a guy asked me to dance. I didn't like dancing to rock, but I did like Bob Seger. Once I started, I didn't stop. I wasn't the kind of girl who lingered at the edges of a room. I moved until my legs hummed.

We danced into the early morning. When the party finally thinned out, the handful of us left claimed floor space and fell asleep where we landed. My friend and I curled up on the living room carpet, using our coats as blankets.

The next morning, the ten of us who'd slept over went to breakfast at a hole-in-the-wall diner. The guy across from me kept staring, so I introduced myself. He said his name was Bob.

"Can I take you out sometime?" he blurted, then shoved a massive bite of pancakes into his mouth, syrup clinging to his mustache.

I told him I was nursing a broken heart and wasn't ready to date. The truth was, I didn't find him attractive. He was short and balding, with a pot belly and a skinny ponytail. Though, he did have nice eyes.

"Can I give you, my number?" he asked. "I'm pretty good with cars and can fix most anything. If you ever need help, call me."

He went back to his pancakes like he'd sealed a deal. I took his number with no intention of calling.

***

My oil-burning Chevy Impala ran fine, until it didn't. I had less than an hour to get to work, and it wouldn't start. I didn't know what else to do. I called Bob.

When I heard him pull up, I parted the drapes. There was still a chance I'd make it to work. Bob stepped out of a powder-blue Mercury Sable wearing flip-flops and saggy jeans.

I met him in front of the house. When he saw me, he grinned so wide his lips disappeared into his mustache. I returned an obligatory smile and thanked him. He lifted the hood and turned his cap backward.

"The engine's dirty, but we can worry about that later. Let's get it running first."

I told him he was saving my ass. He worked for a few minutes but couldn't get it going. It would take longer than expected, he said, then offered to drive me. Desperate, I agreed. I had no money for a mechanic or a cab. It was too late for the bus.

When he picked me up after work, he told me the car was running.

"What do I owe you?" I asked, already feeling obligated.

He laughed nervously. "I'm not taking your money. You don't owe me anything."

After an awkward silence, he said, "I'm taking you out for dinner. When's your next night off?"

I told him I needed to do laundry and clean on my day off. He kept pressing. Eventually, I agreed to Sunday night.

I met him in my driveway. I didn't want him to think it was a real date. I wore high-waisted bell-bottom Lees, pulled my hair into a ponytail, and added a swipe of pale pink lipstick. On any other date, I would've dressed up. I didn't want to lead him on.

Bob scurried around and opened my door. It might not have been a proper date for me, but it clearly was for him. He wore a suit jacket, nice shoes, and expensive cologne.

At the steakhouse, he helped me out of my coat. The attention felt good. We drank and talked. Mostly he talked. He worked construction and learned to fix cars in Vietnam. I asked his age and instantly regretted it.

"I'm thirty," he said, scratching his mustache. "You think that's old?"

I shook my head and swallowed. "No."

He leaned forward. "Well, how old are you?"

"Girls ain't supposed to tell their age." I tilted my head. "But okay. Eighteen."

"Really? I thought you were in your twenties."

"A lot of people think that." I took a swig of beer.

"Order whatever you want," he said, waving his hand over the menu.

"Really?"

"Yes. Anything."

I ordered the ribeye and a glass of Lambrusco. I watched him in quick glances, just enough to show I was listening, never enough to lock eyes. Locking eyes gave men ideas.

He ordered a Brandy Alexander to share, then coffee with Bailey's. By the end, I was tipsy.

"Let's get you home," he said, grabbing my coat. "I'll take you here again sometime."

By the time we got back, I wasn't perfectly sober. He walked me up the steep stairs, purse in hand, his arm around my waist. He didn't ask to come in. He just did.

The room spun. I ran to the bathroom and threw up. When I came out, he'd taken off his coat.

"I'm going to stay to make sure you're alright."

"No, that's okay. I'm fine." He ignored me. You'd think I would've been scared after being robbed and raped. Weirdly, I wasn't.

I woke the next morning to sunlight in my eyes and the smell of frying eggs. I dragged myself out of bed and into the kitchen, hair knotted, teeth unbrushed, wearing green hospital scrubs from Goodwill. My head pounded and my body felt heavy as concrete.

"Coffee?" he asked.

"Yes. Man, I drank way too much last night. You got me drunk."

"I'm sorry." He turned with a pan in his hand. "Was that a bad thing? Should I not have bought you that expensive steak? Should I not have wined and dined you?"

"No, no. I appreciate it."

He chuckled. "Guess you can't handle your booze, huh?"

He put the pan back on the stove, then softened his tone. "I'm just giving you a hard time."

An uneasy silence settled between us.

After we ate, he said, "Some friends are getting together tonight. I'll pick you up later."

"How'd you know I was off tonight?"

"I called and asked your manager."

It felt creepy that he'd called my manager, but I told myself he'd done so much for me. And he really had slept on the couch. He hadn't tried anything.

He kept calling, checking on me every few days. I still didn't feel attracted to him, but I felt obligated—he'd fixed my car, bought me dinner, made coffee while I was hung over. He'd occasionally ask how I was doing with money. I always said I was fine. For a while that was true. Until I took the assistant manager job at Wendy's.

I'd miscalculated how much I'd need to bridge the gap between my tip-based income and my new salaried one. Before long, my wallet held only a few crumpled bills. My stack of unpaid envelopes grew like an accusation.

The next time Bob asked how I was doing financially, the truth slipped out. He jumped at the chance to help. I promised to pay him back, but he waved it off and insisted on covering my bills. He even bought me groceries.

Maybe the Lord sent him to help me. But Mom always said to never rely on a man. Still, I felt the familiar pull of predestination, like maybe this was the part of the plan where he stepped in. I thought about what Mom had taught me, that attraction can grow. That love is a choice. She often told the story of when she met Jack, the father of the baby boy she'd given up for adoption. "I looked into his eyes when we were on the dance floor, and I knew," she said. "Sometimes the Lord puts someone in front of you, and you just have to decide to love him." I told myself Bob and I must have been predestined to meet, though I didn't yet understand the role he'd play.

After Bob paid my bills, he came over almost every night. He held my hand, sang to me, wrote love notes, massaged my feet after work. Since my car still wasn't reliable, he drove me to Wendy's and picked me up at the end of my shifts. He never asked me to be his girlfriend. I just was.

Most girls would've cut off a pinky toe for a boyfriend like him. But something felt off. He said he worked in construction, yet he never talked about work. He was always available. When he paid for something, he pulled a thick wad of bills from his front pocket. He said he didn't trust banks. He'd often stop at friends' houses and tell me to wait in the car. Then one day, it stopped being vague.

We pulled into the driveway of a friend's place we'd visited many times. The house was discreet, swallowed by tall shrubs.

Bob kissed my hand and winked. "Wait here."

I sat listening to the radio, pretending not to notice the dread blooming in my gut. A few minutes later he returned, flushed and cheerful, singing along to Pat Benatar's "Hit Me with Your Best Shot." Without ceremony, he opened the glove compartment.

Then he pulled a plastic bag from his coat pocket, stuffed with smaller baggies—tightly rolled sandwich bags filled with tiny white pills. At least twenty bags. Probably a thousand pills each. White crosses, I later learned. He closed the glove box. Looked forward. Kept singing. We never talked about it. We acted like I already knew. He'd tested me and I didn't run for the hills.

Everything snapped into place: the conservative car, the cash, the stops. In hindsight, I know opening the glove box wasn't an accident. We'd made countless stops like that before. That was just the first time he showed me.

My life became Bob's life. Aside from work, we were always together. The drop-offs and pick-ups slipped into our daily routine. Eventually, he stopped having me wait in the car. I began to recognize his supplier and his buyers—ordinary people, not who I'd imagined drug dealers would be.

His main customer was a single mom with a special-needs child, living in a modest ranch house. His supplier was a middle-aged hippie in a cluttered, musty place that smelled of cats. Occasionally, we ran into a strung-out user desperate for a fix. Bob would shoo them away, saying he was out with his girl and couldn't be bothered.

When we weren't running white crosses, eating out, or going to bars, we were at my place. He never took me to his. He said it wasn't much, just a bachelor pad.

Because I was working fifty-hour weeks and had little time to clean, my apartment slowly turned into a party house: ashtrays overflowing, empty cans and bottles everywhere, rotten milk in the fridge, a three-foot bong on the floor. I didn't know what life I wanted, but I knew it wasn't that.

Bob was always high. Smoking was the first thing he did in the morning and the last thing at night. He said it made him feel normal. Vietnam haunted him. His hands, gray and scaly from frostbite, were a constant reminder of holding his dying friend.

Whenever we saw Asian people, something snapped in him.

"God damn gooks! They better not come near me. I'll kill 'em right here."

At first, I tried consoling him. But I learned quickly not to. He'd turn on me.

"You don't know what I went through in 'Nam," he'd say, "and you should shut up if you know what's good for you."

Mom and Jim kept bugging me about introducing Bob. Part of me wanted their approval. Another part wanted them to hate him, so I'd have an excuse to leave. I finally agreed to bring him to Paledon.

That day Bob came to fix my car, was the beginning of sliding into a reality

I'd only seen in movies—the girlfriend of a drug dealer, trained to keep secrets and override her instincts. I didn't believe I had the power to make choices. I was terrified of interfering with fate. One foot stood in a fragile independence I could barely manage, the other hovered over a life controlled by Mom. Trying to please everyone, I couldn't find myself anywhere.

I wasn't the girlfriend of a drug dealer. I wasn't a zealot. Afraid of choosing wrong, I went along with whatever came.

The Kingdom had felt distant. I stopped examining my thoughts, praying, worrying about the End of Time. I still believed, but belief no longer consumed my days. When guilt flared, when I thought about keeping things from Mom, I shoved it down. I wanted her approval. I needed her to believe I was managing life on my own. If she thought I wasn't, she would've made me come home. And I would have.

***

Bob squeezed my hand as we walked into The Shoppe. We often held hands, but at that time it felt performative—like I was announcing a commitment I wasn't ready to make.

The Shoppe wafted with familiar aromas: baked pizza, fresh-cut fries, sizzling meat. Jim was at the grill. Mom sat at the counter rolling ice cream balls in graham cracker crumbs. She smiled wide when she saw us.

"Coffee?" she asked Bob.

He laughed nervously and said yes, his glasses slid down his nose. She scooched into the back booth and motioned for him to sit across from her. I poured the coffee, then retreated to the kitchen with Jim who wore a greasy cook's hat, clanking a spatula against the grill, shifting sirloin and onions.

Bob was charming. I wasn't worried about Mom. Jim, though, noticed everything.

"Peg, grab that pizza from the oven," Jim asked.

Opening the pizza oven sent a wave of nostalgia through me. The heat on my face, buttery crust, pepperoni crisping at the edges, drunken with cheese.

Bob and Mom were hitting it off. Mom had a slight smile, and a curious look in her eyes. Bob leaned forward and chuckled intermittently. Jim removed his apron and went out to greet him. Beads of sweat appeared on Bob's forehead.

"Peg, go make some dinner for the two of youse," Mom said.

I didn't really want to, but I went back to the kitchen to make use burgers and fries.

I stood at the fryer, watching raw potatoes turn crisp, unsure of what I wanted more—for them to accept Bob or to reject him outright.

Jim returned to the kitchen.

"Peg, something ain't right about Bob."

I cleared my throat. "What do you mean?"

"I get a druggy vibe. And he seems kinda old for you." He ladled pizza sauce on a crust.

I gnawed the inside of my lip, searching my brain for a credible response. "Yeah, he smokes pot, but that's all. He don't do no other drugs."

"I don't know. Feels like he's been around the block too many times."

"He's alright, Jim. He's nice to me. He's better than my other boyfriends. He cooks for me, and he pays for everything."

Jim paused. "I don't wanna see you get into nothing bad."

I didn't know why I defended Bob so hard. Maybe I needed Jim to believe I could make adult choices.

When we got back into Bob's car, he said, "Your mom's cool."

"Yeah. Everybody likes her."

His jaw clenched. "My mom was a drunk and a whore. She didn't give a shit about me. That's why I went into the army. To get away from all that."

"Wow, I didn't know that. You went through a lot, huh?" I put a hand on his shoulder, reflexively soothing.

He shrugged. "Whatchu gonna do?" He kissed my hand, then said, "Seems like the Hoagie Shoppe's in trouble."

"Mom told you that?"

"Yeah. I think she was hinting at asking for a loan."

Maybe that's why God brought Bob into my life.

Later that week, Mom asked me to request fifteen hundred dollars. Bob agreed without hesitation.

***

Deb called asking if she could move back in. My roommate had moved in with her boyfriend, so the timing felt ordained. After that blowup with Mom, I assumed Deb would pay her share. Deb had a steady job and a lift in her voice I hadn't heard in a while—she was in love with Randy, one of Jim's friends from the dojo. For the first time in a long time, she sounded genuinely happy.

She moved into the attic bedroom with the slanted ceiling and the small round window. The place felt fuller with her there, less hollow. But she didn't like Bob. She sensed something off—something I kept pushing aside. "He's controlling," she said. She wasn't wrong, but I defended him anyway. He helped me. He'd helped Mom. Didn't that mean something?

Bob didn't like Deb living with me. He said she stuck her nose where it didn't belong. The tension grew like static in the room—charge gathering, waiting for a spark.

One afternoon, it finally happened.

Bob was in my face, eyes bulging behind his smudged glasses, veins standing like ropes on his forehead. "You're kicking her out," he said through clenched teeth. "Tonight."

"She don't have nowhere to go," I said, inching away.

"That ain't my problem. She only cares about herself."

"That ain't for you to decide."

He backed me against the kitchen table. I nearly lost my footing.

"Oh, is that so?" He said, spit flying as he spoke. Some of his spit landed on my cheek, hot and sour. "Who bailed you out when you couldn't pay your bills?!"

I tried to stand taller, even though my legs trembled. "You need to back up and get out of my face."

Deb must've heard the commotion because she came down from the attic, her nostrils flared like a warning. "Hey, what's going on?"

Bob snapped his head toward her. "Mind your own business."

"No," Deb said, jaw set. "I live here too."

Through gritting teeth, he said, "I don't care if you live here. You need to get…back…upstairs."

"Peg, are you going to let him treat me like this?"

He turned back to me, rage radiating from every muscle. "You're kicking her out. Tonight."

"No, I'm not doing that."

"You owe me. I saved you when you were sinking."

I tried to puff myself up. "Back. Up."

He stayed planted. I tried to get out from behind him, but he firmed his stance, a crazed look in his eyes. "Let's go!" He grabbed my wrist. "We're leaving."

"No, I'm not going anywhere with you when you're like this."

He yanked me. I tore free and dropped into a chair. "I ain't going."

He leaned over me, sweat soaking his thinning hair. "Go to the car, now."

Deb grabbed the wall phone.

"You better put down that phone!"

"What are you going to do…hit me?" Deb said.

"Don't make me!" He ripped the phone from her hand and slammed it onto the mount. "You better get on up the stairs if you know what's good for you."

Deb's lips tightened. She backed up and stood at the base of the attic stairs. She was scared, but she was ready to defend her baby sister.

Bob grabbed my arm and dragged me toward the stairs. I planted my feet, but he overpowered me. He pointed down. "Go to the car."

"Why are you acting this way?"

Bob's face darkened with rage. "I…said…go…to…the…car!"

"You're scaring me."

"Go now or I'll pick you up and drag you there myself."

"Well, I guess you're going to have to, 'cause I ain't going."

He let out a guttural growl, grabbed me around the thighs, and hoisted me over his shoulder in one swift, horrifying motion. I saw the room tilt upside down—the world narrowing to the frantic thud of his footsteps and Deb running for the phone.

"Let me go! Let me go!" I tried squirming free, but he tightened his grip. I tried asking him calmly. He ignored my pleas. I didn't pound on his back or kick like they do in the movies. I didn't want to fuel his anger. He wasn't a big man— five foot eight, wiry—but in that moment he carried me with the strength of Goliath.

When we reached the bottom of the stairs, I sagged willingly, hoping to calm him. He shoved me into his souped-up Chevelle with no seatbelts, and sped onto the freeway, gripping the steering wheel like he wanted to snap it in half.

The speedometer climbed. 80…85…90…100…110

My body didn't react. My mouth didn't open. I didn't scream.

"I want to break up," I said involuntarily.

He floored it. Up to one-twenty.

"If I can't have you, nobody will." He took his eyes off the road. He pointed. "See that pole? I'll crash into it right now and kill us both."

The needle hit 140. He took and exit and headed right for a telephone pole.

Something in me went blank. Thoughts evaporated. My body became a mannequin propped in place. At the last possible second, he straightened the car, pulled into a parking lot, and collapsed over the wheel, sobbing.

"I'm sorry. Please forgive me. I'd never hurt you. I love you. Please don't leave me. I can't live without you." He grabbed my hand and held it to his whiskery, tear-soaked cheek.

I forgave him because I needed to get home alive.

"Don't ever scare me like that again," I said.

He wiped his tears with the back of his hand. "I won't. I promise."

Something inside me shifted that night. I didn't fully admit it yet, but a hairline crack formed between us.

Jim's pickup was in the driveway when we got home. He'd made record time. Bob wasn't a fighter—he was a talker. Jim wasn't a fighter either, but with his training, he could kill a man with his bare hands. Jim and Bob were about the same height, but Jim was solid and confident, his knuckles thick and scarred, his stare unflinching.

Bob kissed my hand. "Let me do the talking."

I assumed Jim would insist I go back to Paledon. Walking up the stairs, my pulse skidded. Bob hesitated beside me.

"Hiya Jim," I said.

Jim's face was stone. "Deb called. Said there was some trouble."

Bob squeezed my hand. "Nah, just a little spat. No reason you needed to come." He chuckled and pulled me against him. "We worked it out. Didn't we, Peggy?" Sweat dotted his forehead. His glasses hung on the edge of his nose.

Jim tilted his head. "Deb said things got outta hand."

Bob glanced at Deb, still standing near the stairs. "Nah. Just a lover's quarrel."

Jim looked at me. "Peg, you alright?"

"I'm fine."

"You sure?"

I hugged him goodbye. The child in me wanted to whisper, *please take me home.* The adult in me clung to independence. And obligation. Bob helped me. He'd helped Mom. I believed I owed him and that God had sent him.

Bob became more romantic than ever—flowers, compliments, breakfast in bed, songs in the kitchen. It all slid off me like water off a tin roof. I watched myself play the role of a girlfriend without feeling the part.

Bob came home one day with an engagement ring. Since it wasn't in a ring case and looked like an antique, I figured he got it in a drug deal. Desperate addicts would sometimes barter with him. He once brought home a complete stereo system. He got down on one knee. Reflexively I said yes.

When I thought about it afterward, I figured it was predestined. I abandoned the thought of leaving him, telling myself the freeway incident was a one-time deal. Plus, Bob had asked for Mom's permission. She granted it. Mom's approval made it God's will. We had a little ceremony at a tavern hall. Bob had the barber cut off his ponytail, and he rented a tux. I wore a second-hand dress. I smiled and recited the vows, my body numb, my mind blank. Bob grinned so wide his crooked nose almost touched his chin. His eyes twinkled and fixed onto mine. I'd never seen him so happy. Forcing the doubts out of my mind, I smiled with him and laughed with our guests. That night, Bob said he wanted to try for a baby right away. Although I was ambivalent, I agreed, figuring it too was predestined.

***

After three months of trying, Bob became impatient and made an appointment at a fertility clinic. They ran tests. His sperm was fine. I was the infertile one. Scar tissue blocking my tubes from pelvic inflammatory disease. My only hope was surgery. Even then, I'd still only have a 30% chance. I had so many contradictory feelings. When I thought of the future, I saw myself getting married and having kids. Mom said we needed to find mates and produce offspring. Part of me was relieved I couldn't have kids with Bob, but another part felt like my womanhood had been stripped. The only future I saw for myself, short as it may have been, dissolved with that one word: infertile.

At Bob's insistence, I quit my job at Wendy's and sold the Impala. He said I didn't need to work. And I didn't need a car because I could use the Chevelle. I gave up my apartment, and we rented a house together. I was stuck at home most of the time because Bob was at his friend's garage working on an old chopper he was restoring. Most days, he'd sleep until ten, have breakfast, smoke a joint, then head over to his friend's. I wouldn't see him until eight or nine p.m. I was bored out of my mind. I spent my days sunbathing, gardening, reading, cooking, and cleaning. All things I enjoyed but not every day. I was trapped, though I hadn't yet admitted that to myself.

A few weeks into the marriage, Mom called asking for another loan. I was nervous to ask Bob, but to my surprise, he agreed. That night, we drove to Paledon to give her the money. We entered a familiar scene: Mom sitting in the corner booth sipping coffee, smoking, and making entries in the ledger. There were just a few customers. Mom smiled when she saw us. We slid in the booth.

"Peg, let your mom and Bob talk." (She often referred to herself in the third person). "Get Bob some coffee. Then, go make youse some dinner."

I stood, feeling excluded and small. I poured their coffee then went to the kitchen to make taco salads. Maybe Mom will scare him off with The Kingdom stuff. Then I'd be off the hook. But the thought of moving back to Paledon snapped me out of that daydream. I switched off the overhead fan so I could hear what they were saying. Though, it was still hard to hear. I tried to put together the bits and pieces of what I could hear. They'd settled on something, but I didn't know what. As I approached with the salads, they shook hands and smiled. Bob had agreed to buy Mom's station wagon for $5,000. She gave us the car that day, promising to hand over the title once she'd paid off the bank loan.

Driving back on Highway 44—a bleak two-lane highway between Paledon and Des Moines—Bob Segar's "Turn the Page" played on the radio. Driving the station wagon, I passed one telephone pole after another, I felt the gravity of what had occurred. Mom and Bob had entered a business transaction. I was happy the money was helping keep The Shoppe afloat, but what did it mean for me? Maybe God was testing him, and he passed. I still wondered if he was my soul mate. I didn't want him to be my soul mate, but I also didn't want to go against the Lord's will.

And there was another conundrum. Mom liked him. She'd smile and throw her head back, laughing at his jokes. She didn't warn me against him like Jim had. She didn't ask where he got his cash. I figured she'd know if he was a bad guy from reading his mind. But I also knew if I'd told her what happened on the freeway, she would've made me move back to Paledon. A domestic violence survivor herself, she had no compassion for abusive men. Mom would've welcomed me home with open arms. But I'd be forced to admit I'd failed at living on my own. I was trapped between two worlds I couldn't escape. It felt like I was being swept down a fast-moving river with no branch to grab. I didn't know if Mom consciously looked the other way to get money for The Shoppe, or if she too thought the marriage was predestined. My mind was in tangles.

Clawing that woman's fingers from Mom's throat that day had left a lasting impression. Although Mom hadn't chastised me, I still harbored the question:

Did I change the course of destiny? I'd vowed to never again interfere with the Lord's will. But even greater than my fear of interfering with the Lord's will was my fear of moving back to Paledon. Twelve-hour days in The Shoppe for no pay and reverting to the only pastime the town knew: the doleful bar scene. Late nights of Mom interrogations, preaching at us, breaking us down. She'd stopped seeking new converts but still expected us to be perfect. There were many good reasons to stay in Des Moines and only one good reason to return to Paledon. But that reason was colossal. The memory of what Bob did on the freeway that day: His raging face, the speedometer, those words: "I'll kills us both right here."

***

Bob and I fell into a routine. Every evening, I'd drop off a hot plate of food for him, but I wouldn't stay. He'd be knee-deep in grease. Truth be told, I didn't mind that he was gone. But I was lonely. Bob gave me money whenever I asked, but it never sat well. I felt okay about shopping for things for us with his money, but I didn't like spending it on myself. I wanted to buy my own things without having to account to him. Not that he would've audited my spending. He never even hinted at it. If anything, he went the other way. He'd give me five or six twenty-dollar bills, and I'd always hand back a couple. He'd refuse. "Buy yourself something," he'd say. I never did. I didn't want to feel any more obligated than I already did. Plus, spending drug money felt criminal. I'd lost touch with my work pals. Bob and I only hung out with his friends. I wanted to earn my own money, and I needed to be around people.

Driving down Euclid Avenue one day, I noticed a HELP WANTED sign on the marquee of the Hawaiian Inn. They hired me on the spot. Bob said we didn't need the money. I said I was going stir-crazy. After some cajoling, he agreed I could work two nights a week. I would've taken the job no matter what he thought. He knew that.

We sat on the couch, a plate full of weed and Zig-Zag papers in his lap. He sealed a joint, then lit it.

"You better not be letting guys look at you."

I whipped my head. "What? I can't control if guys look at me… that's silly."

He offered me the joint. "Well…you know what I mean. Just don't smile at them."

"So, you're saying I can't smile?" I scooted back from him. "At the customers?

The ones who'll tip me?"

He lectured me about how guys want just one thing. I assured him I could handle myself. But he kept pressing. I turned away.

"Come on, baby." He leaned into me. "I didn't mean anything by it." He guided my chin toward his lips and kissed me. I kept my lips taut.

I could never stay angry with Bob for long. He'd tickle me, act silly, buy me chocolates and flowers, whatever it took to get back in my graces. However, I should say that I rarely got angry with him. Life wasn't all bad. We got along quite well most of the time. We'd sing to the radio, dine out, shoot pool, make breakfast together, and go for motorcycle rides. I didn't love being with him, but I also didn't hate it. Still, I couldn't forget the freeway. My view of him changed that day. He was no longer the awkward, romantic guy head-over-heels for me. I became acutely aware of things I'd minimized: his secrecy about his past, the drug dealing, his pot-smoking, his outbursts at the sight of an Asian person. I'd married a shattered, controlling 'Nam vet who sold drugs for a living. And I allowed myself to be victimized by a man, something Mom always warned against.

Even though we had two cars, Bob insisted on driving me to work. I'd call to let him know what time I was getting off. He'd get there early and wait in the car.

One slow night my manager let some of us off early. We all went into the bar to have a drink. Six or seven of us sat laughing as we sipped our drinks and puffed our cigarettes. I hadn't called Bob to tell him I'd gotten off early because I'd planned to call him at the usual time to give myself an hour to hang out with my coworkers. But I lost track of time.

I was starting my second drink when Bob walked in. He took short, rapid steps, his chin jutted. He locked eyes with mine. I smiled, then swallowed hard. I hadn't done anything wrong, but guilt flushed me. Bob didn't return the smile. He had rage in his eyes. My insides contorted, but I tried to act unflappable.

"Hey everyone. This is my husband, Bob."

Everyone greeted him cheerfully. He ignored them.

In the deepest voice I'd ever heard him utter, he said, "Let's go. Now."

"Okay, but I just got a drink. Have a drink with us."

He let out a curt sigh. "I'm going to the car, and I'll wait for five minutes. If you're not out by then, I'm leaving." He stormed out.

Blood rushed to my cheeks. I apologized to everyone, fumbled to grab my purse, then dropped it. I scooped it up and followed Bob, running behind him as if my life depended on it. I'd love to say I considered standing up to him, but my mind blanked. When we got to the car, he didn't look at me. His body was tense, his lips tight.

His hand trembled when he tried to put the key in the ignition. Then he dropped the keys on the floor. "Goddammit!"

I picked them up and handed them to him. "They let some of us off early 'cause it was slow. I should've called. Sorry."

"I saw you flirting with those guys."

I swiveled toward him. "What? No, I wasn't flirting. They're guys I work with. They have girlfriends and wives. I ain't no cheater."

He clenched his jaw, looked ahead, and flew out of the parking lot. "If I catch you flirting again, you'll never go back to that job again. You hear me?"

I raised my voice. "I wasn't flirting!"

He jerked the steering wheel and whipped into a mini-mall parking lot. Before it even registered what was happening, he smacked me across the face so hard everything went white. Then he wagged his finger with gritted teeth, and said, "Don't you ever raise your voice at me." He tore out of the parking lot. I held my burning cheek, turned, and pressed my forehead against the window. I married a wife beater.

After that night, I confronted my unhappiness. Predestined or not, I wanted out. But I had nowhere to go—except Paledon. I wasn't ready to go back.

***

A few weeks later, Deb and Randy got married. They chose Deb's birthday for their ceremony, proof of how certain she was. Mom's yard was warm and bright that day. Deb wore a white dress with lace flutter sleeves and a crown of baby's breath. I was there, but I wasn't present. My mind was in a thick fog.

The night before, Bob had cornered me against the wall, wide-eyed and trembling with rage. He'd accused me of flirting with our waiter at lunch that day.

I kept my eyes locked to his trying not to show my fear. "You can't keep me here," I said. "I'm going to my sister's wedding."

When I grabbed my purse, he yanked the strap, jerking me backward. Then he gripped my jaw, squeezing until my eyes watered. "You're not going anywhere," he said, spit flecking my face.

I tore away from him. He planted himself in front of the door.

"Please move," I said, my voice trembling but determined.

"You're not going to that wedding."

I stepped right up to him, nose to nose, and spoke through clenched teeth. "Let. Me. Go."

He clutched fistfuls of my shirt then hurled me across the room. I tried to catch myself but landed on my tailbone onto the arm of a chair, pain exploding up my spine. Something feral rose inside me. I scrambled to my feet, shoved him hard enough to make him stumble, grabbed my bag, and bolted.

He chased me barefoot into the yard. "Get back here!"

I didn't look back. I fumbled the keys from my purse into the ignition.

I drove to Paledon, shaking so violently I had to grip the wheel with both hands. The hour-long drive gave me space to think, to breathe, to decide. I thought about what I'd been through that year. Cheated on, almost raped and then actually raped and robbed, married an abusive drug dealer. Des Moines had put me through a meat grinder. I was tired of pretending I could survive it all alone. Like an Amish teen returning after Rumspringa, I knew the truth: I had to move back to Paledon.

When I pulled up to Mom's lake house, the windows glowed with warm light. Laughter floated into the yard. I forced a smile onto my face before walking in— Deb deserved joy. I didn't want to be the shadow across her day.

The brick lake house that Mom had rented after Jim, Deb, and I moved out was surrounded by soaring trees. I ambled up the stairs, my overnight bag slung over my shoulder, my stomach twisted. Inside, Mom's guests filled the room— Jack (her husband), Jim and Bev, Randy and Deb. Believing Jack was her soul mate, she'd tracked him down with a couple of phone calls. Within a few weeks, he left Pennsylvania to be with her. Their relationship was rocky. They'd already broken up once since reuniting. But Mom was determined to make their relationship work. He'd gone back to Pennsylvania after a fight. Mom followed him. After winning him back, they came to Paledon just days before my arrival and planned to marry.

Mom's eyes lit when she saw me. She hugged me, pulling back to scan my face like she was reading scripture. I fought the urge to look away.

She pulled in her chin. "What's wrong? And where's Bob?"

I shook my head and swallowed, "Uh, he had some other stuff to do."

She stepped back and crossed her arms. "What's more important than coming to his sister-in-law's wedding?"

I put my hands in my jeans pockets and shuffled my feet. "He doesn't like weddings."

"What's wrong with you?"

I said I was zonked, then went to the kitchen to grab a chair. Sitting on the hard chair, pain shot through my tailbone like I was sitting on a metal spike. Mom told stories from her months in Pennsylvania. How she'd fought for her man and won him back. Jack just smiled, his arms crossed over his chest.

Halfway through the night, Mom turned to me, "Peg, you're acting funny. You've been quiet all night." She pointed her cigarette at me. "Tell me what's wrong."

I tried to deflect. She wouldn't let me.

Finally, I broke. Tears gushed. The whole truth spilled out: Bob's jealousy, his rage, the slapping, throwing me across the room, the death threat on the freeway. Then it was a barrage of questions: Why hadn't I told her? How long had it been going on? Why didn't I leave?

"You should've told me. Jim would've come and got you."

I looked at the floor. "Yeah, I know, but I was embarrassed."

"Embarrassed of what? You didn't do nothing. He hit you."

"I know. But I let it happen."

"Come over here." She motioned for me to sit at her feet. I obliged, calmly detached.

She snapped open her cigarette case, pulled one out and lit it. "I'm not going to let you go through what I went through." She took my face in her hands. Her eyes welled. "Remember that beating I endured?"

I reluctantly held her gaze. "Yeah, of course I remember."

Mom's face went pale, then hard. "Jim," she said, "call Bob. Tell him Peg's not coming back. And tell him he better stay away from her."

Jim adjusted his cap, got up—a Coke bottle he was using for a spittoon in hand—and phoned him from the kitchen. "Yo, Bob. Jim here. So, Peg ain't coming back. You come near her, I'll kill ya. You got that?" After a short pause, Jim slammed down the phone, spat in the Coke bottle, and walked over to me. "He ain't gonna bother you no more, Peg."

Mom reassured me repeatedly that it wasn't my fault. Men like Bob knew how to con women. Even smart ones. Even strong ones. I wanted to believe her.

Since Bob knew Jim was a black belt, I was confident he took his threat seriously. I knew he wouldn't drive to Paledon to see me. But a couple of days later, he called.

His voice shook. "Baby? Is that you?"

My stomach knotted. He begged me to meet him at Denny's when I went back to get my last paycheck from the Hawaiian Inn. Against my better judgment, weighed down by guilt and habit, I agreed.

Driving to Des Moines, I had the urge to turn around several times but kept driving. I felt guilty for leading him on. When he asked me to promise to love him forever, I promised. When he asked me to have kids with him, I said yes.

Walking into Denny's, my legs wobbly, I instantly regretted agreeing to meet him. Bob sat in the booth wearing a wide smile. His smile did little to offset my apprehension. He wore his usual: baggy jeans, a faded T-shirt, and a backwards cap. I gave him a butt-out hug, then slid into the booth.

I lit a cigarette, my hands sweaty and trembling. "Mom and Jim don't know I'm here."

"Well, you're an adult."

My face went hot. "But I told them you hurt me and that you threatened to crash the car on the freeway. They're pissed as hell." I turned away.

"I've been thinking a lot about what happened." He took my hand. "I love you and I won't ever hurt you again. Please come back, baby."

I slipped my hand back and put it under the table. "Well, I don't think Mom and Jim would let me."

"Baby, come on. Don't be like that. I love you so much… that's why I get jealous."

I butted my cigarette, then folded my arms. "I told you. Mom and Jim ain't gonna let me come back."

He tilted his head until our eyes met. "Let me talk to your mom. She likes me. Once I explain, she'll feel different."

"She don't like you no more. She got hit by guys before and she's pissed about you hitting me."

"How many times I gotta say I'm sorry?"

It was clear he wouldn't take no for an answer. So, I didn't give him one, not directly. I nodded just enough to get out of there safely.

When I returned to Paledon, I confessed to seeing him. Mom was furious, not at me, but at him. She told Jim to arrange a trip to Des Moines to collect my things.

A few days later, I rode in Jim's pickup—me squeezed in the middle, Jim driving, Randy shotgun. As we pulled into the driveway, my stomach churned. My waves were wild from driving with the windows down. I waited in the truck while Jim and Randy went to the door. Bob came out, shuffling his feet. I climbed out of the truck and strode across the yard toward them. I didn't feel unsafe, though my tense body spoke a different language. Jim and Randy stood wide with fire in their eyes. I walked between them, glancing at Bob's feet. It hit me where that phrase came from: *shaking in his boots*. He was literally shaking in his boots. I walked up the steps and inside. Jim and Randy followed behind. The drapes were drawn. As usual, it smelled of weed. Flashbacks came from that night when Bob threw me across the room. Noticing my furniture was gone snapped me out of it. To my consternation, my wicker queen's chair, my tweed couch, my plants, even my bed—gone. I turned from anxious to furious, from guilty to enraged.

"Where's my stuff!?" I yelled.

"Sold it," Bob said. "Figured you didn't want it."

"What do you mean I didn't want it? It's my stuff."

"Your dresser's in the bedroom. Your clothes are in those boxes over there."

Rage shot through me—clean, bright, clarifying.

While Randy and Jim loaded what little remained, Jim took one long step toward Bob until they were nearly touching noses.

"Don't call," Jim said. "Don't come around. You got that?"

Bob nodded, sweat snaking down his face.

Randy gave him one long, contemptuous once-over before turning away.

We carried the boxes out to the truck. Each step felt like peeling away a layer of my old life. Yet I felt lighter with every trip. The house behind me—stale weed, dim rooms, the ghost of my own fear—already seemed like a bad dream I'd accidentally lived. That was the last time I saw him.

On the ride back to Paledon my dresser rattled in the truck bed behind us— what little remained of a life I'd tried so hard to convince myself was normal.

The weight of everything hit me in slow waves—humiliation, grief for the girl I'd tried to be, anger at myself for failing.

When we reached Mom's lake house, she stood waiting in the doorway, arms crossed, jaw set. She didn't say I told you so. She didn't need to. She let me walk past her with my boxes, then called after me softly. "Peg, you're home now."

The tenderness in her voice split something in me. Her words didn't comfort me. I didn't cry, not then. But a small breath escaped, something like surrender, something like survival. I thought of the life I'd been living in Des Moines— working double shifts, dropping into party houses, falling asleep next to a man whose anger could swallow a room whole. I thought of the freeway, the moment when I wasn't sure if my life would continue past the next breath. Predestination. Fate. How I'd been taught about how God guided every step. I wondered if I had choices after all.

CHAPTER SIXTEEN
Back to Paledon, 1981

There was an assumed understanding that I'd return to working in The Shoppe, and that the station wagon Bob bought—technically mine—would go back to Mom. She also saw no reason for me to keep the engagement and wedding rings he'd given me. She slipped the wedding band onto her thumb and wore the diamond on her right hand like she'd always owned it. She was still wearing the promise ring she'd taken from me after Ricky left. Later, when money dried up, she pawned all three.

Working at The Shoppe wasn't the worst life. There was always food, always a roof. But it felt like walking backward into a version of myself I'd worked hard to outgrow. I wanted more independence, not less. More space than a town narrow enough to throw a rock from one end to the other. Living that year in Des Moines afforded me freedoms I hadn't had in Paledon. I'd stopped examining every thought and being paranoid about sinning. Out of sight, out of mind, I guess. I was disengaged from the idea that I was the daughter of the modern-day messiah and that the end was coming. The nightmares about the Lake of Fire had stopped too. I felt unfettered, released from the daily pressure of being perfect. I hadn't forgotten Mom's teachings; I just rarely thought about them. Yes, life was thorny, but it was a price I was willing to pay to avoid damnation hovering over me like a tethered helicopter.

Returning to Paledon buried all that. The fear rose up again, sharp, and familiar. Within days, I repented privately, begging God to forgive me for what I'd done in Des Moines. But it wasn't enough. Shame clung to me like a damp coat. I believed forgiveness wouldn't be complete unless I confessed to Mom.

After Brenda moved out, money had been scarce. I'd shoplifted groceries a couple of times, telling myself it was fine because Mom had stolen toilet paper and saltshakers during desperate times. But other things I'd done that year were harder to justify. In the realm of the sexual "nos-nos," I'd failed completely. I'd French kissed. I'd had oral sex. Not because I'd rebelled, not because the line was blurry, simply because I'd wanted to.

I felt like the prodigal daughter returning with her tail between her legs.

I was still shaken from leaving Bob—barely eating, barely sleeping. Everyone assumed the breakup was the cause, and I didn't correct them. Living in Des Moines, I'd expertly employed cognitive dissonance like a superpower. That superpower had left me. My mind was a secret hell. I needed a way out. My soul was in jeopardy.

One night, Mom was already a couple of rum-and-Diet Cokes in, chain-smoking, eyes bloodshot and fired up. She told us we'd been lax with our souls while she'd been in New York, chasing after Jack to come back to her.

"I know some of youse sinned while I was gone," she said, rubbing the sides of her thighs. "I feel it in my legs." She snapped open her cigarette case and took out her lipstick. "I wanna hear some repentance tonight." As she applied her lipstick, she barely paused to breathe. "Bev, you start."

Bev flushed bright pink and stammered through a confession of having an evil thought. Mom forgave her, then hugged her tightly.

She went around the room, calling on each person. The group was small at that point: Deb and Randy, Jim and Bev, Mom and Jack, and me. A tight circle with no air in it.

My heart banged against my ribs. I picked at my fingernails, avoiding everyone's eyes, scrambling for the courage to speak. Sweat gathered under my arms. My tongue stuck to the roof of my mouth.

"If youse sinned, this is the time to repent," Mom said, her raspy voice reverberating like a warning bell.

A lump rose from my chest to my throat. My chin trembled. "I have some things to confess." My voice cracked. I felt everyone's eyes on me though I stared down at my lap. "I did some bad things in Des Moines." Tears streamed hot down my cheeks. "I stole food from the grocery store, and French kissed." I sucked in a ragged breath. "And I had oral sex." My throat tightened, but I pushed the words through. "I feel so ashamed." I covered my face with both hands.

Mom placed her hand on my forearm. "Peggy, Peggy, don't say no more. Your humility says it all. You don't have nothing to be ashamed of. You're forgiven."

The tension left my body like a plug pulled from a drain.

Mom took a sip of her drink, then turned to the group. She pointed dramatically, the lamp illuminating every scar that lined her forearms from years of restaurant work. "Now *that* was a confession. I don't know what that other business was from all of youse, but what Peg just did—" she held her cigarette between two fingers and took a final drag "—was true repentance. Youse can learn a lot from her."

She rested her drink on the table and said, casually, "Peggy, come here and lay across my lap."

"What? Why?" I wiped my face. "I don't understand."

"Come over here."

Her tone, calm but absolute, ricocheted inside me. I'd heard it too many times in childhood. That tone meant: *Obey, or it will be worse.*

"Mom please. Please don't do this," I whispered.

She pointed at her lap, icy certainty replacing the earlier warmth. "Lay over my lap, right now."

My legs turned to rubber. For a split second, I hoped she'd stop me. Declare it a test of obedience, the way God tested Abraham. But her face was stone. No soft harbor anywhere.

I inched toward her and draped myself over her legs. Blood rushed to my head. My arms dangled. With my nose nearly touching the floor and pressure on my abdomen, the scent of nicotine-soaked carpet mixed with Mom's perfume, forced acid to my throat. She pressed one hand onto my hip, holding me steady. With the other, swatted me several times. With each blow, I was crushed with indignity. I felt naked. When it stopped, I waited for a beat, afraid to rise too early. I pulled myself upright, hunched, face hidden by my hair, then slinked back onto my chair. Mascara dripped onto my acid-washed jeans like black raindrops. I stifled the sobs, but tears kept falling. I'm eighteen years old. How could you do this to me? I screamed it inside my skull, but my lips didn't move. I sat, trembling.

Looking back, Mom spanking me is among the most traumatic experiences of my life. She didn't wound my body. It didn't even hurt that much. But she drove a dagger through my will in front of an audience. She broke me. Again.

Then came the next blow, this one emotional.

"Peggy, I'm making you an elder. It took a lot of strength to repent the way you did. You'll be my handmaiden. You'll sit at my feet. Everyone will respect you as an elder."

I didn't want to be an elder. It meant aligning myself with Mom. Helping her seek confessions, keeping her pleased. It meant being closer to power but farther from myself. Deb had once held that title, until she questioned Mom one too many times. Mom stripped it from her like a crown she never deserved.

My job? To serve Mom. Though it wasn't spoken aloud. I just knew. Make her drinks, squeeze her pimples, crack her back, rub her feet, cut her hair. I told myself it was a small price to stay out of the Lake of Fire.

Elders were excused from chores like doing dishes, but I never took advantage. Privilege in Mom's world was a trapdoor waiting to swing open beneath you.

Jim's elder role was different. When Mom was away, he led the get-togethers. "San called. Said we need to get together. Somebody's backslidden," he'd announce, disappointment in his voice. Jim did the prodding but didn't exclude himself as a person who could be the sinner among us. He didn't preach. He'd get right to the point. "Quicker we figure out who's backslidden, quicker we can go to bed," he'd say. My stomach dropped every time. Even eight hundred miles away, Mom felt as close as the next room.

Nobody liked the gatherings. Anxiety warped each of us differently: I gnawed my nails, Deb's nostrils flared, Randy laughed nervously—" letting the Demon of Mockery in," Mom always said. Jim fiddled with his cap. Bev blushed and avoided eyes. Jack stared at the ceiling like he was waiting for divine instructions.

While it was futile, Jim sometimes questioned Mom. She'd call saying she was having leg or back pain and for us to get together to see who was backslidden. One week, she called several nights in a row. She'd been feeling overly emotional and attributed the experience to someone sinning. She wept, begging Jim to find out who was backslidden so she could get relief. "Are you sure, San?" Jim asked. "Don't seem like nobody's backslidden." Finally, after a week, she called saying she'd forgotten to take her hormone pills for her menopause. Jim said she'd apologized for what she'd put us through. That was the only time I could remember her apologizing for anything.

Mom rented a three-bedroom house for her, Jack, and me. Soon after moving in, she and Jack went back east to finalize his affairs. Before she left, she gave me a warning. She grabbed my chin, peered over her glasses, and said, "Now, Peggy. I don't want you going out with no guys while I'm gone. You're too vulnerable right now."

She wasn't wrong. I'd lost ten pounds. My stomach was a pit. No money, no friends, no extended family, no options. I got my shot to live on my own. I blew it. I agreed to her rule. Besides, dating was the last thing on my mind.

That is, until Rich walked through the door.

He stepped into The Shoppe like something blown in from another world—tall, sun-bronzed, muscles cut like stone. When he got closer, I noticed a white powdery substance snaking down his biceps and sideburns. Dried, salty sweat, I figured. His posture slouched slightly, like he was trying not to draw attention to his height. His hair was wild, his face chiseled—a blonde Tom Selleck. He slid into a booth, knees hitting the underside of the table. He pulled out a crushed pack of Kools from his jeans, extracted one with his lips and lit up.

I ducked into the back; grateful I'd worn my contacts. I dabbed on lipstick, smoothed my flyaways, and checked my reflection. Jim was busy at the grill, so he didn't notice my preening. Steeped in delight and thinking, *this town ain't seen nothin' like this guy before*, I sauntered to his booth and greeted him. An electrical charge shot between us.

"I'll have a twelve-inch ham and cheese grinder, a bowl of chili, fries, and a large RC," he said. His deep voice vibrated through me.

"Want your chili first?" I asked, hoping he'd look up. And he did. Just long enough for me to take in his emerald eyes framed by thick blonde lashes.

"Don't matter, either way."

I found excuses to return to his table. Emptying ashtrays, refilling soda, clearing plates. He devoured his food like he hadn't eaten in days, cramming his mouth with fries and mammoth bites of hoagie, then gulping down two jumbo glasses of RC. He left a fifty-cent tip, but that didn't bother me. I just needed him to come back. And he did. That same night.

He smelled like Old Spice, his hair still damp, combed to the side. Somehow the receding hairline made him even more appealing. Imperfect in a perfect way. He downed cup after cup of coffee, each time using three packets of sugar. I'd come by and scoop up the packets. Through the billow of smoke surrounding him, our eyes would momentarily meet.

Finally, he leaned back and looked at me more directly. "Can I buy you a cup a coffee?"

"Sure, but my mom's the owner," I said. "So… I can drink coffee for free." I turned away to put dishes in the bus tub and to hide my grin.

It was getting late. Only a couple of customers remained. I walked back to the kitchen and Jim shot me a disapproving look.

I put my hands in my smock pockets, looked down, and shuffled my feet. "Don't worry, Jim. I'm not gonna do anything crazy."

"Peg, you know what your mom said."

"I know. It's just coffee."

He shook his head. "You're gonna have to deal with your Mom when she gets back."

I finished my work, poured myself a cup, and slid into the booth across from him. I pulled a pack of Marlboro Lights from my smock and smacked it against my palm. Rich kept his eyes on the table, fiddling with his lighter like it might confess something if he worked it long enough. I didn't usually go for bashful guys, but his shyness drew me in. I don't remember what we talked about during the more than two hours we sat there, only that I did most of the talking.

He came in every night after that and waited for me to get off work. Each night, he opened up a little more, until he was the one doing most of the talking. He told me about his failed marriage. About being asked to resign from the police force after getting caught in a squad car smoking weed with locals.

"Stupid. That's what I was. Stupid," he said.

He blamed himself for the divorce and swore he'd get it right next time. His honesty impressed me. From our talks, I learned he had two boys he desperately missed. He'd grown up the son of a farmer in rural northern Iowa, lived in foster care in Germany, then came to the U.S. at five years old. I thought it was destiny that we'd met. We'd both survived hard lives, both fresh out of bad marriages, both full of regret. Me returning to The Shoppe and him working construction outside Paledon didn't feel accidental.

My age didn't bother him. He said I was mature. And at twenty-six, he didn't seem too old. After all, Bob was thirty.

When the weekend came, he went home to Pocahontas. Four hours north. I wanted to follow Mom's rule, but I also wanted to see him again.

Noon couldn't come soon enough on Monday. Rich wouldn't be able to do much more than say hi over his thirty-minute lunch, but it didn't matter. I needed to see him.

That night, he showed up at his usual time for supper. I tried stifling my smile when he walked in but I'm sure he caught on to my delight. He slurped from his mug, beads of coffee clinging to his mustache, then asked. "Uhhh, wanna grab a six pack and drive around in my car?"

"Well, I don't know about that. Pretty sure it's illegal to drink and drive. How 'bout we go next door and shoot a couple games of pool?"

He agreed.

I dashed back to the kitchen.

"Peg, I know what you're gonna ask," Jim said.

"It's just a game of pool." I pressed my hands together in prayer. "Please, Jim."

He wiped his brow with his forearm and sighed. "You said just coffee the other night. Now it's just pool." He flipped a burger. "I ain't responsible if something happens between youse."

"I wouldn't want you to be." I giggled. "Thank you. Thank you."

After finishing my duties, I went to the bathroom, undid my bun, and touched up my makeup. I pushed Mom's parting rule out of my mind.

Walking beside him down the street, I realized just how tall he was. I could feel his eyes on me when I wasn't looking. When I glanced his way, he'd quickly look off. Like we were playing a private game of gotcha.

Everyone turned as we entered the bar. Smoke curled lazily through the air, and Fuzzy, a short, balding man with frizzy ashen hair, stood behind the bar washing glasses.

"Hi, Fuzzy," I said, trying to impress Rich that I knew the owner.

I scanned the smoke-stained ceiling and torn-up-booths, to the pool tables in the back. "Shoot! The best table's taken."

As we walked to the far table, the guys playing snapped their heads toward us. Being seen with a stranger would undoubtedly fuel the rumor mill, but I didn't care. Let 'em talk.

"How 'bout some quarters for the jukebox?" I suggested.

Rich straightened his shoulders and crammed his hand into his tight jeans pocket. He handed me the quarters, his fingers brushing my palm. I masked my delight with a polite smile.

He lit my cigarette and told me I looked pretty, lowering his voice when our faces were close. I watched my drinking. He did the same. I needed my head clear.

I had to tell him about The Kingdom. Mom said the next guy I date had to get saved. I wanted to get it over with.

After a few games, I suggested we go to my house.

Outside, he opened the door to his metallic green VW Beetle. I pegged him for a pickup guy. He said with all the driving he did, he needed something good on gas.

"VWs love the cold. That's the way they build the engine." He turned the key. "Starts every time."

I smiled like I'd learned something. Inside, reality tightened its grip. He might run for the hills once I told him about The Kingdom. On the drive, I rehearsed ways to explain it: My mom is Jesus Christ. My family is chosen. The world is ending any day now. Hearing it in my own head sounded insane.

Inside my house, I snapped on the lamp. We sat on the couch, suspended in an awkward silence. I chewed the inside of my lip. He spoke first.

"Whatcha thinking?"

I looked away. "I hate when people ask that."

"Why?"

"Because. It makes me nervous. What if it's something I want to keep to my-self?"

"Okaaaaay, now I'm really curious."

"Well, if you must know. I was thinking about something I need to tell you."

He cocked his head. "What?"

"Uhhhh, my family is kind of different."

He leaned in, locking his eyes on mine. "Different?"

"Okay, let me see if I can explain."

I told him about Mom's calling, the end of the world, the mates we were meant to find. "If you wanna be with me, you'll have to get saved." I exhaled. "What do you think?"

"About what?"

"What I just said."

His lips curled and he broke eye contact. "Sorry. Wasn't listening. I's just thinking about how pretty your blue eyes are."

I tucked a wave behind my ear and smiled. "Oh, thanks, well…but what about what I just told you?"

"Can you tell me again?"

"Really? Okay. If you want to date me, you gotta be born again. You gotta accept Jesus as your personal savior."

"That ain't no big deal."

"Really?"

"Yeah, it's fine. I'll do it."

My body fizzed like champagne. "You like my eyes, huh?"

"Yeah. They're so blue."

"Do you want to kiss me?"

Without hesitation, he leaned in. His mustache tickled my upper lip. I pulled back and giggled. He tried again.

We kissed. I floated. I'd found my soul mate.

Rich came to see me every night that week. After work, we shot pool at the taverns or hung out in his fleabag hotel room. One night, we made love for the first time.

With my cheek pressed to his chest, I thought about the second thing I needed to tell him: that I was infertile. It felt like a flaw I owed him. Lying beside him on the creaky wrought-iron twin bed, worry pressed down on me. Will he think I'm a freak? Will this be the last time I see him? I sat up, pulled the sheet under my arms, and said, "Rich, I have something to tell you." My voice trembled. "I can't have babies."

"That don't matter. Got two kids already."

I sank into him, wrapping my arm around his chest. He had to be my soul-mate. Almost everything was cleared. Except telling Mom I'd broken her rule. I convinced myself Rich was the kind of man she'd respect. Hardworking, polite, handsome. And best of all, willing to get saved.

✳✳✳

Mom and Jack came straight to The Shoppe the night they returned. They perched at the counter holding hands, sipping coffee. Jack wore Bermuda shorts cinched beneath his bounteous gut. Mom wore a bright tube top under a navy blazer. Her signature look. She glowed, like the sun was touching every part of her. Jack, not a single piece of hair on his head from the ears up, was beaming too, periodically kissing the back of Mom's hand.

"Peg, grab some more coffee for us, will ya?"

"Cute hair, Mom," I said, refilling her cup.

She feathered the wisps at her neck. "You like it?"

I said I loved it, asked about their trip, then turned away.

"Jim said you got a new boyfriend already. I knew you couldn't wait, Peg."

I stared at the floor. "Sorry, Mom. I know you told me to wait. But he came in a couple of days after you left. I got a good feeling about him."

She pursed her lips. "You can't help yourself, can ya?" She turned to Jack. "Always been boy crazy, this one."

Jack grinned. "Like mother, like daughter."

Mom cackled.

"We better meet this guy," Jack said, dragging on his Camel.

"Oh, Peg knows he'll have to go through me."

I went to the back room, heaped a stainless-steel bowl with onions, then carried them to the kitchen to peel. Mom joined me at the sink.

"Look at me."

I turned.

"Remember, if he wants to be with you, he's gotta get saved."

"I know, Mom. I already told him."

"You did?" She blew smoke toward the ceiling. "How'd he take it?"

I told her he'd agreed.

She grabbed a dish cloth and wiped the front of the sandwich bar. "Alright then. Invite him over for supper Sunday?"

I continued peeling, starting to tear up from the onions. "But he goes home on the weekends."

"From what Jim said, he's crazy about you. He'll stay. You'll see."

She was right. He agreed to come.

We'd entertained potential converts many times, so I knew the script. We'd eat a feast prepared by the women. Afterward, Mom would retreat to the room with a rum and Diet Coke while the rest of us cleaned. We'd insist she go sit. She'd resist, then agree. Rich would join her. Guests never cleaned up. When the kitchen was done, we'd gather in the room for dessert and Mom's sermon.

She always began the same way: the government was corrupt, churches kept people in bondage. She railed against organized religion, especially the Catholic church, for turning sex, drinking, and smoking into sins while hoarding tithe money for greed. She warned that families could become enemies through religion and materialism, and that true servants of God couldn't be attached to anyone or anything. She'd read scripture about the apostles dropping everything to follow Jesus. About Jesus dying so we could have everlasting life. Then she'd tout her gifts: reading minds, casting out demons, raising the dead.

Her sermons always, I mean *always*, hooked them. She was charismatic and relatable. She smoked and drank, which people didn't expect from a Pentecostal preacher. "They think they're better," she'd say of nonsmokers. After joining Mom's group, everyone smoked. She knew who to target—people who didn't quite belong anywhere. Rich fit the profile perfectly: divorced, regretful, unattached, unsure of himself.

I wanted time with Rich before the indoctrination began, though I didn't think of it that way back then. I knew Mom would expect him to serve the Lord first. That meant I'd never have him to myself. That was the hard truth.

I worried Mom would scare him off. Because she was happy with Jack, I hoped that it might soften her. Maybe she wouldn't get drunk and sob. Maybe she wouldn't flail on the floor in that Linda Blair exorcist voice. Maybe she wouldn't pick him apart like he was a house searched room by room for what shouldn't be there.

Deb, Randy, Bev, and Jim arrived as they did every Sunday. At dinner, Mom fired questions at Rich. What were his intentions? Was he willing to move here? Did he love me? Was he ready to give up his life for the Lord? He handled her interrogation calmly.

"Don't worry, Ma'am. I have the best intentions. And yes, I'm ready to get saved. Something I've been needing to do, anyway."

I squeezed his hand.

"Rich," Mom said, motioning. "Let's take our coffee to the room."

He winked at me as if to say, *I think she likes me* and followed her while the rest of us cleaned up.

When the dishes were done, I joined them and sat on the floor against the wall. Mom motioned. "Rich, go on over and sit by Peggy." He settled beside me, shoulder to shoulder, our fingers laced.

My wish came true. Mom stayed sober. She didn't mention demons or repentance. She spoke only of grace—Jesus turning water to wine, rescued Mary Magdalene, forgiving sinners. She told the story of becoming the chosen one. Rich listened, with intent.

She preached until three a.m. I kept thinking about his six-thirty shift. I studied his face, searching for doubt, but he stayed fixed, eyes on Mom. I worried he was only being polite.

Finally:

Mom checked her watch. "What time do you work tomorrow?"

"Six-thirty, but no worries. Gone on less sleep."

"You want to come back tomorrow night?"

All eyes turned to him. He smiled and said yes. Relief gave way to fear. He wasn't running. He was stepping deeper in. Mom had once told me, "God will use you as a vessel to bring in a mate." I didn't want to be a vessel. I wanted to be Rich's girlfriend.

He stayed late the next night. And the next. Mom was energized. A new convert. Fresh fire. She could go all night and drink all night too. Rich said he'd never felt so alive. The more alive he felt, the farther away he became.

We stopped sitting together at The Shoppe. We stopped talking and flirting. One night Mom invited him to sit with her. Then it became routine: smoking, coffee, long confessions. He told her about his transgressions. She promised forgiveness, a place in heaven. I'd take breaks and sit with them here and there, but it didn't matter. His attention had shifted from me to her.

Mom became central to our relationship. I pushed down my anger, telling myself not to interfere with the Lord's will. Not to be selfish. Still, I worried she'd run him off the way she had Ricky.

Before the next weekend came, Rich said he was ready to get saved. The whole thing felt eerily similar. When Ricky packed his things into a black garbage bag at the dairy farm that day, he'd decided, even loving me, that it wasn't worth it. I didn't blame him. Mom had taken control of his soul.

The night Rich got saved, we gathered in the room. Randy, Deb, Jim, Bev, and Jack were there, but they were a blur. I saw only Rich and Mom. He and I sat on the floor. His body trembled. I held his moist hand.

Please no demons, I prayed. He'll bolt if she starts casting out demons.

Mom motioned for him to kneel at her feet. He looked impossibly large. Long legs folded, shoulders broad as a doorway. Tears spilling as he whispered for forgiveness. She had us kneel beside him, hands laid on his body. I knew it had to happen for us to be together, but with every second, he slipped farther away.

With one hand raised and the other pressed to his forehead, Mom prayed, "Lord Jesus, we ask you to allow this vessel to receive your Holy Ghost and speak in his own tongue. Lord, only you will know what's on his heart."

We bowed our heads and babbled.

"Receive!" Mom commanded. "Receive!" She shook his head in time with her words.

After a few minutes, softly, Rich began to speak in his own language.

Mom smiled. "Hallelujah. We praise you, Lord."

The rest of us echoed her. I exhaled. It was official. Rich was saved.

***

After that night, my relationship with Rich went through a crash course. Our courtship ended almost as soon as it began. When we were together, it was always at the house with the rest of the family. Once the bridge construction job outside Paledon ended, he began staying only on weekends. I can't remember whether Rich first mentioned moving to Paledon or if Mom suggested it, but suddenly we were talking about living together. The plan was for him to give up his mobile home in Pocahontas and rent the apartment above The Shoppe. He'd see his kids when he could.

Moving in together was fast by anyone's standards, but I told myself it was the Lord's will. It was practical, too. Rent was only $110 a month, utilities included. Far better than the hotel in which he'd been staying. I'd sleep at Mom's during the week and with Rich on weekends. I ate up time alone with him.

The apartment was tiny. Three furnished rooms tucked beneath slanted ceilings that forced Rich to duck in places. From the bedroom window, the small-town rhythm of Main Street on display down below. The living room held a sixties-era puke-green tweed davenport. The kitchen had a speckled Formica table with chrome legs, two wobbly lemon-yellow chairs, a mini gas stove, and a toy-sized refrigerator.

Despite living together, our relationship stalled. I clung to the hope that Rich would reemerge as the vulnerable, affable man who'd pursued me before Mom returned. But with each passing day, it became clearer I'd never see that version of him again. I didn't know how he felt about The Kingdom, about Mom, about the way his life had shifted. He never brought it up. Neither did I. I was afraid Mom would read my mind. I'm sure he feared the same.

We talked about work. Mostly I talked. I told him stories about customers and kitchen mishaps, like dropping an entire pizza on the floor. He'd nod, offer an occasional "uh-huh," then retreat into himself.

Then, something shifted our relationship in an unexpected way. Standing at the bureau one morning clasping my bra, I noticed my breasts were tender. I rushed to the calendar hanging on the fridge. I was a twenty-eight-day girl without

186

exception, and I was ten days late. The doctor had said I was infertile, so I didn't take the pill. And nobody used condoms back then. It was before AIDS. Part of me hoped I was pregnant, proof the doctor had been wrong. Another part of me prayed I wasn't. Our relationship wasn't ready for that yet.

All week, I wrestled with how to tell Rich. It felt too soon, but what if this was my only chance to have a baby? I trusted that Mom wouldn't force me to marry. Mammy and Pappy had forced her when she got pregnant. She'd sworn she'd never do the same to Deb and me.

One Saturday night, Rich and I brought hoagies upstairs from The Shoppe. My stomach was knotted tight. We sat at the kitchen table. I picked at my hoagie, twirling a loose lock of hair near my ear. He ate hunched over, elbows on the table.

"You're quiet," he said, mouth full.

"Actually, I have something to tell you." I cleared my throat. "Remember I told you the doctor said I can't get pregnant?"

Rich set his hoagie down and straightened. "Yeeeaaahhh."

"Well, I'm late on my period."

"How late?"

"Ten days."

He picked up his sandwich, took a bite, and spoke through it. "That ain't that late."

"My body feels weird," I said.

"Then go get a test."

A few days later, I drove to the doctor's office, pummeled by nerves. By then, I'd decided that if I was pregnant, I'd be happy, but I wouldn't get married. Three months wasn't long enough to make that decision. Still, Mom's teachings about predestination rattled in my head. Was this pregnancy a sign that I was supposed to get married? Still, I figured God would understand if we waited. Plus, Mom always said never to rely on a man. I was sure she'd back me about waiting.

After the doctor confirmed I was pregnant, I sat in my car rehearsing what I'd say. Then I climbed the creaky back stairs with resolve in my step. Mom and Rich sat waiting in a booth.

I slid into the booth, knees weak. "So, the rabbit died. But I ain't getting married just because I'm pregnant."

Mom raised her chin. "What? Not getting married?"

My voice quivered. "I wanna get married because I'm in love. No other reason."

She crossed her arms across her full bosom. "No daughter of mine is running around here pregnant out of wedlock when there's a perfectly decent man right here. Oh, you're getting married. Right Rich?"

Rich nodded, a lit cigarette dangling from his lips as he retied his boots. "It's the right thing to do."

I was stunned. I'd expected Mom's support, and Rich's hesitation. He'd just got divorced. We'd agreed to live together for at least a year. We'd only lived together for a month.

I was outnumbered. Overpowered. I boxed up my wants and padlocked them shut. I took what Mom said as a mandate and accepted that it was the Lord's will.

I believed Rich was my soulmate, yet I barely knew him. In part because he was reserved and undemonstrative. But also, because The Kingdom life drove a wedge between us. We couldn't speak openly. We were too afraid of being put in the hot seat for doubting. We didn't steer our relationship. Mom did. It was like trying to get to know someone while wearing gags.

Once I realized I had no choice, I embraced the wedding. Mom ordered a cake and flowers in lavender and celery green; my selected wedding colors. A secondhand cream-colored dress with brown stitching fit my swelled belly perfectly.

Deb was pregnant too, about a month ahead of me. We shopped garage sales for baby clothes, planned nurseries, and took progress photos. Our shared pregnancies drew us closer.

Rich and I had no friends to invite. Mom invited a few Shoppe regulars. Rich's parents came. He didn't invite his siblings. Because it was his second wedding, he said. A robust Justice of the Peace with a meaty double chin and silver curls officiated.

Everyone waited in the living room while I got ready. Bouquet clasped in my hands, I ambled out from the bedroom and joined Rich. He wore the dressiest outfit he owned: blue polyester pants, a dingy white belt, and a powder-blue button-down. Even with his hair pasted flat and his worn clothes, he was the most handsome groom I'd ever seen. He wore that intoxicating smile and smelled of Old Spice, a scent I grew to love.

The Justice gently guided us into place. My stomach churned. My body felt like dough. If I'd had a voice I trusted, I would've said, *Stop. I'm not ready.* If I'd had a place to go, I would've dropped that bouquet like a hot matchstick and bolted. But I stood beside Rich, holding my body steady. Mom told me to marry Rich, which was the same as God Himself telling me.

"Do you take this man to be your lawfully wedded husband?"

I forced myself to look into Rich's eyes. "I do."

I smiled for the camera, but in the candid shots, my face revealed my true emotions. Sober. Wondering. Would I grow to love him? Would we have more children? Would I work at The Shoppe forever? Would the world end before I became anything more than a wife and a mother?

Then, the next command came. It was the Lord's will that Rich and I move in with Mom and Jack. Privacy was not part of the plan.

***

Unsurprisingly, Mom's relationship with Jack began to unravel. She swung between rebuking and adoring him. One moment he was lazy, doubtful, drinking too much. The next, she was fawning over him. Watching him grill with his cook's hat plastered to his sweaty, bald head was catnip to her. They stole kisses, slow danced to oldies, drank at Fuzzy's after closing. Mom strutted like she'd landed the best man in town.

When she wasn't doting over him, he was just another convert. He didn't work at her pace. He'd begun slipping off to the bar on slow nights. At first, Mom was okay with it, even shooing him away to go play a hand of cards or have a couple of beers. But that sentiment quickly shifted.

Once night after work, she gathered us together because "Jack was backslidden." He'd let in the Demon of Laziness. He'd gone to the bar that afternoon to play cards and had left Mom alone to handle the slow stream of customers. As the evening approached and it got busier, she called the bar. "I'll be right there," he said. She called again. Same thing. By the time he got there, the rush was over. He'd bowed to fleshly desires. And because of his tight lips, he'd also let in the Demon of Stubbornness.

"I have the right to have time to myself," he argued, his arms crossed over his inflated chest. "I get tired. And my feet hurt."

"How do you think Jesus felt hanging on that cross? Nails in his feet and hands. His side cut open. A crown of thorns on his head." She leaned forward and pointed at him with her cigarette. "You don't think *I* get tired? You don't think *I* have pain? I always have pain."

189

Jack rolled his eyes. "I don't have to put up with this shit." He stormed out, went to The Shoppe, took cartons of cigarettes and cash from till, and drove back to New York.

The next day, Mom went to Fuzzy's and got wasted.

The house was dark and eerily quiet when I got home from work that night. I turned on the light. That's when I saw the state of the living room: mud splat on the walls from potted plants, glass everywhere from shattered pictures, lamps broken, furniture flipped. I found Mom upstairs passed out, fully dressed, eyes swollen and smeared with black mascara. I removed her shoes and pulled the covers over her still body.

I spent hours washing walls, picking up shards of glass, cleaning and vacuuming the mess she'd made. She never said a word about it. To this day, I'm not sure she even remembers what she did.

***

Mom spiraled. After closing each night, she drowned her pain in booze, wept, and talked about not wanting to live. I felt helpless. Her suicide talk terrified me.

Three months before I gave birth, she left for Pennsylvania for good. "There's nothing here for me," she said. I wondered why she didn't consider *us* a reason to stay. She took money from The Shoppe, her clothes, and some kitchen wares. "San, are you sure this is a good idea?" Jim asked a few times. She'd always give the same stock answer: "Jim, I know what I'm doing."

Per Mom's order, Jim and Bev moved in with Rich and me. We didn't question it. I'd given up hope for privacy. Sharing rent made sense, but practicality didn't reduce the awkwardness. They'd been unsuccessfully trying to get pregnant for a couple of years, There I was, supposedly infertile, nineteen, and pregnant.

Mom tried to dictate how we should manage the house, but after she left, we figured out our own system. That was our first step toward independence.

The four of us settled into a routine. Bev and I worked at The Shoppe. Rich worked bridge construction out of town. Jim did handyman jobs and cooked at The Shoppe on weekends, funneling money from his handyman work into the business each month. The soaring utility bills during frigid winters kept us on the brink of bankruptcy. It didn't matter what specials we ran or how much advertising we did, the Hoagie Shoppe was going bust.

One night at supper, Jim brought up selling it. "It ain't turned a profit in over

190

a year," he said. None of us objected. It felt futile to keep it going. Jim ran the idea by Mom, and to our surprise, she agreed.

Only one buyer showed interest, so we had to "drop our pants" and were left with an outstanding loan balance that included the station wagon. Mom worked at Perkins back in Pennsylvania and was barely eking by. She took the station wagon, but the odds of her making the payments were slim.

Life was simpler after we offloaded The Shoppe. Bev and I spent our days planning meals, cleaning, and preparing for the baby. She never said it outright, but I knew she was heartbroken about not getting pregnant. She lived through my experience instead. Feeling my belly when the baby kicked, rubbing my feet, helping me lift heavy things. Despite all that time together, we didn't become friends. I suspected it was the forced closeness, her infertility, and the quiet resentment of me being the one who cut her hair.

***

Before Mom left, she told Bev the Lord wanted her to cut her hair. "That hair keeps you proud," she said. "The Lord wants you to sacrifice it for Him. Peg'll do it. She cuts hair good."

I'd been cutting everyone's hair for years, but I hated the idea of chopping off Bev's long, golden hair that cascaded down her back to her thighs.

I'll never forget that day. Bev slumped in a kitchen chair, shoulders tense. At Mom's direction, I ignored her anguish and started. I pinned sections like I'd seen in the salon and spritzed the rest with water.

Sitting at the kitchen table with her thumbnail between her teeth, Mom leaned toward Bev and ran her fingers through her hair. "Take about six inches off."

Tears slid down Bev's cheeks.

"Bev," Mom said, "you're only giving up your hair for the Lord. I had to sacrifice a lot more than that."

I inhaled and snipped across the first row. Her hair fell to the floor. With every pass, my heart sank. I don't want to do this. This ain't right. Afraid Mom would read my thoughts; I rebuked Satan and told myself it was the Lord's will. The thoughts kept coming. I pushed through until six inches were gone.

Mom stood back and put her hand on her chin. "Uh…take some more off."

Bev's tears turned into sobs. "Isn't that enough? You said six inches."

"It's only hair, Bev. It's still too long."

191

I puffed my cheeks and sprayed her hair again. "How much more, Mom?"

She placed her hand higher. I swallowed everything I felt and kept cutting while Bev cried. When I finished, her hair barely brushed her shoulder blades.

"It looks bee-you-tee-ful," Mom said.

Bev sat frozen, lashes soaked, lips trembling. I felt like a piece of shit. But I was no stranger to sacrifice.

***

While I was pregnant, I made myself a blazer as an incentive to lose the baby weight. I chose brown corduroy with a satin lining and leather buttons. It took weeks. I made mistakes, ripped out seams, and started over multiple times. In the end, it turned out beautifully. I couldn't wait to show Mom. I was sure she'd be proud of me.

When Mom visited from Pennsylvania, I brought it out.

"Peggy. It's so bee-you-tee-ful! It looks store-bought," she said, sipping coffee at the kitchen table.

"It took a long time to make," I said. "I can't wait to wear it."

She peered at me over her glasses, eyes pleading. "Oh, Peggy. Faye's birthday is next week. That would look perfect on her. She's your size. Oh, Peggy, can I have it to give to her?"

Faye was a young woman Mom had taken in. Her "adopted daughter." Mom had taught us that when someone asks for something, you give it selflessly. She'd asked me for things before—my diamond rings, my wedding band, but this was different. I'd made it clear how much the blazer meant to me. It hadn't even occurred to me she'd ask for it. If I'd known, I never would've shown her.

My hands shook as I handed it over.

"She's going to love this," she said, holding up the blazer. "I'm gonna tell her you made it for her."

How could she do this? *I'm* her daughter. Panic surged. No. Don't think that. This must be a test. I needed to show my loyalty. I breathed shallowly and sipped my coffee.

Smiling like she'd won the lottery; she packed it into her suitcase.

After that, I put away my tape measure and straight pins. I shut the sewing machine lid. I no longer ran my hands along fabric at the discount store or looked through McCall's patterns. Other than mending, I retired from sewing.

Deb and I had our babies six weeks apart. She had a girl. I had a boy. We named him Mathew. Matthew from the New Testament, but with one "t." We called him Matty.

When my water broke two and a half weeks late, it wasn't a gush like in the movies, it was just a slow drip. Rich reclined my seat and timed contractions on the drive. He'd told me—confessed was more like it—that he'd left the hospital and got high with friends when his ex-wife delivered their boys. He deeply regretted that and promised he'd stay by my side. A nurse met us at the curbside. Rich held one arm, the nurse the other as they hoisted me into the wheelchair.

I held my big belly. "I wish Mom was here," I said.

"Well, she ain't, but I am," Rich said.

Despite everything, I still wanted my mother. A mother.

Rich stayed by my side through eighteen hours of labor. With Rich's arm around me, gazing lovingly at our son nursing, I was overcome with immeasurable love.

I dove into motherhood full throttle. Everything went smoothly, until six weeks, when Matty developed colic. He screamed like his tiny lungs might burst. I paced, rocked, drove him around. Sleep came in two-hour snatches. Only if I held him. The crib was useless; twenty or thirty minutes, and he'd wail again. Most nights, we camped in the rocker-recliner.

Desperate, I called Mom. I'd seen her beat Jill and Lissa until their bottoms were black and blue, but I'd also seen her rock them and hum lullabies. Aside from the doctor, who offered no advice, Mom was my only lifeline.

"Feed him, change him, bathe him, and let him cry," she said. "He'll wear himself out."

I followed her prescription. He fell asleep in my arms. I laid him in the crib. Thirty minutes later, the screams shredded the silence. I whispered, I soothed, I resisted picking him up. I tried joining Bev and Jim, pretending normalcy. Matty's cries ripped through the house, twisting my gut.

An hour later, I called Mom. Answering machine. Another hour passed. Matty was purple, breath jerking between wails. I rocked myself, my hands clamped over my ears. "He ain't wearing himself out," I muttered.

"How long did she say it would take?" Bev asked.

"She didn't. That's it. I'm getting him." I went to his nursery and scooped him up. His belly was distended, face dark, chin quivering. I held his belly against my shoulder to help him burp out some of the air. I kissed him and spoke softly. I gave him my breast. He calmed down and fell asleep. I held him in the rocker all night. Every whimper piercing my heart.

When I told Mom he needed to be held, she said, "Okay, Peg. If that's what you think is best. You're the mom." I stared at the phone, stunned. But it didn't matter. I was Mama Bear. I would do whatever my baby needed.

I'd learned to care for Matty on my own, questioning Mom's advice without fear. She suggested remedies: Karo syrup for constipation, whisky for teething. I could take them or not. For the first time, I felt agency. I was the one making the calls.

***

Life in Pennsylvania was a grind that never let up for Mom. She would call for money when bills piled up. Since we lived paycheck to paycheck, every call frayed us tighter. Groceries got trimmed, corners cut, everything stretched thin. But the real weight was the emotional avalanche: collect calls, slurred and raw, crying and drunk, spilling loneliness and talk of wanting to die. I'd cradle the phone like it was a lifeline, telling her it would be okay, reminding her that Mammy and Pappy loved her in their crooked way, reminding her of God, of anyone who cared. Hours bled past, more than one, sometimes two, three, until she'd finally agreed to sleep it off.

We were on a payment plan with AT&T. Every time we chipped down the balance, the phone rang. One call could spike the bill a hundred or two hundred dollars. Mom never asked. We never mentioned it. We didn't think we had the right.

When Matty was four months old, we flew her home for Christmas. At first, she was great. Jumping into his care, rocking and singing, making faces that he tried to mirror. My heart swelled. And then, just a few days in, I remembered: she wasn't just a grandma.

I sat at the end of the couch, folding diapers, hair wrapped in a bandana, when a sharp popping cracked the room like a whip.

"That's the Demon of Lust trying to get him," Mom said, cradling four-month-old Matty in the rocker. His gasp sliced through the quiet, a tiny chest trembling like a leaf in a storm.

"Peg. Bev. Come over here."

Bev stepped in from the kitchen. The room froze. Anger coiled inside me, a

194

snake ready to strike. You better not hurt my baby. Bev and I hovered by the chair. Our eyes met. No words, but she felt it, too. She hadn't seen Mom's violence firsthand. I had. Too many times.

"Girls, you gotta make sure the demons stay away. Babies are very vulnerable." Mom hollered, then popped Matty on the mouth again. "See, you gotta teach him now." She rocked him like she was casting a spell. Eyes locked on his tiny face.

What the hell? He's, my baby. You have no right. I willed the Demon of Doubt out of me. Praise Jesus. Praise Jesus. Praise Jesus.

Mom fussed with his socks. "Remember, the Demon of Lust manifests itself by making us stick out our tongues. So, you gotta tap him on the mouth like this—," She popped him again, "—when he sticks out his tongue."

Praise Jesus. Praise Jesus. Praise Jesus.

"It's just a little pop," she said, "to let him know he needs to keep his tongue in."

I told myself she was protecting him, keeping him pure. I told myself to have faith. I told myself I didn't want the Demon of Lust to claim him. Every pop made my heart hammer. Every time she touched him, I wanted to roar, "Get away from my baby!" and snatch him from her arms, but my body froze, caught between horror and disbelief.

Thankfully, it lasted only minutes. And he didn't cry. Had this been one of her marathon-spanking episodes, I would have torn through the room. My mama-bear instinct was awake, claws unsheathed, fire in my veins. Lake of Fire or not, I would have protected Matty, even if it meant taking on the devil himself.

***

Mom came home for another visit when Matty was eight months old. I wasn't as thrilled this time. We had a rhythm now: mornings and bedtimes, bills and chores divvied up, Matty on his schedule. But Mom arrived like a storm, scattering our order. Some nights she preached into sleeplessness; others, she hit the bar, stumbled home drunk. Woke Matty. "I need to see his bee-you-tee-ful face," she slurred. I spent hours coaxing him back to sleep while she slept off her drunken stupor.

The first day, she claimed her dominance.

"Girls, come in here," she barked, that iron voice we knew too well. Bev and I dropped our tasks and rushed to the kitchen.

"Look at the grease on these cupboards," she said, hands on her hips. "And when's the last time youse took down the light fixtures for a good soaking? Huh?"

We exchanged glances, bracing ourselves. Mom stalked to the mudroom. We followed.

"Look at them shoes. How can you expect Matty to put his shoes on the right feet when they're back-wards like that?" She bent and lined them up meticulously, then motioned for us to trail behind her. Room by room, she cataloged our neglect.

Who do you think you are? You don't live here no more! You left! I swallowed the words like jagged stones, but they thudded against my ribs anyway. You can't tell us what to do. You're a guest in this house. As hard as I fought, the anger lingered. The thoughts prevailed. Something was changing in me. A flood gate opened. For years, Bev and I slaved at the Hoagie Shoppe while you drifted free, paying for trips, draining us with drunk, collect calls. We sacrificed. You sacrificed nothing. We need a washer and dryer, but we can't afford it because of you! I fought the thoughts with prayer, rebuke, replacement, but they dug in like claws. The house wasn't perfect, but we had a baby. It wasn't her business.

Bev and I scurried, cleaning and straightening as Mom circled like a hawk. Though, she wasn't idle herself—sloth enraged her. Then fear replaced fury. Part of me still believed she was God's chosen instrument. Maybe Jesus was testing us. I feared she could read my mind. My independence felt like smoke slipping through my fingers.

That night, the nine of us sat for supper: Jim and Bev, Randy and Deb, Rich, Mom, Matty and Missy (Deb and Randy's baby). The babies babbled, forks clinked, but the air was thick as tar. When Mom was quiet, we knew she was pissed. Deb's nostrils flared. Randy's aviators slid. Bev teetered on tears. Jim fidgeted with his cap. Rich devoured food with surgical focus. I chewed the inside of my cheek.

When we finished, Mom snapped open her cigarette case, lit one, and retreated to the room. Deb and I got up to tend to Matty and Missy. The men washed dishes. Later, we all joined Mom.

She sifting her teeth, a sound she always made after eating. "Things are out of control around here."

I rocked Matty, chest tight, heart pounding.

"I guess I've been gone too long. While I'm here, things are gonna get whipped into shape. The house," she pointed at us, "and your souls." Bible open, she recited: "Blessed are the poor in spirit: for theirs is The Kingdom of Heaven. Blessed are they that mourn, for they shall be comforted. Blessed are the meek: for they shall inherit the earth..." She lectured on humility, on our lack of it. Guilt lodged in my throat. Confession lingered on my lips. Last time, my confession ended with a spanking in front of everyone. A ticking time bomb pulsed in my chest.

"San," Bev said, voice quivering, "I had doubtful thoughts today."

Mom rubbed her hands together, a predator sensing a catch. "What'd you doubt?"

Tears gushed down Bev's cheeks like a levee breaking. "Well...when you were chastising...Peg and me...about the house, I had doubtful thoughts. I thought...that...it wasn't your place to tell us how to clean."

"Well—" Mom tightened her lip, chin raised. "—you want to learn, don't ya?"

Bev raised her eyes. "Yes."

You're not gonna make it in this world if you can't handle a little chastising." Her gaze softened. "Come over here."

Bev knelt. Mom cupped her face in her hands. "Bev, I feel your humility and your remorse. You're forgiven."

Tension drained from Bev like water from a sink. Guilt filled my pores. I'd betrayed Bev. Mom said nothing to me. That night, I repented privately and wondered why she hadn't read my mind.

***

Later, at Fuzzy's, Mom revealed she saw what I hadn't yet known. We had a beer while the men watched the babies. When I stood to go use the bathroom, I unbuttoned the top of my jean skirt, which was a bit tight.

"You're pregnant," she said, eyes sharp, pointing at my stomach.

I hadn't thought about it. Rich and I hadn't discussed another child. Yet I'd always pictured a boy and a girl. Sitting there, I decided it would be a girl.

Back at the table, I whispered, "I think it's a girl, Mom."

"I knew with you girls," she said, arm across her belly. "I prayed for a blonde-haired, blue-eyed girl, and the Lord gave me Deb. Then a red-headed, blue-eyed girl, and the Lord gave me you. Jack and I prayed for a son, and the Lord gave us Joseph."

I said I hadn't prayed, but I still had a feeling it was a girl.

"Well, Peggy, the Lord knows what's on your heart." She signaled the bartender for another round. "Let's celebrate."

"I'll have a Diet Coke," I said.

"Oh, I smoked and drank with you girls and youse turned out fine. That's a wives' tale."

"Are you sure?"

"Yeah, look at you girls. Perfect." She held up her glass for ice. "It's not like you're getting drunk. It's only a couple."

I changed the subject. "Mom, if I am pregnant, will you come back for the birth?"

She snapped open her compact, dabbed her nose. "We'll see."

I felt like a child. I can't count how many times Mom said, "we'll see," when I was a kid.

So, I wouldn't contradict her, I sipped that second beer but didn't finish it. It didn't feel right to drink.

***

The doctor later confirmed I was twelve weeks. I'd hoped for a girl initially, but the moment Matty was born, I fell in love. His curls, cheeks, ocean-blue eyes. He was unstoppable, fearless, defiant. Crawling at six months, he zipped through the house like a little tornado, defying every "no" and "don't." Toddlerhood brought chaos. He tested boundaries relentlessly. I couldn't take my eyes off him. My experience babysitting Jill and Lissa provided little training for the likes of Matty. Frenzied, I called Mom for advice.

"Peg, that baby came into your life. You don't change nothing. He needs to adjust."

"But the ashtrays, the plugs?"

"I didn't put nothing up with you girls. Just said 'no.' Slap his hand, yell 'no.' He'll learn fast."

One day, folding diapers, Matty toddling around the coffee table, reached for an ashtray. I popped his hand and yelled, "No!" To my horror, he slapped my thigh with all his might. Oh my god. I just taught my baby to hit. I picked him up. "Matty, we don't hit." As soon as the words left my lips, I realized I was a hypocrite. How could I expect him not to hit if I hit him? That Friday, I told Rich we needed to baby-proof the house.

198

Matty split me in two: fear of the Lake of Fire, and a need to protect him. Babyproofing was my first true act of defiance.

Parent's Magazine confirmed my instincts: protect, teach without hitting, avoid smoking and drinking in pregnancy. Surprisingly, I wasn't worried about displeasing Mom. I was prepared to defend my position if she questioned me. Rich wasn't on board with no spanking at first. But when I explained that spanking can accidentally injure kids, create mistrust, and put them at risk of molestation, he agreed.

Mom reminded me that children need to be shown who's boss. I assured her that I planned to use timeouts and removing privileges. I could almost hear her eyes rolling through the phone, but that didn't dissuade me.

***

The closer my due date approached, the more I thought about Mom coming home. There was still a part of me that yearned to feel close to her, to feel like she saw me as a daughter who needed her. We bought her a flight to come for Christmas Eve. My due date was December 7th. I figured either we'd have a new baby when she arrived, or she'd be there for the birth.

By then, I was as robust as a rhinoceros—feet swollen, barely sleeping, getting jabbed in the ribs around the clock. I propped a pillow behind my back to lift my chest and elongate my torso. Otherwise, it felt like a knife pressing into the inside of my ribs. On top of that, I suffered maddening heartburn. At times, I drank baking soda water just to make myself vomit.

In anticipation of Mom's arrival, Bev and I cleaned the house—every corner, crack, and crevice. We weren't going to risk a repeat of the last visit. We didn't speak of it. We just knew.

Jim went to get Mom from the Des Moines airport that frigid day before Christmas. We gathered in the room, the TV on while we waited. Missy and Matty, pudgy bodies dressed in their Sunday best, sat toes-to-toes on the floor, playing with blocks. I sat in the rocker-recliner, chewing my thumbnail.

You nervous?" Rich asked, sitting near me on the couch.

I shrugged.

"Relax. It's your mom. Ain't that big of a deal."

I adjusted my glasses and looked away. "I know. I'm just excited to see her."

Deb sat reading while Randy chain-smoked. Bev brewed the coffee Mom would expect. Then we heard Jim's truck pull up.

"Mom's home," She hollered as she came in.

I hoisted myself out of the chair and waddled to the back door. "Here," she said, shrugging off her coat. Bev scurried over and took it.

"Hiya sweet babies," Mom sang in a high-pitched voice. "Grammy's here." She bent down and opened her arms. Matty stood and hid behind my leg.

"Ahhhhhh." Mom stuck out her bottom lip.

"Just give them time," Deb said. "They'll warm up."

She took each of our faces in her hands, searching our eyes with her signature gaze. When it was my turn, I interrupted her and asked if she wanted to feel my belly. Waves rolled beneath her palm.

"You're gonna have a big baby."

She settled in with coffee and a cigarette and retold—again—her birth story with me: forty-five minutes, barely made it to the hospital, little pain, dark hair that later turned red.

After supper, we gathered in the room to listen to Mom preach her sermon-threaded with an undercurrent of *I'm back now*. I gave her the rocker-recliner and sat on a straight-backed kitchen chair to stretch my ribs. I shifted throughout the night, heartburn burning up my throat, eyelids heavy as lead.

Then she surprised me.

"Peg, go on to bed."

I hesitated, wondering if it was a test.

"You're about to have a baby. Look at you." She waved her hand. "Go on."

I shuffled to the bedroom, changed into my nightgown, and hoisted myself onto the bed. I drifted in and out of sleep, trying to tune out Mom's gravelly voice filtering through the burlap curtain dividing our room from the living room.

Part of me resented her disruption. A bigger part needed a mom. I didn't realize it then, but this was the test, whether she would make me a priority.

At three a.m., Rich fell into bed and immediately fell asleep. I stared at the clock, praying to go into labor.

The next day, we women prepared Christmas dinner. Despite my discomfort, I was happy. The house filled with the smell of turkey basting in its own juices, hot cider, and holiday seasonings. Swept up in the joy of watching Matty discover the wonders of Christmas, my heart swelled. His golden locks bounced as he toddled around. He'd stand in front of the tree and point at the shiny bulbs and say, "pitty" (for pretty) with a grin that bore his chiclet teeth.

The babies ripped open gifts while Deb and I snapped photos with our 110 cameras, Johnny Mathis playing on the tape player. Matty loved the camera, and the camera loved him. It was a good day. But beneath it pulsed my fear that I wouldn't have the baby before Mom left.

As her departure date approached, I grew more anxious. I wanted independence, but I also wanted my mom, crying tears of joy, helping me after the birth. I was twenty days overdue. Mom was set to leave in a few days.

I asked Rich if we could pay the $50 change fee to extend her stay. He didn't understand why it mattered so much, but he agreed.

I barely slept. I teetered between fantasizing about Mom being there for the birth and fearing she wouldn't stay because maybe it wasn't the Lord's will.

I got up at six a.m. to change and feed Matty. I busied myself playing with him and tidying up waiting for Mom.

Finally, she sauntered down the stairs with smeared mascara and hair standing on end. I got her a cup of coffee and offered her some eggs. She insisted I sit and rest and that she'd cook her own breakfast. I poured myself a cup and sat across from her. She lit a cigarette and grabbed the Time magazine lying on the table, flipping it open to the page she had doggy eared. Unable to hold back, I asked her if she would stay a few more days.

"Can you Mom?" I begged.

She sipped her coffee. "Oh, Peg. I don't know."

"Please."

"I wanna get back. I miss my friends."

My head twisted like an impossible mathematical problem. What? You miss your friends? I'm your pregnant daughter! I never asked you for nothing until now. I thought you were Jesus. I thought we were God's chosen people. What do friends have to do with it? The world's supposed to end any day.

Then it hit me: She's just an ordinary person. She ain't Jesus. This is bullshit. Like the boom of a Roman candle lighting the sky, my whole body was illuminated with revelations: I don't have to be perfect. The end of the world ain't coming. I'm a grown woman. I can make my own decisions.

Ten years of fear and oppression left my body. We sat, sipping our coffee, in silence. Her attention on the magazine. My attention on her. As I stared through her, I decided to say nothing and lay low until she left.

Unable to sleep that night, I lay replaying what she'd said: she had to get back because she missed her friends. It was like being injected with truth serum.

Thoughts I'd suppressed for a decade shot through me. She ain't special. She's a forty-one-year-old single mom from Pennsylvania who drinks, smokes, and craves attention. Then, I promised myself: I'm gonna open my mind and let myself think any thought that comes. Fury saturated me, my emotions unearthed, the taste of liberation on my tongue. I siphoned and spat out the delusions I'd been forced to believe.

I didn't know it then, but asking Mom to stay had been a test. And she'd failed. Everything I believed collapsed inward. At last, I surrendered to the voice that had long whispered something was wrong. She'd torn apart families, abused children, lied, wielded control like a weapon. I finally admitted the truth: Mom wasn't right in the head. I gave myself permission to think freely. No more shoving thoughts aside. No more betraying myself.

My life reassembled in a mosaic of memories. I saw how Mom had controlled my thoughts, my actions, where I lived, how I lived. I thought about the education I'd been denied, the teenage years stolen from me, the chance to make my own choices about my future. I thought about the danger and trauma I'd survived, the holes in my heart left by all the goodbyes.

I realized I could get a job. Go to college. Live where I wanted. Buy things without guilt. I could laugh at funny movies without fearing the Demon of Mockery, lick my lips without fearing the Demon of Lust, furrow my brow without fearing the Demon of Hatred. Did demons even exist? I could do whatever I wanted in the bedroom, and it would be between my husband and me. And most of all, I could be imperfect.

I watched the minutes tick by, waiting for Rich to wake. I didn't care whether he agreed. He could stay if he wanted. As soon as he stirred, I jumped up and flipped on the light.

Rich yanked the covers over his eyes. "What the hell?"

"Sorry, but I need to tell you something. I made a huge decision last night."

He rubbed his eyes. "What are you talking about?"

"I'm leaving The Kingdom. I thought about it all night. The end of the world ain't coming. Mom ain't Jesus neither. It's all bullshit."

Rich pulled back the covers, grabbed his crumpled pack of Kools, and lit one.

I paced our tiny bedroom. "For all these years, I didn't let myself think. I blocked out every doubt because I was scared shitless of going to the Lake of Fire. You know what? I don't even think there *is* a Lake of Fire." I paused, staring at the wall. "I'm leaving, with or without you."

His cigarette dangled from his lips as he squinted at me. "What do you mean, without me?"

"If you wanna stay, that's fine. But I'm still leaving, and I'm taking Matty and our new baby with me. I'm not letting them grow up like I did. I want them to think for themselves. They're going to graduate high school. They're going to make their own choices. I ain't forcing them to believe nothing. And if they believe something I don't, that's okay. I want them to stand on their own two feet without being scared all the time."

He looked at me, wounded. "You don't think I want that for our kids too?"

"I didn't know what you thought."

He flicked ash into the tray. "I had doubts from the beginning, but I kept my mouth shut. 'Cause of you and Matty." He pointed at my belly. "And now this baby." He met my eyes. "I want out too."

I could hardly breathe. It was exactly what I needed to hear. We decided we'd see Mom off, say nothing, and tell the group after she left.

***

We gathered in the kitchen to say goodbye. One by one, we hugged Mom. I lifted Matty so she could kiss him. She kissed me on the lips, as always. I thanked her for coming.

"You already had Mathew and got through that, and the first baby's the hardest. You don't need me. You're strong."

I forced a smile.

She placed both hands on my belly. "It's gonna be any day now." Her glassy gaze swept the room. "I'm gonna miss youse."

Her tears didn't move me. I wanted her gone. Before, I would've given anything for her to stay. Now, I wanted to shout *Fraud! Liar!* to her face.

Once she left, relief curdled into anxiety. I didn't know how the others would react, whether we'd be kicked out, pressured, or if they'd jump on the freedom train with us. Jim worried me the most. He was the only positive male figure I'd ever had. I couldn't bear to lose him.

That night, Deb, Randy, and baby Missy came for supper. Deb was pregnant again, three months along. Despite my nerves, I felt energized, lighter than I had in years. We made small talk. When the food was ready, I strapped Matty into his highchair, fastened his bib, and spooned diced green beans, chopped meatloaf, and mashed potatoes onto his tray. I filled his sippy cup with milk. Deb did the same for Missy. We served ourselves, but I had no appetite. A pit formed in my stomach.

At the table, my fork screeched against the plate as I pushed food around. The room felt distant, voices muffled, walls closing in. I swallowed hard then blurted, "I don't believe no more."

Everyone froze.

Jim, hunched over his plate, asked, "What don't you believe no more?"

"Mom. I don't believe Mom no more."

Forks clanked onto plates in unison.

I tucked my hair behind my ears. "Before last night, I didn't let myself think about it. Too scared—"

Everyone, still as statues, kept their attention on me.

"—but I ain't scared no more. Mom hurt people. Destroyed lives. And she controls ours. Mom ain't Jesus. The End of Times ain't coming."

Rich leaned back. "I was only part of it 'cause of Peggy. Had to be. Some of Sandy's preachings are okay, but a lot of it's crazy." He shoveled meatloaf into his mouth.

Jim removed his cap and scratched his head. "Well, Peg, I've been thinking the same thing. For a long time."

I stared at him, stunned.

"Mo Mama," Matty chirped, flapping his hands.

I added more meatloaf to his tray. "Really, Jim?"

"Yup. A lot didn't sit right. I trusted San. Thought she knew best. But there was a lotta shit that shouldn't have happened." He wiped his mustache and dug a toothpick into a molar. "Forcing me to be with Maryanne. That broke me. She said it was the Lord's will, but I never saw it. Going back east didn't help none. I thought I was gonna lose my mind."

Rich motioned Jim for a beer. Randy too.

I told Jim I was surprised he had doubts. That I always thought his word was as good as Mom's.

"Yeah Peg, like you, there was things in the back of my mind that nagged at me."

"I never believed any of it," Deb said, then spooned potatoes onto Missy's tray. "I went along 'cause I thought that's what Randy wanted."

Randy adjusted his glasses. "Really?"

Deb widened her eyes. "Yes, that's how I feel. I never believed any of it."

"Well, wish you woulda told me."

Deb said she didn't know how he felt and was worried he'd rat her out to Mom. He said he had the same worry. He leaned back in his chair, lacing his hands behind his head. "Okay, then. I'm out too."

I got up and refilled Matty's sippy cup. "I was scared to think anything that went against Mom. Thought she could read my mind. And no way I was gonna talk about it. I thought Rich was into it, big time."

Deb folded her arms. "I never believed she could read minds. You guys, she drinks and takes muscle relaxers. Don't you guys know that most of the time when she's preaching, she's drunk? The muscle relaxers make her more drunk."

Hearing that stripped away the last bit of her mystique. She wasn't divine. She was broken.

Rich spoke up. "We're leaving Paledon. Starting fresh."

Silence fell.

"Us too," Deb said.

Jim pulled his hanky from his back pocket and blew his nose. "We'll stay. Our life is here."

Bev smiled close-mouthed, then studied everyone's faces. "Well…I *did* believe." She pulled her napkin from her lap and dabbed under her eyes.

Jim put his hand on her shoulder. "She fooled all of us, Bev. Except Deb, I guess." He chuckled.

We all laughed—deep, belly laughter—the kind that shakes loose years of fear. The babies joined in, giddy with us.

"What are we going to tell San?" Bev asked.

"The truth," I said.

For the rest of the night, we confessed our fears and dreams. We wanted our lives back. Our minds back. No more being responsible for Mom's back pain. No more sending her money we didn't have. No more late nights in the circle. No more fear of the Lake of Fire. No more battling our own thoughts. No more shame for having desires and wants. No more fear of not being perfect.

On January first, I gave birth to Amanda Louise—Mandy. Nine pounds eight ounces, dark wavy hair. Born at one twenty a.m., the first baby of the year in that county. Our photo made the front page. Mom was right. I didn't need her there. I was strong. Rich took care of me.

But I couldn't break free over the phone. She knew how to trap me. So, I wrote her a letter.

Dear Mom,

I'm writing to tell you something very important. I'm leaving the kingdom. I'm not doing this to hurt you. I'm doing this for my family and me. After you left the other day, I let myself think for the first time. I kept hearing you repeat, "I miss my friends." You miss your friends, Mom? What about me? I'm your daughter. But you know what? I'm glad you didn't stay because then I wouldn't have come to my senses. I'd still be controlled by you.

I'm not going to let you control me no more. I couldn't sit back and listen to the lies no more. You lie about raising people from the dead and about reading people's minds. You tell people you perform miracles like healing people's ailments and making the rain stop. You never healed nobody. You tell people you're Jesus come in the flesh and that you can give them eternal life. You can't do none of that, Mom. You're just a regular person like everyone else. After you said you missed your friends, I realized you're not Jesus. I'm not sure why you think you are. Maybe because you want to believe it.

You said if I wasn't perfect when Jesus came, I'd be cast into the lake of fire. I don't believe God would do that to me. How could He torture the people He created, for eternity, just for making mistakes? I don't think God would burn people alive because they weren't perfect.

For all these years, I went along with things I knew were wrong, all because I was afraid of going to the lake of fire. I don't believe there is a lake of fire. And, I don't believe we have to be perfect to get into heaven. Mom, you ain't perfect. You've never been perfect. You do whatever you want, whenever you want, without thinking of nobody else. You broke up families. You made Diane leave Ron. You made David leave Sharon when she was pregnant. Thank God he went back to her. I pray she took him back. You tried to get Maryanne to leave Lissa with you. Mom, that's her baby, not yours!

For ten years, I lived in fear of saying or doing the wrong thing, constant torment in my mind. I realize now that none of what you taught me is true. The world ain't ending in three and a half years.

Mom, you controlled so many parts of our lives. Deb didn't want to smoke, but you forced her by telling her she thought she was better than the rest of us. Maybe she didn't like it. Maybe it made her feel bad. How can forcing someone to smoke be Godly? And the way you beat Jill and Lissa was wrong. That was child abuse.

You even controlled what we did in the bedroom. You made Ron sleep in the barn for a week because he admitted to having oral sex with Diane! That was his wife. They have the right to do whatever they want in the bedroom and it's not your business.

You forced Jim and Bev to live with us. They deserve to have their own place, and so do we.

You wouldn't even let me and Rich have a door on our bedroom! Why wouldn't the Lord want us to have a bedroom door?

And I can't believe how many people you kicked out. You brought them into the Kingdom and forced them to give up their families, and when they didn't do what you wanted, you kicked them out. We don't even know what happened to most of them. You kicked Diane out, and she was left in Kansas City by herself to take care of Jill with no family. How is that Godly? You forced Jim to be with Maryanne even though he said repeatedly he didn't want to be with her. People should choose their own mates.

You made us believe that when you had pain in your body, it was our fault. You got pain in your body for the same reasons the rest of us do, sore muscles, tiredness, or whatever. You made us feel guilty for that. That's crazy. There were so many things that were crazy that it makes my head spin. I'll stop here and end by telling you that I'm going to start living my life on my terms. I know this hurts you, but this is what needs to happen. I hope you can find happiness.

Love,

Peggy

The only response I got from Mom was a collect, drunk call in the middle of the night, sobbing and asking, "why are you doing this to me?"

CHAPTER SEVENTEEN
Denison, 1984

After leaving The Kingdom, we agreed that Mom should be the one to pay off her car loan. When we sold The Shoppe, she'd said we could keep her furniture in exchange for what she owed. We didn't think that was sufficient compensation, so Jim went to the bank, explained the situation, and they agreed to go after her for payment.

The day Mom got the letter from the bank, she called late—collect—and drunk. I dragged myself out of bed and answered, fully knowing it was her. She asked why we were hurting her. I said we needed our own lives and that we weren't trying to hurt her.

After a long pause, she said, "Well, I guess there's no reason for me to live no more. Then, I might as well just die."

My chest tightened. "Don't say that, Mom. You'll be okay. You always are." My hands trembled.

"Youse don't care about me." I heard her exhale smoke.

"We care, but we can't live the way you made us live no more."

Click.

I stood motionless. What if she does it? What if she kills herself this time? I dialed her back—no answer. I sat on the couch, my stomach churning. I dialed again—no answer. I crawled back into bed, guilt and worry gnawing at me. I got up and dialed again—no answer. My mind volleyed between panic and self-talk.

She was a broken record. Drunk dialing and talking about dying was her M.O. You'd think knowing the pattern would've eased the fear. But each time it felt brand new.

***

Several weeks later, Rich took a job in Denison, pop. 8,000, a town about ninety minutes away. We struck an arrangement with Jim and Bev to divide the housewares, rented a truck, and set out to start our new life.

I'd hoped Rich and I would grow closer. Instead, the opposite happened. We'd rarely had sex while living with Jim and Bev, but once we had our own place, it was even less frequent. And aside from the coordination of daily life, we didn't talk. I wanted to talk about what we'd been through. He didn't see the point. "Don't matter now. It's done and over with," he'd say. Drive forward. Don't look back. That was how he lived.

I'd thought escaping Mom's grip would bring us closer, but leaving The Kingdom didn't fix everything. Rich was a troubled man. Trouble that went far beyond what we'd lived through under Mom's rule.

He came home from work every day wound tight, yelling at the kids, picking fights with me, then storming out to the bars. Or he'd come home, smoke pot, and pass out on the couch, ignoring all of us. I'd never felt so lonely.

Desperate, one night I called Jim and asked if I could move back home. I didn't want to return to Paledon, but I had nowhere else to go. Jim was all I had. He reminded me I was an adult, married, and needed to stay and work it out. He offered a little money, but I said it wouldn't help. I hung up, defeated.

It took me many years to understand Jim's stance. He was right to turn me away. He and Bev needed to rebuild their lives. I did need to face mine.

Rich went back to bridge construction and was gone all week. For our second vehicle, we bought a double stroller. I took the kids out nearly every day. The park, the ice cream shop, the grocery store, hanging bags from the stroller handles. Sometimes I had to jog home because Mandy was ravenous or had a dirty diaper.

My days were spent caring for Matty and Mandy. My nights alone, watching TV and knitting.

After four months, Rich got tired of being on the road and took a job at IBP as a lugger. The guy who unloads sides of beef and hoists them on his back like

209

Sylvester Stallone in *Rocky*. It paid the same as bridge construction, but at least he was home every night.

Mandy was six months old and sleeping through the night, so we agreed I'd go back to work. I took a waitress job at a steakhouse on weekends to avoid paying a sitter. It helped. It kept Rich out of the bars and eased our finances. I came home to fed, clean, sleeping children. He didn't drink at home. He promised to only smoke pot after the kids were asleep. I chose to trust him.

The stroller no longer worked as a second vehicle, so we bought a 1960s Chevy for $200. Rich spent an extra twenty bucks registering it and got a vanity plate: LUGGER.

A few months later, we rented a three-bedroom double-wide. I decorated it with garage-sale finds. Rationally, I knew it was okay to want nice things, but I couldn't shake the fear that desire itself was sin. Mom's conditioning lived in my bones.

My wardrobe was tiny, worn, and dated. I couldn't remember the last time I'd bought new underwear or bras. Our furniture was ancient. The couch was faded and sagged. To get the box TV working, we had to bang the side and wedge tin foil around the antenna. I stretched the food budget with cheap cuts and ingenuity. "During the Depression, we didn't throw nothing away," Mom would say. "We drank powdered milk and ate boiled potatoes every night."

Even with my paycheck, we couldn't get ahead. We were still paying off Rich's debts from his ex, and he'd started gambling. He didn't contribute his winnings, but he covered his losses with our money. Twice, we took out bank loans to pay off gambling debts. The bank required my signature. He said the bookies would break his legs if he didn't pay, so I signed.

Some weekends, he went north to Pocahontas to drink with his buddies. I worried he was doing more than smoking pot. He'd stay up all night, sometimes with a wild look in his eyes.

Our marriage was circling the drain. Drinking. Gambling. Drugs. Probably cheating, though I had no proof. I suggested marriage counseling.

"I ain't going to some stranger to talk about our personal business," he said.

The future with Rich looked bleak. Still, it felt better than being controlled by Mom. And yet, I wasn't fully free from her grip. Since leaving The Kingdom, the only contact I had with her was through drunk, collect calls in the middle of the night. We talked about making our number unlisted but worried about emergencies. So, I answered. Stayed on the line. Still believing, somewhere deep, that her needs came before mine. More than that, I feared she'd sink into depression and kill herself.

The phone rang around two a.m. one night
I rushed to answer so it wouldn't wake the kids.

"Peg, it's Mom," she said, slurring.

I let out a discreet sigh. "Hi, Mom."

After a long pause, she said, "Peg, why don't you love me?"

"I do love you, Mom."

"Peg, everything I did, I did out of love."

"I know, Mom. But I must live my own life."

"You guys broke my heart."

I sat on the couch; hand pressed to my forehead. "I'm sorry, Mom. I didn't do it to hurt you."

Her crying intensified.

"Drinking always makes you sad. Go to bed. You'll feel better in the morning."

"No, it won't feel better in the morning. My life is over. There's no point in living. I just wanna die."

Thunk.

"Mom? Are you there? Mom. Mom. Mom."

My mind raced. Did she take something? I hung up and scrambled for someone to call. What was her name? Her real name? Think.

Then it came. Betty. Betty Meyer.

I dialed 411 for Northumberland, Pennsylvania, got her number, and called. She agreed to check on Mom.

Half an hour later, she called back. Mom was passed out drunk on the couch, the phone off the hook on the floor. I went back to bed, furious and exhausted. I felt compassion for her pain, but I was worn down by the suicide talk and the drunken calls.

The next day, I left a message on her answering machine while she was at work. I said I wouldn't accept collect calls in the middle of the night. "We got two kids to feed and bills to pay. I don't get enough sleep as it is." Then, sharper: "I thought you were dead the other night. Call me during the day, sober, and on your own nickel."

I didn't hear from her for weeks. When she finally called, it was still drunk, still collect, still in the middle of the night. I refused the charges. Before the line went dead, I said, "Mom, call me tomorrow when you're sober."

She tried once more weeks later, not collect, but still drunk and still late. I reminded her of the boundary.

Not answering at all wasn't an option I would consider. What if that was the time she did it?

Eventually, she stopped calling.

The quiet was a relief. Life was hard enough.

Most days, I didn't think about her. No bandwidth. But sometimes—a mother and daughter on TV, a passing moment—I'd feel the hollow ache. I didn't miss *her*. I missed having a mom.

***

As angry as I was with Rich for nearly bankrupting us, for being emotionally absent, not a day went by that my heart didn't ache for him. On the rare nights we went to bed together, I lay facing his massive back, longing to be touched. When I put my arm around him, he shrugged me off. Eventually, I stopped trying.

At work, I made new friends, but I kept my marriage and my past locked away. Too much shame. I talked about daytime soaps, funny things my kids did. To them, I was a mom married to a handsome man who lugged beef at IBP and was a good dad. That's what they knew.

On job applications, I wrote that I'd graduated from Lewisburg High. Actually, I'd only attended junior high, but no one questioned it. I worked hard and kept my head down, always afraid of being found out.

Terri, the bartender, was easy. We drank after work and complained about men. I kept it light. Underwear on the floor. Dirty dishes. When asked about family, I said I had an uncle in Iowa. The rest lived in Pennsylvania.

One night, after getting off early, Terri and I went uptown. At the bar, smashing lime into her gin and tonic, she ranted about her loser ex. After a couple of beers, I joined in.

"I need to get laid. It's been way too long." I slammed my PBR down. "I'm married; God damn it. And I'm only twenty-two." I lit a cigarette and blew smoke from the side of my mouth. "I'll bet there's plenty of guys who'd have sex with me."

Terri nodded, adjusted her A-line skirt, and crossed her leg. "Yeah, for sure. With that red hair, Rich don't know what he's got."

212

"Well, he don't even notice me no more."

"You're changing that tonight." She pointed at me with her cigarette. "Go home and jump his bones."

"I don't know. He's impossible to wake up."

She grinned. "Crawl on top of him. No man can resist that."

"Okay. Before I go, I need something stronger than this." I scooted closer.

Terri ordered two shots of peppermint schnapps. "This'll do the trick."

I downed mine. "You're right. I'm his wife. Husbands and wives are supposed to have sex, right?"

"Damn right." She raised her glass. "Now git before you lose the nerve."

At home, I checked on the kids, showered, shaved, brushed my teeth, dabbed perfume behind my ears. Naked, I slipped into bed and pulled back the covers. You can do this. I climbed on top of him and kissed his chest. He wrapped his arms around me. Encouraged, I kissed his lips. He kissed back. Then he flipped me over.

"What's gotten into you?" he asked.

I smiled.

Afterward, he fell asleep. I went to the bathroom. Sitting on the toilet, panic surged. Did I take my pill? I checked the pack. I'd missed two days. I counted back. My last period was fifteen days ago.

Oh shit.

***

Not a day went by that I didn't think about leaving Rich. Our one night together faded quickly. Life returned to its pattern.

We co-parented well, found moments of joy. Mandy's first steps, Matty riding his Big Wheel. Sometimes we even did things together, like the spring day when the local paper snapped our photo on a walk. We looked perfect. But, inside, we were imploding.

I'd pushed the missed pills out of my mind until one afternoon, months later, when I banged my breast on the refrigerator handle. They were tender. Fuller. I knew that feeling. Because I was on the pill, my periods were light and easy to forget. I realized I hadn't had one in a while. I didn't bother with a pregnancy test. I knew.

The worry consumed me. We were barely surviving. Rich already had four

213

kids. And I didn't want to bring another baby into our broken life.

One sleepless night, I made tea and wrote Deb. I needed the thoughts out of my head. Deb and Randy had moved to Minneapolis for more job opportunities, but we'd stayed in touch. I told her I'd considered abortion, then dismissed it. Afraid it would haunt me the way giving up Joseph haunted Mom. I said I wanted to leave Rich but didn't know how. A third child made it feel impossible. We'd only had sex once that year. Was that a sign I was supposed to stay?

I hadn't figured out what I believed yet. There was no time for that. Rich and I agreed on one thing: no religion. What we taught the kids was simple: be kind, nonviolent, respectful, expressive. Everything I wasn't allowed to be.

Mom hadn't preached since I left The Kingdom, but I still believed in signs. I decided the pregnancy was one. I needed to tell Rich.

I sat at the kitchen table, staring out the window, waiting. This announcement felt different. Our marriage wasn't healing, it was collapsing, like a star being pulled into a black hole.

When Rich got home, Matty ran to him. "Daddy!" Rich hugged him with one arm, lunch cooler in the other.

I ladled some leftover tuna-noodle casserole into a pot and turned on the burner. "There's something I need to tell you."

Rich furrowed his brow. "You're making me nervous."

I sat at the kitchen table then put my hand over my brows. "I'm three months pregnant."

"You sure?"

"Yep."

"When? We haven't been—"

"Remember that night?" I cleared my throat. "I missed my pill a couple days."

"Ahhhhh, Peggy." He exhaled.

I set his plate down.

"Well, we ain't got room for another kid. We'll have to move." He took a bite. "Matty, come here."

Matty went to him. Rich swung him up onto his knee. "You're gonna get a baby brother or sister."

Matty grinned. "Okay."

I clung to pregnancy like a life raft. A sign. A reason. A new beginning.

Rich and I talked about sterilization throughout the pregnancy, the conversation circling us like a low-flying plane we couldn't ignore. He didn't want to get a vasectomy. He worried it could affect his performance. We decided I'd get my tubes tied. The doctor suggested doing it during my hospital stay. Convenience framed as kindness. I nodded, though my stomach clenched. It was a colossal decision. One I was only ninety-five percent sure about. Five percent doubt doesn't sound like much, until it's about something irreversible.

The night before the surgery, a social worker came to my room. I was propped up in bed nursing Joshy (we named him Joshua Michael), his warm weight anchoring me to the present. The social worker, a thin woman with salt-and-pepper hair, sat on the edge of the empty bed across from me, a clipboard balanced on her knees. We exchanged pleasantries. Then she glanced down at her paperwork and said, "So, Peggy, you're twenty-three, right?"

I nodded.

"You're so young. Are you certain you want to do this?" She paused, her eyes sharp with intention. "You have a lot of childbearing years ahead of you."

Without hesitation, I said I was sure. I shifted Joshy to my other breast, his mouth finding its mark like instinct knew more than I did.

"Well, it's just that—," she wrote something on my chart, "—well, of course I hope nothing would happen, but if something were to happen to one of your children, you may decide to have more."

I averted my eyes. I didn't want her to see even a flicker of doubt. "I thought about that, but my husband and I hardly ever have sex, so it don't make sense for me to take the pill. Besides, I'm holding my pill baby right here. Only missed a couple of days, and boom: pregnant."

"What about your husband? He could have a vasectomy. That's less invasive."

"My husband's too nervous to do it, so—" I shrugged. "Besides, I've been thinking about leaving him. Him having a vasectomy don't do me no good." I tightened my bottom lip and nodded. "I want to go through with it."

I held her gaze. She handed me the clipboard. The papers felt heavier than they should have.

Sleep never came that night. The hospital hummed, beeped, and whispered. Nurses came and went. Joshy nursed every two hours. My vitals were taken around the clock. I lay awake, staring at the ceiling, my thoughts running laps. Was the social worker, right? Scenarios unfurled like cautionary tales, but no matter where they lead, I always circled back to the same place. Go ahead with it.

The doctor said it was minor surgery, so Rich didn't need to be there. A nurse rolled me down fluorescent corridors to the operating room, where a team waited, efficient and distant. Blue sheets rose around me like water. The anesthesiologist leaned in and told me to count backward from one hundred.

"100, 99, 98…97…96…95…"

I came to. Alone. Pain ripping through me, the lights above harsh and unforgiving. Blue curtains boxed me in. I pressed the call button and waited, clutching my belly, moaning. My mind snapped back to the ER years earlier, after the dog bite. I screamed, "I want my mommy! I want my mommy!" I remembered the moment Mom burst through the doors, and how her presence revived me like oxygen. I wanted her next to me. Her voice steadying me. Her authority ensuring I was cared for. Then reality settled in. Having her would have come at too high of a cost. The comfort wouldn't have been worth the price.

I moaned louder. Still nothing. I pressed the call button again. And again. No one came. They'd said, "mild discomfort." It was not mild. It felt like my insides had been branded with a hot iron.

Eventually, a nurse appeared and gave me pain medication. They told me I'd be sore for a few weeks. They didn't say it would feel like my core had been unplugged. I couldn't use my abdominal muscles at all. Getting out of the rocker-recliner required strategy. When Rich was home, he'd lift me by the elbows. When he wasn't, I'd roll onto my side, Joshy bundled in my arms, scoot inch by inch to the edge, shift my weight, and push up with my legs. Every movement was deliberate, like learning to walk again.

In the quiet moments, when all three kids slept, I wondered about other new mothers. Were they alone like me? Did their moms bring casseroles, fold laundry, rock babies so they could nap? I knew I needed distance from Mom, but that didn't erase the hollow ache she left behind. There was a space in my life shaped exactly like a mother, and nothing else fit.

When Deb called to congratulate me, we talked about how Mom hadn't been there for any of our pregnancies, and how little interest she showed in our kids. I told her about the woman I'd shared a hospital room with whose mother had traveled from out of state to stay for a month.

"I wonder what it feels like to have a mother that cares," I said.

Deb sighed. "Guess we'll never know."

For a while, Rich was more attentive. Then old patterns crept back in. He started going out again, funneling overtime pay into drugs. Weed and cocaine gave way to crank—meth by another name.

He unraveled. So did we. The fights were on repeat: drugs, money, gambling, his absences, his emotional vacancy. We were hanging on by tissue paper. He slept on the couch most nights. When he did come to bed, he turned away immediately. No kiss. No touch. I'd lie there staring at his bare back inches from my face, aching for him to turn around. To pull me close. To let me rest against his chest and match my breathing to his heartbeat. It had been years since he held me like that.

I tried to imagine life alone with the kids and couldn't make the math work. Tips were unpredictable. Even with child support, it wouldn't be enough. I needed out of restaurant work, but with an eighth-grade education, my options were thin. I needed my GED.

The classes were easier than I expected. Time was the problem. I traded sleep for study. I missed classes because of sick kids, work, Rich's double shifts. One night, the teacher pulled me aside, her hand warm on my forearm, concern softening her eyes behind thick glasses. I explained my situation. She suggested I test out. Fifteen dollars for the full set. If I failed, I could retake them. For fifteen dollars, I could try.

She did more than her job required. She made my life lighter when few people had.

I passed on the first try. Even math. Despite bombing most of the algebra. I was elated. It was the first goal I'd achieved purely for myself. Independence felt closer. No longer theoretical.

The steakhouse owners divorced and sold the restaurant. The new owner offered me assistant manager. I agreed. But with the condition that I could keep waitressing for tips. A three-dollar raise put me at five an hour—still not enough to leave Rich. It was no longer a matter of *if* I'd leave; it was a matter of *when*. I was biding my time, waiting for, I don't know—a sign.

Then two men walked in one night, suits crisp, cologne expensive. I took their drink order. An Old Fashioned for the ginger, middle-aged man, and a bottle of Bud for the tall, younger one. After I served their steaks, the ginger one asked, "Have you ever worked in sales?"

"Me? No. I wouldn't be good at sales."

He laid his fork on his plate and wiped his mouth with his napkin. "Well, actually, you're selling right now."

And just like that, a door cracked open.

World Book. Encyclopedias. A draw. Bonuses. A path that didn't run through the restaurant floor. After paying their bill, the ginger winked at me and said, "I'm going to make you a star," and the tall one mouthed, "call me."

Make me a star? What does that mean? I tucked the card into my purse like a secret.

A week later, I called.

I imagined myself in hose and heels, a blazer on my shoulders, a briefcase swinging at my side. But more than that, I could see a path out of my ailing marriage. Was this the sign I'd been waiting for?

That night, I told Rich. He said it sounded too good to be true, but we agreed I'd shadow. If it were legitimate, I'd start part-time before quitting the steakhouse.

After shadowing Lester, the tall one, a couple of times, he had me take the lead. I mimicked what I'd observed and added anecdotes about my own kids. To my utter delight, the couple bought. What a rush. Waves of hope and possibility fluttered through me.

Next, Lester gave me a few school leads, and I went out on my own. I sold to those couples too. When I received a commission check for over two hundred dollars, I signed the area manager contract and quit my job at the steakhouse. Rich was on board, though by then, I didn't much care. I was taking the job with or without his approval.

Selling World Book was easy, but about half the parents got buyer's remorse and returned the sets—something Lester had failed to mention. I worked nearly every night. With the returns, I wasn't selling the three sets needed to make the promised, two hundred eighty draw. After a few weeks, I became discouraged and quit. Still, the experience wasn't for naught. It taught me I had choices. And that I was smarter than I'd realized.

Next, I took a job as a Residential Advisor at Job Corps, where troubled kids could finish high school and learn a basic trade. High school had been denied me. So, helping kids graduate felt meaningful. The pay wasn't great, but it was full-time and steady. If I proved myself, I could be promoted to Lead and earn a decent raise.

Even though Mom was no longer in my life, the lessons she'd taught me proved useful. Her philosophy was simple: if you worked hard, you'd always have a job. I showed up on time, smiling, with a cheerful outlook. Volunteered whenever opportunities arose. I led aerobics classes. I organized dances on Friday and Saturday nights to keep residents from sneaking off campus. I learned that going beyond the call of duty earned privileges. I was given nearly complete autonomy. When I needed time off for sick kids, my supervisor never hesitated.

Meanwhile, at home, things continued to deteriorate. Rich went to the bars every weekend and worked double shifts to fund what he put up his nose. I was starting to hate him.

One Saturday night, as he got ready to go out, something in me shifted. My future flashed before me. A life of frustration, heartache, and anger. I gave him an ultimatum: move out or go to rehab. At first, he refused to choose. He said he didn't have a problem, that I blew everything out of proportion, that I was little miss perfect— "Perfect Peggy." I didn't argue, though I hated the nickname. I repeated the ultimatum. Finally, I told him I'd pack his bags and change the locks if he didn't decide. He chose rehab.

With Rich gone, the house was peaceful. No arguments. No lying awake wondering when he'd come home. No more staring at his back, yearning for him, knowing he'd reject me. Though temporary, I savored the respite.

A couple of days into rehab, his counselor called. After introducing himself, he launched into a recruitment speech. He said it was essential for spouses to be involved—group therapy twice a week, individual therapy once a week. I told him I couldn't afford a sitter and reminded him I was the sole support for our kids during the six-week program. He brushed past my objections and said they'd cover childcare.

"Why do I have to be the one to sacrifice?" I asked. "For once, I feel peaceful. It's been nice not worrying whether he's dead in a ditch somewhere. I need a husband I can count on. My kids need a sober father."

"You need to heal too, Peggy," he said.

To get him off my back, I agreed to think about it, though I had no intention of calling him again.

He called a few days later to follow up and convinced me to sit in on a group session "just to see how it felt." I conceded, on the condition that he stop calling.

***

I arrived right on time. The Styrofoam-tiled ceiling and stale ashtray smell gave the room the feel of a basement tavern hall. I threaded through the cigarette haze and spotted Rich, his hands laced over his abs. I sat beside him. He reached for my hand. I pretended not to notice.

The facilitator introduced himself and asked us to go around the circle. Spouses identified themselves as wives or husbands of alcoholics or addicts. When it was Rich's turn, he said, "Name's Rich. I'm an addict."

"Hello, Rich," the group responded in unison.

"I'm Peggy," I said, "Rich's wife." I deliberately left off *wife of an addict*. I wasn't going to follow along just because everyone else did. I vowed to think for myself. Always.

The facilitator opened the floor, asking patients to share one thing they were ashamed of. After a slow start, confessions poured out: rape, robbery, even a hit-and-run. Some cried. Others spoke with eerie detachment. It felt unsettlingly familiar, like the circle nights back in The Kingdom.

I avoided eye contact with Rich. I resented being pressured into attending. I believed sobriety was his responsibility.

Rich raised two fingers to signal the facilitator. He stared at the floor. "I've been lying to my wife a long time. I downplayed how much I used—"

"Look directly at Peggy," the facilitator said.

Rich lifted his gaze. I couldn't remember the last time he'd truly looked at me.

"I've lied about so many things. You didn't deserve that. You probably should've left me a long time ago." He smiled. "But I'm glad you didn't."

A soft laugh rippled through the group.

"I know I've said it before, but I'm gonna change. This time, I mean it." His eyes filled.

I felt the urge to comfort him but stayed silent. I didn't want him to think a few words could erase years of damage. Still, it was hard not to feel hopeful. He seemed sincere.

I left that night conflicted. Maybe he'd get better. Maybe we'd be happy. Or maybe he'd relapse the moment he got out. I reminded myself he was the father of my children. I decided to give him another chance.

The following week, the facilitator paired spouses and patients, pulling chairs into the center of the circle. Patients read their regrets; spouses read their resentments. Tears flowed. Voices shook. One person stormed out. We watched each other transform from distance to closeness, anger to acceptance, pain to peace. My resistance wore down. The counselor was right. I needed to be there. Not just for Rich, but for me. I did need to heal.

We sat knee to knee. My legs and hands trembled. Rich smelled of Old Spice. That familiar scent softened me. He rubbed his mustache, then pulled a folded sheet of paper from his back pocket. Both sides were filled. He held my hand with one hand, the paper with the other, and looked into my eyes after each regret.

"Peggy, I regret hurting you. Peggy, I regret lying to you." A tear splashed onto the page. "I regret—" he paused, inhaled deeply, then met my gaze. "Peggy, I regret cheating on you."

I pulled my hand away and broke eye contact. Forgiveness was not forthcoming.

When he finished, the facilitator signaled me. I swallowed hard and began.

"Rich, I resent you for choosing drugs over me and the kids. Rich, I resent you for trapping me into signing bank loans for your gambling debts."

Each resentment felt like a link sliding off a heavy chain. Anger surged, then despair. By the end, our eyes were swollen, our noses running. We embraced.

In individual therapy, the counselor asked me to write my life story. The process unearthed feelings about Mom I'd buried for years. He said I'd been so consumed by survival that I'd never addressed my trauma. It had never occurred to me that I might need healing. My childhood was a twisted mess. But I thought I should just move on. I'd never considered how deeply it had damaged me.

The connection Rich and I had in the beginning returned, this time with depth. He was vulnerable and attentive. I learned more about him in those weeks than in all our years together. The kids and I were eager for him to come home.

After three weeks, he visited for the weekend. The kids screamed his name and raced to the door. He gave Matty a gentle noogie and crouched so Mandy and Josh could climb onto his knees.

"I missed you, Daddy," Mandy said, pressing her cheek to his chest.

"I missed you too," he said, voice catching. "More than you know."

That weekend Rich played with the kids, helped around the house, and made love to me.

After six weeks, Rich was discharged. The first two weeks were like the weekend home visit. He attended AA meetings three times a week, and I attended Al Anon. He was home more, not just because he'd quit going out, but he'd also all but stopped working doubles. He was the husband and father I dreamed he could be. Still, I couldn't silence the skeptic in my head.

Two weeks after discharge, he announced he was going out. He promised he'd only have a couple beers. I lay awake until he crawled into bed around one a.m.

He curled against me, apologetic, claiming he'd been helping a friend get sober. I wanted to believe him.

The following week, he went out again. This time, he didn't come home.

By dawn, I was calling hospitals and police stations, drinking coffee to stay upright for the kids. At ten a.m., he walked in. With my best friend. And just like that, whatever hope I'd been holding shattered.

Linda and I had become friends shortly after she started waitressing at the steakhouse. We were both young mothers trapped in bad marriages, treading water in lives that felt too heavy for our age. She was my closest friend.

I leaped to my feet, the chair scraping backward and toppling behind me.

She stopped in the entryway, hesitating as if the threshold itself might save her. With a nervous smile stretched too thin, she said, "I know what this looks like, but it ain't that."

I seared a hole through her with my eyes. "Oh yeah? Then what is it? I'd like to hear what—" I pointed at them, "—*this* is."

She said her car broke down at a truck stop outside a nearby town and she ran into Rich. "Rich waited with me. We drank coffee all night. That's all. We talked and drank coffee."

I pointed to the kitchen clock, its hands screaming the truth she wouldn't touch. "It's ten o'clock. How is it that it took until ten a.m. the next day for the tow truck to come?" I planted my hands on my hips, grounding myself. "Besides, you're supposed to be my friend. Do you think it's okay to spend hours in the middle of the night with your best friend's husband? Wouldn't you tell him to call me?"

She dropped her gaze to the floor and said nothing, wrapping herself in her cape like she was naked underneath.

I crossed my arms and turned to Rich. "So, why didn't you call?"

He stood a few feet away, closer to her than to me. "I didn't want to wake you," he said, his face was smeared with guilt, "then the time got away from me."

"Bullshit!"

"Nothing happened," Linda said.

I pointed to the door. "You need to leave."

"I'm sorry."

"Get. Out."

Linda's cape flew behind her as she fled through the doorway. I never saw her again.

After that, my plans to divorce Rich surged to the forefront. I hung on as long as I could. I had to. We had three children together. And we'd escaped The Kingdom. That counted for something. I didn't want to raise my kids in a broken home. I certainly didn't want to be a twenty-six-year-old single mother unable to give them the stability they deserved. But Rich and I were already a sinking ship. Him sleeping with my best friend wasn't just another leak. It was the gaping hole that finished us.

After that night, Rich went back to using, just as he had before. The loneliness settled into my bones. Still, I couldn't afford to give up hope. Three little lives depended on me. I pasted on a smile every day, even when it felt brittle. Nights off were the hardest. By the time I put the kids to bed, Rich would already be passed out on the couch. I'd sit alone in the kitchen, smoking cigarettes, staring at the walls, calculating my future. I didn't want my children to witness my despair the way I had watched Mom unravel. I refused to let them shoulder emotions that weren't theirs to carry. Instead, I focused on the small, steady joys of motherhood and the work in front of me.

I found ways to move my pain through my body instead of letting it rot there. On my days off, I squeezed into a leotard, cranked the music, and danced through the house, practicing choreographed steps. The kids joined in, bobbing their heads and wiggling their bodies, laughter filling the rooms. I fantasized about dancing on stage alongside Paula Abdul and Whitney Houston—big hair, toned thighs, spotlights burning away doubt. When I was little, play had been my escape. At twenty-six, dancing carried me somewhere else, if only for a while.

I had excommunicated myself from The Kingdom to escape Mom's drinking and chaos, and there I was, married to an addict. I was biding my time, surviving, waiting for the opening that would let me leave cleanly.

It came one afternoon in a phone call from Lester, the World Book manager. He told me he'd been promoted and they wanted to offer me the District Manager position—four hundred dollars a week, still a draw, not a salary. I felt flattered and irritated all at once. I voiced my concern about returns. "Denison's a low-income town," he said. "Carroll County's affluent. Families there consider it practically child abuse not to have a set of World Book in the home." He guaranteed I'd meet or exceed the draw for six months. If I didn't, he'd cover the difference out of his own pocket. I accepted.

Leaving Job Corps was bittersweet. I'd grown attached to the girls. It was my first job in a helping profession, proof I could matter in someone else's life.

Lester was right. I had no trouble selling the expected three sets a week. I booked two appointments a night and closed half the time. Within weeks, I climbed to the top of the leaderboard. My thirteen-week bonus was a couple of thousand dollars. I exceeded quota and won an all-expenses-paid trip to Chicago for the semiannual conference. I'd never been to Chicago.

For the first time, I felt confident about my future as a single mother. I ran the numbers. One extra sale a week meant six hundred dollars saved each month. Freedom suddenly had a price tag. And it was within reach. Then it dawned on me: it made more sense to ask Rich to leave. The kids needed the house. I was their anchor.

I not only met quota. I was named top District Manager. I was elated and terrified. I worried they'd discover my eighth-grade education, my chaotic adolescence, that I was an imposter. Around educated people, I heard my accent sharpen. I noticed my grammar. I scrubbed "ain't" from my vocabulary, corrected myself mid-sentence when I spoke like a hick, laughing it off while fear simmered underneath.

What I learned was that World Book didn't care where I went to school. They cared how I performed. No one asked about diplomas. People congratulated me and asked for advice. I wasn't used to anyone seeking my guidance.

Selling came naturally. My adaptability, my work ethic, my ability to read a room mattered more than credentials. If this didn't last, I could sell something else.

On the final day of the conference, the vaulted ceiling and gold-patterned carpet felt unreal. Chuck, the ginger, introduced me as his "new star." Hands shook mine. Admiration washed over me, unfamiliar and dizzying.

I chewed the inside of my lip raw, relieved no speech was required. Just walk up, smile, take the plaque, walk back. Simple.

The M.C. introduced Chuck, then stepped away from the microphone to shake his hand. Chuck spoke into the microphone. "And the newest District Manager in Iowa with the highest sales in Nebraska, South Dakota, and Iowa is…Peggy Hobmeier."

I held my head high, walked up to the stage, my legs feeling like noodles, my heels clanking against the wooden steps. The movie theater-sized screen behind us projected a photo of me. Awkward. I walked across the stage, my pits damp. Chuck, wearing his usual swag smile and crisp suit, handed me my plaque and shook my hand. The room rumbled with applause. The photographer motioned us to pose. For the first time ever, I was part of something.

***

I ended my marriage to Rich just weeks later. I knew if I stayed, my life, and my children's, would orbit his addiction. My anger faded into indifference, my sorrow into pity.

Rich saw the kids a few times after we separated. But after a couple of months, he took a construction job in Des Moines and stopped visiting, calling, and paying child support. It was painful to hear "When is Daddy coming to visit?" and not have an answer. I made excuses. Soon, they stopped asking. Even though I had good reason, I felt shame for divorcing. Given Mom's insistence on us marrying, I'm not sure she would've supported my decision. The pressure to be perfect still existed in me.

***

I met and married Jeff, a six-foot-five, Jeff Bridges look-alike who gave me my first orgasm at twenty-six. Jeff—college-educated, teetotaler, vegetarian, meditator, homebody—was nothing like the men I'd known. He was divorced with three kids, but somehow that only added to the sense of order he brought into my life.

Life felt steady, almost luxuriously so. World Book awarded me a brand-new company car for my sales accomplishments. The hum of its engine was like a victory drum, a quiet anthem of everything I'd clawed my way through. Jeff and I were in love. The kids were happy. For the first time in what felt like forever, hope didn't feel fragile—it glimmered, solid and bright.

Jeff became a stepfather in the way I'd never dared imagine. Firm when needed, gentle when it mattered. Loved without conditions. The kids responded to him immediately. He worked for World Book too. Our Branch manager thought it prudent to put him in my sales organization. My world, once a storm of chaos and doubt, was now a landscape I could shape.

Two years later, we were promoted and moved to Council Bluffs. The city stretched before us like a blank page, the promise of a future we could finally write together. The weight of past failures had lifted enough to let me breathe. I was no longer just surviving; I was building.

But as I watched Jeff helping the kids with homework one evening, the sun

225

casting long shadows across the living room floor, a tiny flicker of unease danced at the edges of my chest. Life was good. Maybe too good. I had learned the hard way that even the brightest light casts shadows. Something, somewhere, was waiting to test us. I just didn't know it yet.

CHAPTER EIGHTEEN

Council Bluffs, 1989

We piled into the car, a convoy of hope and luggage, and set out to look at rentals. Matt held his hand out the window, letting the wind tug at his fingers.

"Look, Mom! Look!" he shouted, exhilaration etched across his face.

"Yeah, honey. I see," I said, glancing back with a soft smile.

As usual, Mandy had a book in hand, her eyes devouring every page, and Josh balanced a jumble of toddler toys on his lap. Outside, the red bluffs rose like smooth shields, guarding the outskirts of the city.

"Is that why they call it Council Bluffs, Mommy?" Mandy asked, tilting her head.

Jeff reached over and took my hand, squeezing it. His warmth grounded me.

But the reassurance dissolved as we drove deeper. Broken buildings sagged under layers of grime; trash scuttled across the streets. Toothless men shuffled past with the stench of factory smoke clinging to them. The city's veneer of promise was thin, fragile, and already flaking. Jeff and I decided we'd stick to our appointments. If we found an affordable house in a decent neighborhood, that would be the sign we needed. And we did.

The job quickly revealed its bite. Council Bluffs was poverty-stricken. Few people bought the books, many returned them. Pink checks—meaning I owed the company money—arrived monthly, mocking our efforts. Jeff and I worked more independently than ever. The extra hours doubled the strain. But working apart chipped away at him. His confidence eroded; some days he wouldn't leave the bed until noon. And he'd secretly started smoking. He'd avoid kissing me when he came home and would go straight to the bathroom to gargle. Didn't matter. His clothes reeked and the odor oozed from his skin. Having been a smoker, I was ultra-sensitive to it.

He grew isolated, irritable, and explosive. Bills stacked higher than we could manage. Child support payments went unpaid, my car payments lagged. I followed Mom's philosophy—send what you can to show effort—so I mailed ten dollars a month. But we were sinking. World Book wasn't the lifeboat we'd hoped. We decided that Jeff would find steady work while I kept chipping away at my sales.

He took a job at a meatpacking plant, the only decent-paying choice. Every day, he came home stressed, his conscience gnawed by the slaughter he despised. Anger and frustration clung to him like his own skin. He was either depressed or angry. And he'd started having insomnia. I'd wake up in the middle of the night and find him downstairs watching TV or outside smoking. "I just have a lot on my mind," he'd say. Nights became exercises in patience. I wanted the old Jeff back. The attentive, health-conscious, visionary man. But it was as though a stranger had occupied his body while he slept.

In hopes that Jeff would find himself, after two years of ten-hour days, six days a week, we made a daring choice. I resigned from World Book and Jeff quit the plant. We had no ties, no roots. Jeff suggested Fairfield, Iowa, a place he'd dreamed about for years because of its Transcendental Meditation community. He'd practiced TM since he was eighteen, chasing "enlightenment" and "cosmic consciousness," claims I quietly dismissed. I learned the technique too, but my belief ended at relaxation. I vowed never to blindly follow again. Jeff respected my skepticism.

We rented a house sight unseen, cashed out our 401(k)s, packed a U-Haul, and drove straight into the unknown. Despite the hope, anger simmered beneath my optimism. I didn't want my kids to grow up as rootless as I had, moving constantly, holding only fleeting memories of each place. Mom and I had counted: from birth to eighteen, I had moved twenty-five times. Already, my children had six homes to their names. This, I swore, would be the last move until they were grown.

We got a new phone number. Mom didn't have it. So, obviously the calls had stopped. Relief and guilt collided in me. I told myself: three children, my responsibility. Her needs would no longer take precedence over theirs. She was a grown woman, capable of managing her own life.

And so, we arrived in Fairfield. Hearts heavy with uncertainty, yet alight with possibility. For the first time in years, I allowed myself to imagine stability, roots, a life built, not just survived.

CHAPTER NINETEEN

Fairfield, 1991

The moon hung in an inky sky as we drove into Fairfield. From Highway one, the two golden domes appeared in the distance, like gigantic breasts dusted with gold flecks, glowing against the dark.

"See, kids? Those are the golden domes," Jeff said, smiling wide. "Every day, men go into one and women into the other, and they levitate."

Matt spun his Teenage Mutant Ninja Turtle, its arms circling wildly. "What's levitate?"

"When your body comes off the ground all by itself," Jeff said.

Matt stopped mid-spin. "That ain't true."

"That *isn't* true," I said, correcting his grammar.

"But it *is* true," Jeff insisted. "I've watched people do it."

"You have?" Mandy asked, pushing her glasses up her nose.

Jeff ran his fingers through his wavy pompadour. "Yep. And Maharishi teaches that when enough people practice TM together, it creates heaven on earth."

Matt turned to me. "What's heaven on earth, Mom?"

"Well," I said, cupping his chubby cheek, "I don't know about heaven on earth. That seems a little far-fetched. But we're here. I bet it's a great town."

Jeff jumped back in. "Heaven on earth is when people are nice to each other all the time and everyone lives in harmony."

That opened the floodgates. Questions flew from all three kids at once.

"Jeff," I said quickly, "why don't you tell them about the school?"

I wasn't comfortable with him teaching my kids the tenets of TM, but I swallowed it. I loved him. I told myself love required flexibility.

When we pulled up to the house, we'd rented sight unseen, relief washed over me. "Thank God the house is decent."

The kids tore inside, racing through the rooms, their feet pounding upstairs as they claimed bedrooms. Watching their excitement, my heart swelled. For a moment, it felt like we were finally safe.

Jeff had friends in Fairfield, people he'd met through TM courses, and within days he landed a job at a local print shop. It paid $7.50 an hour for twenty hours a week. It wasn't much, but it was steady. I hadn't found work yet, but I was confident I would.

Once we were settled, I hit the pavement. Restaurant work was my last resort. I wanted evenings with the kids. I didn't want to miss the moments my mother had missed with Deb and me.

Daytime jobs were hard to come by. I applied everywhere: receptionist, secretary, customer service. I lied about graduating high school. I was used to that. Mom had us lying about our ages since we were twelve and thirteen. She'd taught us, "Unto the pure all things are pure." Lying wasn't a sin if it was for God.

After a month, I landed a job as an assistant at a small insurance company. During the interview, the owner asked how many words a minute I typed.

"How many do I need to type?" I asked.

"Thirty-five."

"I can do that," I said, despite never having typed a single word in my life.

She hired me on the spot.

I checked out a typewriter from the library and asked Jeff to take care of the kids for the weekend. I practiced obsessively. Nearly every waking moment. By Monday morning, I could type thirty-five words a minute.

With our low-paying jobs, we were barely scraping by. Jeff wasn't paying child support. I still couldn't make the car payments.

One morning, standing in front of the kitchen sink looking out the window sipping my coffee, a black truck pulled up, screeched, and kicked up dust. A skinny, blonde guy jumped out, then unlocked the door to my Dodge Aries with a Slim Jim, faster than I could register what was happening.

I dropped the cup. Glass shattered. Coffee splattered everywhere. I ran. "Wait! Please!" I screamed, running down the gravel driveway. "I need that car!"

They didn't stop or even look back. It was the oddest feeling ever, like my dignity was driven away with my car.

Growing up, we often didn't have a car. We borrowed shopping carts to haul groceries home. I knew how to live without one, but I wanted better for my kids.

I shielded them from my childhood. When they asked questions, I gave answers that satisfied without inviting more. Even though I had no relationship with Mom, I didn't want to ruin any chance they might have with her someday. I planned to tell them the truth when they were old enough to understand.

I heard about a telecommunication company with good pay and benefits. I was determined to work there. I kept applying until they hired me. After a couple of months in customer service, they offered me a job in the sales department. A position with commission.

Things improved financially. But Jeff slipped again. Sometimes I'd come downstairs in the middle of the night and find him sitting inches from the TV, a wild look in his eye, watching the same clip repeatedly. Siddhas "levitating" on *The Phil Donahue Show*. Thin men in lotus position hopping on mattresses.

It felt hauntingly familiar. Reminiscent of Mom disappearing into fanaticism.

***

Jeff and I routinely meditated together late afternoons. One day, while sitting on a pillow, the buttery afternoon light warming my face, repeating my mantra to the rhythm of my breath, I sensed something intrusive. Not physically. Something else.

It felt like Mom. Her presence swirled around me, heavy and unmistakable. I could almost smell her musky perfume. I opened my eyes and shook my head.

Jeff looked at me. "You, okay?"

"Yeah." I adjusted my ponytail. "I'm fine." I shut my eyes and resumed meditating. A few minutes later, I was hit by another wave. I tried drowning it with my mantra. The feeling undulated for a few minutes more until it finally dissipated.

But it kept happening. Every day. The feeling grew stronger each time, lingering longer and longer. Eventually, I surrendered to it, convincing myself it was a sign. God telling me it was time. I knew the day would come; I just didn't know when. I'd escaped her, but I hadn't stopped feeling responsible. I was still that little girl who comforted her when she was drunk, weeping in my lap.

I ran the conversation through my mind repeatedly while making dinner that night. Then after everyone was in bed, I psyched myself up for the call. Except for the tick-tocking of the clock, I sat in silence on a kitchen bar stool, wringing my hands. Just do it, Peggy. Just pick up the phone and dial. I climbed off the stool and paced back and forth. I sat, rubbed my thighs, and took deep breaths. Finally, I dialed her number. A glob formed in my throat. I swallowed it. I shifted my weight from one foot to the other.

She answered.

"Hi Mom."

"Peggy? Is it you? Is it really you?"

I felt guarded. "Yeah, it's me."

Crying tears of happiness, she said she'd missed me and knew one day I'd call. She said her prayer was answered. I gave no response to that.

"I thought I lost you."

"I know Mom, but I had to make my own life." I wanted to say I had to get away from that crazy life, but I didn't because I wanted our reunification to go as peacefully as possible.

"I'd like to see you, Mom. And I'd like the kids to meet you."

"Oh, Peggy. You made me so happy."

"But Mom, I want us to talk for a while before you come out."

"Why?"

I cleared my throat. "Well, because I need to make sure you're not fanatically religious anymore."

"I wasn't religious," she said, defensively.

"You know what I mean, Mom."

"You don't need to worry. I don't preach no more."

"That's good. But I still want to talk for a while."

She sighed. "Okay, Peg."

She asked if she could talk to the kids. I told her she could the next time we talked. I wasn't ready yet. She was disappointed but agreed to wait. I hung up feeling like I'd been handed a fragile gift that I was happy to receive, but worried about breaking.

After a couple of months of weekly phone calls and having saved enough money for airfare, I felt comfortable enough to fly her out for a visit. The kids were eager to meet their grandma from Pennsylvania. They had questions. Lots of them. Where had she been all those years? Why hadn't they met her before? Why hadn't she sent birthday cards like their other grandma had? I told them she loved them and had been going through a lot, but she wanted to be part of their lives now. That satisfied them.

The day her visit arrived, I'd slept maybe two hours. My mind ran through different scenarios on repeat. In one, Mom would run to me with open arms, hollering, *Peggy, Peggy*. In another, she'd be bawling, making a scene. I planned to hug her; I just didn't want a spectacle. Not because I cared what people thought, but because her intensity made me uneasy. She'd grab my face. Force eye contact. And cry. She'd always cry.

***

The sun was high and blinding on that frigid day. Dirty heaps of snow sat piled at the corners of the airport parking lot, remnants of the massive storm we'd just had. My body tensed the moment I walked through the automatic doors. As I approached the sign that read ALL GATES, my stomach dropped. What if she hasn't changed? What if this is a mistake?

I sat on a vinyl seat and watched the monitor. Finally, it read: ARRIVED. I went to the ALL GATES waiting area and stood, chewing my lip. Passengers spilled out, rolling carry-ons, scanning faces for their person. Gradually, the crowd thinned. Then they stopped altogether. No, Mom.

I checked the monitor again. Then the paper with her flight information. I asked a flight attendant. She said everyone had deplaned. I paced. I talked to an airport staff member. They checked the computer. Mom had boarded the flight. I didn't know what else to do. I sat near the entrance and tried to think. Did she pass out in her seat? Did someone steal her ticket and take her place? I paced again. Checked the monitor at least ten more times. I was in the middle of begging a staff member to check the plane when Mom appeared.

She smiled, exposing the space between her teeth, and moseyed toward me. A bloated beige purse hung from one shoulder and a large, overflowing quilted floral bag from the other. I thought I'd be excited to see her. I wanted to be. But my body felt stiff. And I was confused. She'd appeared twenty minutes after the last passenger had deplaned.

I hurried over and slid the quilted bag from her shoulder to mine. She took my face in her hands, tilted her head, and looked at me through her bifocals. Steeped in the smell of cigarettes and Tabu, her eyes shifted back and forth, forcing close-up eye contact. Finally, she let go and stepped back.

"Ahh, you're so bee-you-tee-ful. Mom missed you."

I broke eye contact. "Missed you too. Where were you? The other passengers got off a long time ago. I was worried."

"I was on that plane all those hours with no cigarette. I couldn't take it no more."

You haven't seen me in almost ten years, and you had to have a cigarette? I thought it but didn't say it. I told myself it wasn't worth it. Some things never change.

***

Mom and Jeff hit it off. I wasn't surprised. He was likable, and so was she. She was warm, charismatic, and commanded the room. She often said she didn't like attention, but that couldn't have been further from the truth. When attention drifted away, she pulled it back with a story or a bit of wisdom. If that didn't work, she'd get up to do the dishes or go outside for a smoke. She had to be the center of everyone's attention, or she grew bored.

I was working my ass off, working two jobs and raising the kids. Mom was between jobs and struggling financially. She'd had fallouts with friends, which deepened her depression. I decided, and Jeff agreed, that we'd move her to Fairfield. I saw it as a way to pull our family together. She'd help with childcare, and I'd help her financially.

I wasn't afraid of her controlling me. I wasn't afraid of her being around the kids. I'd taught them to question, to stand up for themselves, and that respect begets respect. I wasn't worried about her dominating them or even hitting them. If she tried, they'd tell me immediately. My kids were assertive, outspoken, and occasionally sassy. Mom wouldn't approve of the liberties I allowed them, but I didn't care.

A few weeks later, I flew back to help her pack and drive to Iowa. The long hours alone in the car would give me a chance to say what I'd never said, something I dreaded but needed to do. I needed her to know how she'd hurt me. I wanted to tell her about the mental torment I'd carried for years, and how hard life had been. I wasn't seeking an apology. I just needed her to listen.

Sitting on the plane, I tried to imagine what life would be like with us under the same roof. My guard was up. I wouldn't let her control me again. I was prepared to fly home alone if I felt it wouldn't work.

When we parked in front of Mom's duplex, I wasn't surprised to see a manicured yard bursting with flowers. Mom beautified every place she lived.

That night, she invited several girlfriends over for a goodbye dinner. Before we ate, she asked everyone to join hands and pray. I followed along, but my thoughts flashed to The Kingdom days. Is she trying to restart her ministry?

After packing the car, we went to Point Township Fire Company. "The Point," as everyone called it, where Mom tended bar. It was a private club on the edge of town that funded the volunteer fire company. You needed a key to get in, but Mom had turned hers in the night before, so we rang the bell.

I hated The Point. The smell of cigarette smoke soaked into every dark pore of the place. My eyes burned. My tongue tasted like an ashtray. But I went because Mom said it mattered.

Carl, her boss, a thin, silver-haired man with a craggy face, answered the door. Mom didn't like him. He'd tried to get her fired, but the board refused. She was their top-earning bartender. "He don't like me because the customers like me more than they like him," she said.

"Sandy, come on in," Carl said with a half-smile. He turned toward the bar. "Hey, everyone. Look who's here. Sandy and her daughter."

Heads turned. People emerged from the pool room, leaning on their cues.

Carl hollered, "Get Sandy and her daughter a drink. Whatever they want. This might be her last drink here at The Point." He climbed onto his stool, clicked the TV remote, and took a gulp of beer.

Throughout the night, people hugged Mom and said their goodbyes. Some teared up.

"The place ain't gonna be the same withoutcha," one raspy-voiced woman said.

I wasn't surprised. Everyone loved Mom.

She hadn't preached in ten years. No one there knew about that chapter of her life. Even during The Kingdom days, she didn't preach to her friends. I remember being shocked and confused when she didn't preach to a childhood friend who came for supper one night back in New Columbia.

She'd lived a double life. In one, she was chosen by God to prepare for the End Times. In the other, she was just a hardworking, generous woman who was deeply loved. The latter was the version The Point knew.

Mom fussed over me, telling everyone I was her baby from Iowa. "I bet you never saw such bee-you-tee-ful red hair."

Feeling flaunted, I held a thin, obligatory smile. We finished our beers, said goodbyes, and turned in early.

On our first day on the road, I didn't think much about the conversation I needed to have with her. The miles passed easily.

But by the second day, the pressure began to rise. Slow at first, then insistent, like air filling a sealed room. Mom didn't notice. She was fine. I wasn't. All day, I scanned for the right moment, my chest tightening with each hour that slipped by. I'd made peace with much of the past, but I didn't want a relationship built on polite silence. I wanted honesty. And I knew that without speaking about The Kingdom, honesty was impossible.

We stopped at a motel outside of Chicago. They upgraded us to a room with a Jacuzzi, an unexpected mercy after the long drive. The room had a king-sized four-poster bed draped in green velvet, with curtains that could be pulled shut like a stage set. We dropped our bags and fell back onto the bed.

"Oh my god!" Mom said. "Couples watch theirselves having sex in that mirror."

We lay there staring at our reflections, laughing, our faces doubled and suspended above us. For a moment, it felt easy. Like a pause between storms.

That night, in the pale shadows of the room, sleep wouldn't come. Instead, memories did. They crept in like fog. Late nights in the circle. Mom forcing Ricky out. Being held at gunpoint, my hands clawing a woman away from Mom's throat. Babies beaten. Mom spanking me at eighteen in front of everyone. Maryanne pushed to eat grass off the floor. The goodbyes. The losses. Each memory pressed against me until I felt pinned beneath them.

After breakfast, we merged back onto I-80. Despite barely sleeping, I was wide awake. My mind wouldn't slow. Mom popped in one of her '50s tapes, and for a while, we sang together. Then we stopped at a rest area and switched drivers. My throat tightened. I couldn't sing anymore. Mom noticed and turned off the radio.

"What's wrong, Peg? You got serious."

"No, I didn't."

"It's written all over your face. What's wrong?"

I took a few deep breaths. My hands trembled on the wheel. "I wanna talk about The Kingdom years."

She flicked ashes out the crack in the window. "Oh, Peggy. We don't need to bring up that stuff. I don't think about it no more."

I tightened my grip. "Well, I do, Mom. A lot. Do you know how much I've struggled because of the stuff that happened?"

"That was a long time ago." She rolled down the window and tossed out her cigarette butt. "Wasn't that bad. Look how good you turned out."

"Yes, it was that bad, Mom."

She folded her arms and turned away. "Well, it didn't hurt ya none. You just gotta forget about it."

The hair rose on the back of my neck. "That's the thing, Mom. I thought I had. But when we reconnected, I realized I still needed to tell you how I feel. Mom, you've never let me talk about it."

"What?" She jutted her chin. "What do you need to talk about?"

I stared at the road. "I don't know… I just." My throat closed. "I *need* to tell you how I feel."

I hadn't planned what to say. I'd rehearsed the opening, not the aftermath.

She drew her eyebrows together. "Everything I did, I did out of love."

"You didn't even let me go to high school."

"Well, I only went to the tenth grade."

"You dropped out, Mom. That's not the same."

"Well, look how good you're doing. You didn't need to go to high school."

"You said the end was coming. And back at the dairy farm, you pushed Ricky until he left. Do you know how that hurt me? You said we were married. You did horrible things to people."

She clutched her chest. "Oh, Peggy. Stop. Don't say no more. Please stop."

I gripped the steering wheel harder. "We can't just pretend those things didn't happen."

"I can't take no more. Please, Peggy. Please stop."

Something collapsed inside me. Hope drained away, leaving only the hollow echo of it. I finally understood. She would never hear me. If I wanted to survive her living with us, I'd have to bury my needs. Again. I feared her depression more than I needed the truth. So, I locked the feelings away, sealed them up like contraband.

I dabbed the tears from my cheeks and swallowed my feelings. Then I cut the umbilic cord to my requirement for validation. My breath shuddering. I clicked on the radio and flipped through the stations stopping at a song I knew she'd like. I gave her a close-lipped smile. She returned the same.

***

Life moved forward. Mom took a job cleaning houses while the kids were in school. After school she baked cookies and made home-cooked meals, like when I was a kid. She got after the kids about their chores and chastised them for talking back. They loved the desserts and food but didn't like her. She hated that they spoke freely and thought they should be slapped for being sassy. I said I was raising them without hitting, and I allowed them to freely express themselves. Still, she tried to assert her dominance. She hung a paddle on the wall, which she named Charly. The kids giggled when she threatened them with it. "Mom won't let you hit us," they told her. They were right. That infuriated her.

After a few months, she'd saved enough to move out. She hadn't demonstrated any religious fanaticism or tried controlling me in any way. I was thirty-one, a mother, and a successful manager at a telecom company. I was guarded against even a hint of control.

***

Meanwhile, Jeff never bounced back. I'd hoped moving to Fairfield would shake him loose from the funk he'd been trapped in for more than three years. But it didn't. Instead, the fog of his moods thickened. Erratic sleep. Anger outbursts. Long stretches of silence that felt like invisible walls pressing in. One day, without warning, he shaved his head "to solve 108 spiritual dilemmas." The absurdity would have been funny if it weren't so unsettling. The kids didn't know what to make of him. Nor did I.

He showed little interest in the kids, except to bark at them. They complained endlessly. "He's mean, hogs the TV, and eats all the food." Frustration and fear braided together in their voices. He was no longer the playful stepdad who crouched down to their level and shared little truths. He was no longer the man who made their mom smile. Instead, he had become a presence that hovered. Volatile. Unpredictable. Heavy. I had lost a partner and inherited a storm.

He refused help. Refused even to admit there was a problem. When I begged

239

him to go to couples counseling, he waved me off. "We just need to meditate more." As if serenity could magically repair the fractures he was widening every day.

After a year in Fairfield, I faced a hard decision. I asked him to move out. My children needed safety, boundaries, stability, things that had no chance under his shadow.

Divorce was the right decision for all of us. Jeff would no longer bear the weight of father or husband. He was free to descend further into the TM movement. Maybe, somehow, that would heal him. The kids would no longer live under his unpredictable wrath. And as for me, something in me had shifted. I no longer imagined a future with him. I only saw a life without him. It felt like stepping into daylight after years of being in the dim.

Because we didn't have children together, the divorce was swift. Clean on paper, but the echoes lingered. Three marriages. Three divorces. I was done with marriage. I was ready to go it alone.

For the first time in years, I could feel the possibility of breathing freely. Untethered from another person's unpredictable will. The years stacked up like sediment. Layer upon layer of adaptation, compromise, and endurance. No more. It was my first taste of sovereignty since The Kingdom.

***

Mom came and went. Pennsylvania. Iowa. Pennsylvania. Iowa. When she couldn't pay her taxes or fix her car, I'd send her money. She never asked. Instead, she'd say, "I'm going to need..." I was doing better financially. A quiet guilt gnawed at me for having more than her. So, I sent the money. Always. But I couldn't resist a small, pointed reminder about the cash she squandered on cigarettes and beer. After her gluten intolerance diagnosis, I'd caution her about what the beer was doing to her body. She carried a litany of ailments: asthma that rasped through her lungs, stomach ulcers that twisted her insides, chronic pain that made her movements jerky and tense. Most calls were punctuated by hacking fits, phlegm rattling like chains in her throat. My pleas, no matter how urgent or impassioned, washed over her like rain on stone. She clung to smoking and drinking, as if they were only friends.

We talked weekly. She spilled the same catalog of complaints: coworkers plotting, men disappointing, the old wound that Mammy never loved her. I listened.

I offered comfort. Even though I no longer believed she was God's chosen one, tending to her felt less like care and more like walking the tightrope of obligation she'd spun decades ago. A rope that tethered me to her whims, her chaos, her suicide talk, her never-ending storms. Resentment grew quietly, like mold behind a wall. I told myself this was love. This was duty.

Frustrated with her life in Pennsylvania, Mom returned to Fairfield a few years later. I helped her get a job at my workplace. I figured if she had structure, a steady paycheck, she'd be less dependent on me. And maybe even a little happier. Although I'd left The Kingdom over a decade before, its echoes still clung to me, like faint chants in the corners of my mind. I felt guilty for feeling joy, for savoring peace, while she wrestled with her chaos.

She proved herself quickly in the job. Within months, she was promoted to Manager. I thought the arrangement would work a second time. But the cracks appeared almost immediately. She clashed with the kids, especially Matt. Mouthy, spirited, sharp-tongued—he collided with her rigid, do-as-I-say-not-as-I-do parenting style. One day, Matt called me at work. "She told me to F off," he said, voice tight with frustration.

I asked Mom about it. "Well, he said it first," she replied, as if that excused everything. That was the moment I knew: she had to move out. I couldn't take it anymore—her complaints about the kids, the kids' complaints about her. The old rhythm of dominance was creeping back in.

The next day, I put down first month's rent and a deposit on an apartment and moved her out. She sulked. I reminded her firmly that she was a fifty-something woman and it was time to model self-control. She didn't speak to me for a month. I'm sure she imagined she was punishing me, but her silence became a shield, a rare reprieve from the relentless drama.

With her living on her own, the kids' relationship with her improved. Not perfect, but better. She came for birthdays, holidays, sometimes dinner. They teased her, she teased back. Life finally held a steadier rhythm. She was content, financially independent, and woven into a community. And I wasn't losing my mind.

Eventually, she admitted she loved the apartment and thanked me for it. But a couple of years later, her job went overseas, and she was laid off. Rather than seeking another position, she returned to Pennsylvania. Again. Mammy's health was failing, and she wanted to be near her in those final years. She'd hoped they'd grow closer, and she'd get the validation and love she'd craved her whole life. She visited her often in the nursing home. She got her closure before she passed.

***

While Mom lived in Pennsylvania, I met Steve. From the start, I felt a kinship I'd never known with another man. Witty, thoughtful, tall with dimples, he made me feel safe and seen. I told him my story. The Kingdom, my childhood, the failed marriages, and he didn't flinch. He didn't judge; he admired my survival. He was no stranger to trauma. Losing his father to suicide at three had carved its own deep scars.

In under two years, we were married. The kids—seventeen, sixteen, and fourteen—were wary at first, but eventually they grew to love him. Mom and Steve were cordial, though she sensed he knew more than I'd ever admitted.

Marrying Steve expanded my small tribe. I gained in-laws who treated me as their own, a network I quickly cherished. My life grew fuller. For the first time, I felt completely secure with a man, not just romantically, but in how he valued me. He became my best friend. The greatest allure of being with Steve wasn't just love, it was how fully he allowed me to inhabit my own worth. Free from the shadows of past control.

He proposed at Regina's, our favorite restaurant. The other diners cheered as I said yes. I realized I'd found something rare: a love that both held me and let me stand tall. I wasn't just marrying a man I loved. I was marrying someone I liked. Being with Steve was easy. For the first time, it felt like home. Warm, steady, and mine entirely.

***

Mom returned to Iowa at seventy-one, her body a ledger of decades of heavy smoking and drinking. COPD and severe arthritis had added to the toll. A routine gallbladder surgery nearly ended her life when her lungs shut down. Three surgeries to stop internal bleeding and three months in the hospital. Steve and I decided it was easier to coordinate her care living near us. Again, I flew out, helped her pack, and drove back with her. A fragile shadow of the woman who had once ruled my world.

I was stunned when I saw her: willowy, gaunt, knees turned inward, a few inches shorter, hair thinning, shoulders curved in defeat. Compassion mingled with obligation, a heavy chain in my chest.

After three long months under our roof, she moved into a senior living apartment down the street. Steve and I exhaled with relief. She'd been drinking nightly, chatting on speakerphone while playing Yahtzee with herself. Sleep became a rare currency for those first few nights. I negotiated: Ten o'clock, lights out, lower level for her Yahtzee and tele-drinking. She told her friends I had given her a "curfew," like a parent of a delinquent teenager.

I took her to doctor appointments, grocery shopping, out to eat, included her at dinners and holidays, though she dominated every conversation, especially when the alcohol loosened her tongue. She reshaped the past to her liking. Debating why Deb and I had been pulled from school, romanticizing the dinners in The Kingdom. I wanted to scream; *those dinners were hell!* But her frailty and the invisible line of caution kept my tongue pressed to the roof of my mouth.

Her depression still haunted me. I feared her sadness might tip her toward something worse. An abyss I could not hold open. Years before, she had shut me down in the car, on the road back to Iowa. Why would this be any different? I locked my feelings away again, shoved them into that box I had carried for decades.

Then one Christmas, the lid blew off the box.

We had a couple of drinks during our Christmas festivities at Matt's house. Just as we were getting ready to leave, Matt blurted something I'd shared in confidence. Mom's eyes snapped into lasers, her bony finger stabbing the air. "You're either for me or against me," she hissed. Words older than memory, sharper than glass.

Time rewound. Back to the circle. Back to that phrase that I heard countless times. Back to the threats of the Lake of Fire. But that night, something shifted.

I straightened, inhaled, and let the words tumble out like a landslide. "Okay, you wanna go there, let's go there." Ten minutes of emotional expulsion followed, breathless sentences pouring out of me. Steve, Matt, and Ingrid (Matt's wife) disappeared into the living room, the TV clicking on, leaving the room Mom and I stood in anesthetized, the rest of the world a blur. She clutched her chest, begged me to stop.

I stretched taller. "I've been listening to you for over fifty years. Now you're going to sit there and listen to me," I said.

She folded her arms.

I came around the kitchen counter, perched on a stool beside her. "Mom," I leaned in. "Now we can have an honest relationship."

She turned her face.

"Mom, please look at me."

She turned up her nose.

"Mom, listen to me. It's out in the open now. We can be honest with each other."

She held her posture.

I stood. "Well, I guess we should go," I said to Steve, feeling myriad of complicated emotions.

Mom got up, retrieved her coat, and said nothing.

On the drive home, a tidal wave of emotion crashed through me. Pain rose from my belly, into my chest, bursting into the world through my mouth.

Steve asked softly, "You, okay?"

I couldn't answer. The grief poured like molten iron, wailing from the depths of my body.

"Please, please stop crying," Mom leaned forward from the back seat. "I'm sorry. I'm sorry. I'm sorry."

Steve, eyes in the rearview mirror, said calmly, "Sandy, leave her alone and let her go through what she needs to."

Mom slumped back, folded her arms, and stared out the window. "I guess you're the boss now."

I wailed until the sound drained from me, leaving a hollow numbness. Silence filled the rest of the drive.

At her apartment building, she flung off her winter coat, a gift from Matt and Ingrid. "I don't deserve this."

"Mom," I said, picking up the coat and handing it back. "This is your coat. Don't be ridiculous."

We rode the elevator in silence. Inside her apartment, I hugged her. She held her arms rigid, a wall I could not breach. I stood for a long moment, hoping for a crack, a glimpse of something salvageable. Nothing. Tight-lipped, eyes averted, she was still unreachable. My heart weighed lead, heavy with what I could not fix.

That night, I sobbed in Steve's arms.

A few sleepless nights later, I wrote her a letter. Concise and direct. I told her I had pushed down emotions my whole life. I said I didn't want a fake relationship anymore. I didn't ask for an apology. I asked for honesty. Finally.

Her response arrived as a text: *"Not interested. I wish you the best."* We never saw each other again. At fifty-four, I'd lost my mother for good.

I drove past her apartment often. Guilt stabbing me sharp. I should've let it go back to the way it was, I'd think. Her younger, terrifying face would flash across my mind. Then her older, frail version would come into focus. The two faces hauntingly ping-ponged between past and present. I could've avoided the flashbacks by taking a longer route, but I needed to know she was okay. I checked the parking lot for her car; a small confirmation she still existed. Relief calmed me when I saw it.

Two years later, her car disappeared from the parking lot. She had moved to Seattle to live with Deb. They'd reconciled, grown close, and I was glad. Many nights, I'd been the one to comfort her when she cried about missing Deb, who'd been no contact for years. Her happiness had always felt like my relief, a pressure valve finally releasing.

We exchanged a few texts over the years. Brief, careful tendrils of connection. An acknowledgment of a death. A condolence. A shared memory reduced to a sentence or two. Enough to say we still existed to each other. Yet, not enough to reopen the door.

I survived The Kingdom. I survived Mom. I accepted what happened to me. I learned I could heal without her validation, and that I was strong enough to live without her. As a child in The Kingdom, I feared her wrath and her depression. I feared my own thoughts, the End Times, the Lake of Fire. That fear followed me for decades, shaping my choices, tightening around my throat when I tried to speak. But over time—slowly, painfully—I reclaimed myself. I found my own beliefs, my own identity, a life I could command.

There was a time when I would have changed the past if I could. But I see now that the road I walked, every detour, every collapse, led me here: to a husband who cherishes me, children I adore, a granddaughter whose laughter fills rooms, and in-laws who love me as their own. To a life that feels inhabited. To work that matters. I climbed the steep mountain of education the hard way, hoisting myself up with a GED, then earning a master's degree in clinical social work in my forties, dedicating my work to trauma survivors. People who know what it means to endure.

When I was twenty-one and pregnant, I believed my happiness depended on Mom's approval. In my thirties, I thought it depended on her being a grandmother to my children. In my forties, her survival felt like my responsibility. In my fifties I grieved her. In my sixties, while drafting this book, I finally understand that she loved me the only way she knew how.

I rose from the ruins of my past like a tree grown through cracked concrete, roots tangled with memory but reaching toward sunlight. My mother's voice, her wrath, her love twisted and broken, had shaped me, yes, but it no longer governed me.

For decades I wore the weight of her depression like a wet cloak, heavy and inescapable. But I learned to set it down and build a life of my own making. And in that reclamation, in the quiet triumph of surviving, I learned, at last, that I am sovereign over my own story.

The Kingdom of my childhood is gone. I survived the fire, the chains, Mom's depression, suicide talk, and fear of damnation. And from the ashes I became the ruler of my own life. Determined. Unstoppable. Unapologetic. I will never shrink myself again.

In my own therapy I realized Mom loved me the best way she could. Now, as she's nearing the end of her life, I understand that I can love her from afar, see her (if she'll agree to see me) without needing to talk about what happened, and be grateful for the gifts she gave

CHAPTER TWENTY

Thank You, Mom

Thank you, Mom, for teaching me how to cook
Thank you for modeling generosity
Thank you for saying, "I love you," every day
Thank you for teaching me compassion for the less fortunate
Thank you for teaching me perseverance
Thank you for instilling patience
Thank you for modeling a good work ethic
Thank you for teaching me frugality
Thank you for the cast iron skillet you gave me (I still have it)
Thank you for instilling in me nonattachment to material things
Thank you for teaching me how to be adaptable
Thank you for fostering in me the importance of order
Thank you for teaching me how to apply makeup
Thank you for teaching me to stand up for my rights
Thank you for modeling racial justice
Thank you for teaching me about women's rights
Thank you for teaching me how to take care of babies
Thank you for teaching me resourcefulness
Thank you for rescuing me from Bob
Thank you for teaching me selflessness
Thank you for modeling the value of community and family
Thank you for teaching me self-control
Thank you for modeling sharing
Thank you for teaching me survival skills
Thank you for teaching me to be content with little
Thank you for teaching me how to dance
Thank you for teaching me how to keep a clean home
Thank you for expecting independence from me
Thank you for working hard all those years to provide for Deb and me
Thank you, Mom, for loving me in the best way you knew how

Before you close this book…

If something in these pages felt familiar, I want you to know you are not alone.

After I finished writing this story, I sat down and wrote a letter to readers about what came next and what healing has looked like in the years since.

If you would like that letter, send me an email at contactpeggy@peggy-sharr.com and put "letter" in the subject line, and I'll send it to you.

If you'd like a printable version of the discussion guide, put "guide" in the subject line. If you'd like both the letter and the printable guide, put "both," in the subject line

I would be honored to stay connected.

Peggy

Acknowledgements

This book exists because of the people who stood beside me—sometimes quietly, sometimes fiercely. Through both the writing of it and the life that made it necessary.

First, my deepest gratitude goes to my husband, Steve. Your steady love, patience, and unwavering belief in me never faltered, even when my own did. Your thoughtful edits, sharp eye, and calm presence gave me the courage to tell this story honestly and to finish what I started.

To my children, Mandy and Josh: you show up with unmeasured love, and your presence in my life has been a reminder of why telling the truth matters.

To my granddaughter, Inez: thank you for bringing truckloads of joy into my life, and for pushing me to create stories on the fly, even on days when I am not in a storytelling mood. You remind me why stories are so important.

To my dear friends, thank you for listening without judgment and for reminding me, repeatedly, that my voice matters. Your faith in me helped me trust my own truth when it felt risky to do so.

I am sincerely grateful to my critique groups and beta readers. Your insight and careful attention strengthened this book immeasurably. You helped shape it into something clearer and more grounded than I could have achieved alone.

To my chosen parents—my in-laws—Beth and Nels. Your love reminds me that survival can lead to healing, and that family can be redefined. Beth (Mom 1943—2025), may you rest in peace. You will always live in my heart.

To my spoiled cat, Waylon, who curled beside me during countless writing hours, and often insisted on sitting on my laptop instead of my lap: thank you for the quiet companionship and the much-needed interruptions.

To my dog Daisy, who saw me through multiple tragedies. You felt my pain and my joy and were by my side through all of it. May you rest in peace. You will forever be my favorite fur baby.

I also acknowledge those whose actions indirectly shaped this story. To Tim and Richard, owners of the Historic Ausadie Building in downtown Cedar Rapids, Iowa: thank you for the generous use of your beautiful apartment, which gave me the quiet, uninterrupted space to do some of the deepest work of this book.

To my editor, Katie Bannon: thank you for helping mold this story into something far stronger and more cohesive than when it first came to you.

Finally, to the reader: thank you for being here. If these pages help you feel less alone, more seen, or more empowered to reclaim your own story, then this book has done what it was meant to do.

About the Author

Peggy Sharr is a psychotherapist, writer, and survivor of a childhood shaped by instability, poverty, and a family system that ultimately evolved into a fear-based belief structure she would later recognize as deeply damaging. *Surviving the Family Kingdom* is her story of growing up inside that world, and the long, nonlinear journey of disentangling from it.

Raised by a mother whose unresolved trauma and hunger for belonging gave rise to an insular, authoritarian family culture, Peggy learned early how loyalty, love, and fear can become dangerously intertwined. As a child and young adult, she experienced homelessness, emotional manipulation, captivity, and the quiet erosion of personal agency. Leaving did not bring immediate freedom. Instead, it set off decades of learning how to trust her own voice, build healthy relationships, and reclaim a sense of self that had never been allowed to fully form.

As an adult, Peggy earned a college degree, became a licensed clinical psychotherapist, and built a private practice devoted to helping others heal from trauma, dysfunctional family systems, and relational wounds. Her professional work deepened—not softened—her understanding of how easily people can be shaped by fear, and how courageous it is to choose something different.

This memoir is not written from the distance of resolution alone. Peggy brings the reader into the emotional immediacy of her experience while also offering the clarity that comes from years of reflection, therapy, and lived repair. Her perspective is both deeply personal and informed by decades of clinical insight, making this story as much about relationships, boundaries, and resilience as it is about survival.

Peggy lives in Athens, Georgia, with her husband. She is the mother of two adult children and a proud grandmother. After the devastating loss of her eldest son to suicide, she learned—again—that grief reshapes a life but does not have to end it.

In addition to her clinical work and writing, she finds healing and joy in painting portraits and landscapes and in Latin dancing.

Surviving the Family Kingdom is her testament to the quiet strength it takes to leave what harms you, the patience required to rebuild, and the possibility of creating a life rooted in truth, connection, and self-trust, no matter where you begin.

Facilitator's Introduction

Discussion Guide for *Surviving the Family Kingdom*

Thank you for choosing *Surviving the Family Kingdom* for your book club or discussion group. This memoir explores themes of family, belief, control, survival, and self-reclamation. While the story is deeply personal, the questions it raises are universal—about loyalty, silence, identity, and what it takes to find one's way out of systems that no longer serve us.

This discussion guide is designed to support thoughtful, respectful conversation, not debate or diagnosis. Readers may arrive with a wide range of reactions, including curiosity, anger, grief, empathy, recognition, or confusion. All of these responses are valid.

As facilitator, your role is not to interpret the "right" meaning of the memoir, but to create space for reflection, connection, and curiosity.

Suggested Guidelines for Discussion

Remind the group that sharing personal experiences is always optional. Allow silences when they arise; some moments need time to settle. If strong emotions surface, gently ground the conversation in the text. Respect differing perspectives and lived experiences.

This memoir does not offer tidy resolutions or simple answers. Instead, it invites readers to consider how people adapt, endure, and gradually reclaim agency—often in imperfect, nonlinear ways. Discussion may naturally touch on topics such as family dynamics, belief systems, trauma, resilience, and chosen identity. Let the group move at a pace that feels right for them.

You may wish to remind participants that stepping away from the discussion, taking a break, or simply listening is always an option.

Closing Thought for Facilitators

At its heart, *Surviving the Family Kingdom* is a story about finding one's voice after long silence. The most meaningful discussions often arise not from agreement, but from honest reflection and attentive listening. Your role in guiding that space matters. Thank you for holding it with care.

Book Club Discussion Questions

Opening & First Impressions

- What drew you to this memoir, and what expectations did you bring into the book?
- How did your understanding of the story shift as the memoir progressed?
- Was there a moment early on when you realized this book was going to be different from what you expected? What was it?

Family, Control, and Belief

- In what ways did belief—religious, familial, or ideological—function as a form of control?
- How did the family structure reinforce loyalty, silence, or obedience?
- Were there moments when you found yourself empathizing with characters whose actions were harmful?

Power, Fear, and Survival

- How does fear operate in the memoir—both overtly and subtly?
- What strategies did the author use to survive emotionally and psychologically before she was able to leave?
- Did you notice moments where survival required compliance rather than resistance? How did that complicate your view of "strength"?

Identity and Voice

- How did the author's sense of self change over time?
- What role did silence play in shaping her identity?
- Were there moments when the author reclaimed her voice in small, quiet ways before doing so openly?

Leaving and Aftermath

- What did "escape" actually look like in this memoir? Was it a single moment or a long process?
- How did leaving the family system create both freedom and new forms

of loss?

- Did you notice how the author carried remnants of the past into adulthood? Which ones stood out?

Trauma, Memory, and Healing

- How does this memoir portray the long-term effects of trauma?
- Were there moments where memory felt unreliable, fragmented, or emotionally charged?
- What does healing look like in this book—was it resolution, acceptance, ongoing work, or something else?

Choice, Agency, and Reinvention

- How does the author redefine agency over the course of the memoir?
- What role did education, work, and chosen relationships play in rebuilding her life?
- Did this memoir challenge any assumptions you held about why people stay or return to controlling environments?

Broader Reflections

- In what ways is this memoir a story about systems, not just individuals?
- How does this memoir expand or complicate common narratives about cults, abuse, or family loyalty?
- What conversations did this book open for you that you didn't expect?

Personal Connection (Optional, Use with Care)

- Did any part of the memoir resonate with your own experiences or observations of family, belief, or control?
- How did reading this book affect the way you think about silence, complicity, or survival in everyday life?

Closing Question

- What stayed with you after finishing the book?

The Burning Mouth Syndrome Survival Guide

If you, or someone you know suffers from Burning Mouth Syndrome, please know this first and foremost: you are not alone, and there is help and hope.

Living with ongoing burning or unexplained oral pain can feel frightening and isolating. Burning Mouth Syndrome (BMS) is still widely misunderstood. Most doctors have never heard of it, and many people living with BMS are told their symptoms are "all in their head," or something they should simply learn to live with or not think about. Too often, people are dismissed or unintentionally gaslit, left feeling confused, isolated, and without answers.

After years of living with unexplained burning pain and navigating a medical system that could not help me, I spent months researching medical literature and studies, alongside documenting my own lived experience, to write *The Burning Mouth Syndrome Survival Guide*. This book is not about a cure. Instead, it is about surviving this elusive condition by reducing suffering, and regaining quality of life.

Inside the guide, you will find:
- Clear explanations of what Burning Mouth Syndrome is and isn't.
- An overview of commonly used and emerging treatments
- Practical strategies that many people find helpful in reducing symptoms
- A special diet designed to reduce triggers and significantly lower burning.
- Guidance for advocating for yourself with healthcare providers
- Reassurance that your pain is real and deserves attention and care
- Ways to care for your mental health
- Which types of doctors to see, and so much more!

In addition to the book, I also offer a monthly BMS newsletter that shares the latest research, helpful resources, recipes, and encouragement for living well, despite chronic pain.

You can learn more, sign up for the newsletter, and order *The Burning Mouth Syndrome Survival Guide* at **www.peggysharr.com**.

Surviving the Family Kingdom tells the story of emotional survival. *The Burning Mouth Syndrome Survival Guide* is about caring for the body that carries emotional and physical pain.